A LOUISIANA
GENTLEMAN

AND OTHER
NEW ORLEANS COMEDIES

Order online at: www.trafford.com/07-2541

Note for librarians: A cataloguing record for this book is available from Library and Archives
Canada at www.collectionscanada.ca/amicus/index-e.html

Printed in Victoria, BC, Canada.

ISBN 978-1-4251-4522-4

 www.trafford.com

North America & International:
Toll-free: 1 888 232 4444
phone: 250 383 6864 fax: 250 383 6804; email: info@trafford.com
The United Kingdon & Europe:
phone: +44 (0) 1865 722 113 • local rate 0845 230 9601
facsimile: +44 (0) 1865 722 868 • email: info.uk@trafford.com

10 9 8 7 6 5 4 3 2 1

Book Design: Karen Engelmann | www.karenengelmann.com

PLAYS BY
ROSARY HARTEL O'NEILL
VOLUME 1

A LOUISIANA GENTLEMAN

AND OTHER NEW ORLEANS COMEDIES

DEDICATED TO:

New Orleanians
the bravest people I know;
my children
Rachelle, Barret, Rory, and Dale
who shared me;
and my enthusiastic husband,
Bob, who believed in me.

BRAVO!

TABLE OF CONTENTS

THE PLAYS

APPENDICES

FOREWORD

Rosary O'Neill, whose work you may be encountering for the first time in these pages, is a sterling example of what used to be called a "regional" writer, in the tradition of Lynn Riggs and Paul Green, though she doesn't write Riggsian "folk plays" or Greenian historical pageants. Her work examines the hopes, dreams and mores of people who live in and around New Orleans, a beleaguered city which has been much in the news of late.

New Orleans has never been what you might call a hotbed of theatrical activity. Before Katrina, you went to New Orleans largely for the food and for the music, or to immerse yourself in the spectacle of Mardi Gras. Not for the theater. There have, of course, been fine plays set in the city, the most notable of which is *A Streetcar Named Desire*; but I know of no other playwright who is actually a New Orleans writer other than Dr. O'Neill, who grew up there and who founded almost 20 years ago what still is, to my knowledge, New Orleans' only professional theater, Southern Rep, which was hit hard by the hurricane but will no doubt rebound in time. The plays in this book had all their premiere productions at Southern Rep, whose audience saw in them an amusing and often poignant reflection of their own lives.

Here you will find comedies and dramas. I myself prefer the comedies, such as *A Louisiana Gentleman* and *Wishing Aces*. Who isn't amused by those eccentric, daffy southerners? But all plays herein are well-crafted and very stageworthy. Can they travel beyond the region in which they are set? Well, that may just be up to you.

D. L. LEPIDUS
Freelance theater critic and editor,
Brooklyn, New York

ROSARY HARTEL O'NEILL

INTRODUCTION / VOLUME 1

Volume 1 contains modern plays set in pre-Katrina New Orleans, the City that Care Forgot. I was born and raised in New Orleans, living between my parents' house and my grandmother's mansion on the streetcar line. My grandmother was a brilliant widow terrified to enter her house alone after five. Evenings she turned off all the lights on the screened gallery and told ghost stories, convinced that the dead haunted us through life.

My grandma's mansion on Carrollton Avenue, New Orleans. Photo by Dale Nix.

My parents were big encouragers of theatrical talent, being very active in the New Orleans carnival balls, which were known for their parades and for their extravagant stages and performance skits. They built me a marionette theatre and urged me to write skits and put on puppet shows with my sister and brothers for family parties. They built a teen house next to their summer

ix

mansion on the Gulf of Mexico, where we children were encouraged to put on plays.

Bored to death for three months in Mississippi each summer, I staged plays with my cousins, so many that my family and visiting guests often paid us not to have to come. Yearly Grandma took me via the Panama Limited to Broadway plays and weekly via her chauffeured Cadillac to B movies frowned on by the Catholic Church, so as to provoke my mother. Grandma believed in doing the minimum to get into heaven, while Mother, a daily communicant, believed in doing the maximum.

I went to an all-girls Catholic high school, the Academy of the Sacred Heart, where the nuns encouraged me to direct and stage plays (my production of *Little Women* won the state rally and I was afloat), and belong to clubs like Valencia, where women urged me to act and stage scenes. My parents took me to plays at the wonderful theatre department at Tulane University, which had semi-professional theatre of the finest quality.

Because New Orleans is somewhat isolated and European, her people are very exotic, like rare birds and different; they love to party, to put on airs, and to act unique. Everyone has a story. Everyone is related, and everyone could be and wants to be a character in a Tennessee Williams' play. The exotic, bizarre, sensual flavor of that Mississippi River city made me want to write.

My playwriting did not take off until I had worked as an actress and director in California and New York, become a university professor, written two books on theater, *The Actors Checklist*, and *The Director as Artist: Play Direction Today*, and founded a theatre, Southern Repertory Theatre. Southern Rep, the first equity theatre in New Orleans in twenty years, was dedicated to Southern drama. We rehearsed in real locations on pre-built stage sets for two months and used top directors from around the world. We initiated a new play festival to develop new voices, and a friend challenged me to write. My play, <u>Wishing Aces</u> won me a Senior Fulbright Research Specialist grant to Paris. From then on, I stopped writing textbooks and wrote plays, primarily about New Orleans.

Having my own theatre allowed me to explore new artistic opportunities, and invitations to Europe gave me hope that my stories could reach a broad market. When I first wrote plays, I was fascinated by how bizarre my family and friends seemed, after having lived away for fifteen years in California and New York. They were so different from average Americans —flamboyant in the face of a very hot, steamy and broken New Orleans. They kept telling me to write about them and bring them onto the stage.

ROSARY HARTEL O'NEILL

My parents summer home on the Gulf of Mexico, near New Orleans.
Photo Mary Brent Anderson

In 1991, New Orleans, a premier city of the South, was holding on with its claws but rank with problems, such as illiteracy, crime, and weak levees. While I was writing the early contemporary plays over ten years, I recorded what I saw from a positive point of view. People talked about the big hurricane wiping the city out. But there was no sense it really would. So, I wrote from a sense of hope and admiration of brave, decadent, and driven people, living in chaos, confusion, extreme pleasure and delight.

New Orleanians enjoy food, clothes, love, dancing, music. Even in the celebration of death, there is much singing and rejoicing. My early plays relate to the city as I knew it. After Hurricane Katrina, I have been so stricken by its loss that I have not been able to go back, especially to places that I wrote about, that no longer exist.

Now I write from memory, hoping that this luscious city with its steamy architecture, charming French Quarter, local parishes, river plantations, and fascinating people will rebound. That people will come back and the European roots of the cosmopolitan city will flourish. That people still holding on, trying to make a difference in all the various industries education, food, entertainment, that these people will be cherished and supported because they are staying in a stricken city for the love of the past and the hope of the future.

I would like my plays to communicate to audiences worldwide that New Orleans is a unique city in America and should be cherished.

When shaping a play, I take a question that disturbs me that I can't figure out, such as: why can't this professor and this student communicate in a profound way? Why can't this mother set boundaries for her out-of-control son? What would it take for that to happen? I then look at voice and structure, using the names of people from my life (I may change these later) to get the right phrasing and tone. I put these ghosts in my play, pick the most haunting place in New Orleans, and use cards to come up with an outline of scenes. Place inspires that sense of mystery that is so important to the theatre: an abandoned train station in the Louisiana swamps, a Baroness Pontalba apartment in the Quarter, a Garden District mansion. Place, weather, time, sounds inspire designers who are critical to creating the images the story requires. I try to fill my plays with details from New Orleans: the heat, the rain, the light through the oaks, the phantom gallery of a plantation house at dusk.

I write twelve to twenty drafts, cutting out lines of scenes that bore me and adding ones that are hopefully more interesting. I have read-throughs throughout the draft process. Having worked as an actress, a director and an artistic director, I try to trust my instincts when things get boring, are drifting, or are confusing. I search for the fewest words, and the most interesting language to make something happen, often cutting every other line or giving each character only one line of dialogue or less until an explosion occurs.

I keep a journal of interesting thoughts, language, places, and events, so when I find a scene that looks flat, I explore if there isn't a more interesting way to present the same situation. Once in rehearsal, 10-15% may be cut for a play. But by reading my work out loud, doing many drafts, and writing about real questions, people, and places, I hope to avoid too many changes for the actors.

A play is a puzzle. The missing pieces are the director, designers, actors, and audience. I try to keep in mind what they are experiencing as the script moves relentlessly toward the finale. It is a juggling act to write a play, but it is probably the most fun thing I have ever done.

ROSARY HARTEL O'NEILL
New York, New York

THE PLAYS

Wishing Aces

A PLAY IN ONE ACT

First performed in June 1996
Théatre du Marais, Paris

CAST OF CHARACTERS

KITTEN LEGERE: About thirty-six, Ph.D. grad student, married to new money. Dressed all in bonny blue, SHE wears a Laura Ashley ensemble a bit tight in the waist and bust, and a hat. SHE carries a ribboned basket of supplies and food. SHE is gorgeous like a china doll from Paris but sometimes SHE stutters, especially when talking about her son.

JAMES BEAUREGARD (BEAU) ELLIS: About thirty-eight, professor of English Literature, HE will inherit his family's plantation and sugar business. Right now, HE is broke. HE is dressed from toe to crown in Ivy League blue and gray: an Oxford cloth shirt, the university club tie, Bally loafers. HE carries worn Gucci luggage, a London Fog raincoat, an umbrella, and a briefcase.

BUNKY LEGERE: Kitten's son, fifteen, small for his age. HE is poured into jean cut offs, tee-shirt, leather jacket, and boots. HE carries a knapsack with books, shoes, a bandanna, patches, and pins hanging from it, and a fencing sword. HE wears his hair over his face like a mask.

HETTY WILLIAMS: the porter, late twenties to early fifties, Afro-American. Her leg starts acting up whenever anybody criticizes her. A big strong woman, from rural Louisiana, SHE wears a porter's uniform with a name tag and a rhinestone necklace, earrings. Perhaps a nose ring.

SETTING

The play takes place in a train depot in the Pearl River Swamp in Louisiana: an outpost not far from New Orleans. The waiting room of the abandoned way station is filled with signs of decay: dirt, cobwebs, bugs, and is near the train tracks.

ROSARY HARTEL O'NEILL

SCENE 1

(Ninety degrees at nine a.m. in mid-September. BEAU ELLIS leads KITTEN protectively into the depot. Every now and then, SHE looks back hysterically toward her son, on the train.)

KITTEN: Bunky. Get off the train. It's broken down.

BEAU: Careful, sugar.

KITTEN: Don't sugar me. *(Calls)* Come out here, son.

BEAU: You call this a train station? Whoa. We're on stilts in the water. Looks like a ghost town that went under the marshes. Careful, darling.

KITTEN: Don't call me darling.

BEAU: The floor's broken through.

KITTEN: Where?

BEAU: Over there. Shh. A water moccasin.

KITTEN: That brown thing?

BEAU: A cottonmouth moccasin. It's opening its mouth. Hand me that board.

KITTEN: That filthy wood?

BEAU: Hurry. *(BEAU grabs a piece of wood and smashes the snake.)* I got it. It's dead. *(BEAU dumps the snake through the hole in the floor.)*

KITTEN: I hate assisting you with these lectures. You wouldn't fly.

BEAU: Aw, sugar. Warm water coaxes all the animals out. Alligators float up. Crawfish tunnel over.

(Noise heard from offstage. KITTEN jumps up and crosses to the door.)

BEAU: Come here.

KITTEN: My son's at the door!

(The porter pokes her head in the door.)

KITTEN: How bad is the hurricane?

HETTY: We'll know at the next stop.

BEAU: Marvelous.

KITTEN: What's that crying sound?

HETTY: Blind sheep dog. Beating against her cage!

KITTEN: Bring her inside.

BEAU: No. I'm allergic. Give her a Valium. Porter, I need an iced coffee.

KITTEN: Coffee has five hundred chemicals in it.

BEAU: That's why I like it. Coffee increases sexual activity.

KITTEN: I prefer decaffeinated.

BEAU: It's probably got a thousand chemicals—five hundred more to deactivate those in the coffee. One tall coffee, porter.

HETTY: Hetty Williams, the name. *(Exits)*

BEAU: Ever heard of a porter with rhinestone earrings? A porteress?

KITTEN: *(Removes his lecture notes)* Nice. Have you revised this talk?

BEAU: There's a gigantic cobweb—

KITTEN: What, lord?

BEAU: By your leg.

KITTEN: The Faulkner Conference, remember?

BEAU: That web's got moths stuck in it. See?

KITTEN: Your editor will be there.

BEAU: He's canceling my contract. I'm not working unless you sit by me. I'm depressed.

KITTEN: Why not open with a quote from Lillian Hellman?

BEAU: I'm not quoting marginal women because you like them.

KITTEN: This is our decade. "American Women in Popular Fiction."

BEAU: Our department has its token feminist. The chair. Impeccable resume, but she's a pig. An aging breast feeder. She pops out her boob at the commencement exercises and lets this little suckling hang from it. Everyone stares at the floor.

KITTEN: There's something sick about you.

BEAU: These breast feeders have these massive, pie-shaped kazoos. Those piglets have gnawed them out of shape.

KITTEN: Don't come so close.

BEAU: What is too close?

KITTEN: So I can feel your breath.

BEAU: This far?

KITTEN: Don't talk about breasts. If you don't make an impression, Tulane's going to fire you.

BEAU: Is that why you came, honey?

KITTEN: The university wants to pay somebody to doctor your paper; why shouldn't it be me?

BEAU: Sit by me.

KITTEN: You resent waiting for tenure.

BEAU: No, I hate being broke at thirty-eight. A teacher is a hired slave. My colleague Smith's created a gadget to conserve on his electric bill—this stick with a Styrofoam cup at the end for unscrewing his porch lights. This Fulbright scholar goes around unscrewing light bulbs. Come here.

KITTEN: Shh. Start working. When I brag about your classes, I feel like I'm stepping over land mines. The department chair says—

BEAU: That wench. To quote Faulkner, "I make it a point never to speak

5

harshly of females, but that woman has more ways like a bitch than any lady in these sovereign states and dominions."

KITTEN: You don't like having a woman as the boss?

BEAU: No one survives that barbarian. She's a Visigoth. But you're the antithesis of her.

(BUNKY pushes open the door, and runs. KITTEN jumps up.)

KITTEN: *(Continued)* Oh, no. He follows me about—

BEAU: I don't blame him, honey.

KITTEN: Damn it. Bunky was supposed to stay with my husband.

BEAU: Profanities are for people with limited vocabularies.

HETTY: *(Enters, forcing the door against the wind)* Delay an hour.

BEAU:Fabulous.

KITTEN: Where's everyone?

HETTY: They got off at the Crawfish Festival in Hammond.

BEAU: The engineers have left?

HETTY: They hitched a ride on a patrol boat to the next station.

BEAU: We're by ourselves? Don't forget the iced coffee.

HETTY: Hard ass. *(Exits)*

BEAU: Did you hear that? Some feminist militant from… Who ever heard of a female porter anyway?

KITTEN: *(Removes a cellular phone)* Should I call my husband, Beau?

BEAU: Sure, love. Maybe he'll join us.

KITTEN: *(Into the phone)* Quint, the train's stalled.

BEAU: My wife and I are expanding our sensations.

ROSARY HARTEL O'NEILL

KITTEN: Oh, you're back together again?

BEAU: I got Elsa something new—an exercise man named Scot.

KITTEN: *(Into the phone)* Bunky and I are fine.

BEAU: This blonde stud arrives at seven a.m. to work her out.

KITTEN: *(Into the phone)* Yes.

BEAU: I'm in bed—gossiping on the phone. Elsa greets him with, "I don't like to be pushed."

KITTEN: *(Into the phone)* Yes.

BEAU: The first day, Elsa's knees collapsed.

KITTEN: Not so close.

BEAU: The second, her eyes snapped.

KITTEN: Don't touch.

BEAU: And she couldn't see. Twenty thousand dollars later the hospital found nothing wrong with her. She had a divine rest, and we both loved those fabulous pills. Elsa and I have been getting along great. We just don't speak.

KITTEN: Too bad. She is so rich. I mean, fragile.

BEAU: Fragile. "I'm talking about cruel fate in eight yards of apricot and more metal pound for pound than a galley slave." Faulkner.

KITTEN: *(Hanging up the phone)* I miss you too. *(Looks out)* My son's at the window. *(Screams)* Bunky. Come in. Act normal, Beau. Nothing scares Bunky, I swear. Last week when I grounded him, he shimmied from the attic on two king size sheets. Start reading.

BEAU: Did I tell you about my editor's lousy note? "About the only good thing about your novel is the typing." I'm writing about my grandmother, who died at ninety, and my editor says her entire life lacks progression. Aw. *(Ducks)* Ooh. A flying cockroach. Size of a bird.

KITTEN: Where?

BEAU: Must have come through the wood.

KITTEN: Don't chase it.

BEAU: Give me your shoe. *(BEAU grabs KITTEN'S shoe.)*

KITTEN: You'll stir things up.

BEAU: Victory. *(Kills the roach)* Let me slide your slipper on.

KITTEN: Stop touching me. Don't look around and find nasty things. Don't expose your limited view to these red-neck intellectuals. Yeek, what's that?

BEAU: A sac full of caterpillars.

KITTEN: Auowl ...

BEAU: *(Holds up a sac)* You got to burn these sacs to get rid of—Ever seen something so disgusting?

KITTEN: Stop.

BEAU: If you kiss me.

KITTEN: Time to dictate. *(Takes out a tape recorder)* A birthday gift.

BEAU: From him?

KITTEN: From Kitten to Kitten. Gifts to myself. Talk into the speaker.

BEAU: I won't work, if you won't sleep with me.

KITTEN: I'll type up a politically correct version later.

BEAU: I've lost the capacity for rejection. I grew up in a hick town on my Mamma's sugar plantation, St. Ursula. I was just hanging there like a bat with no place to go.

KITTEN: *(Drinks from a flask)* Bourbon for breakfast?

BEAU: I collect jiggers like silver spoons from universities across the South. Line them up on my armoire: Alabama, Baylor, Chattanooga State. I used to mount the wings of birds which I'd shot: blackbirds, blue jays, cardinals, pigeons, even robins. Chopped them off, stretched

8

them out, and tacked them against my bedroom wall.

KITTEN: A butcher?

BEAU: No, a champion. Bird wings were trophies.

KITTEN: Why can't you fix this speech?

BEAU: Because I'm roasting in a hot box—disconnected from the universe.

KITTEN: What else do angry boys do on St. Ursula?

BEAU: Besides shooting birds, and… pursuing bored wives? You order the servants about. You become a drunkard. Like Faulkner. The South is an exile.

KITTEN: Why not talk about your life?

BEAU: This stranglehold. Philosophy without application is meaningless. I'm trying to get lost in my past… to project a reality. I don't want to see what's happening. Reality is an insecure place.

(HETTY limps in with a cup of hot black coffee and two ice cubes.)

HETTY: Wind's up to forty miles an hour.

BEAU: Fabulous. *(Picks up the cup)* What is this?

HETTY: Coffee with ice.

BEAU: I said iced coffee. It should come in a tall glass with ice. I don't drink from paper.

HETTY: You said a glass, doc.

BEAU: I meant a glass-glass.

HETTY: Hmph.

KITTEN: Please send my son out here.

HETTY: *(Exiting)* Iced coffee. A glass.

BEAU: *(Removes photo)* Most men seem to have wives they love. I wonder what it would be like to have that. I can't even picture it. I accept a loveless

9

marriage. Most men have never gotten over it. I carry this photo, over my heart.

KITTEN: I'm almost nude in that picture. Tear it up.

BEAU: Wonder who else would like to see this?

KITTEN: Put it away.

BEAU: I want to feel you.

KITTEN: My son suspects something.

BEAU: I lie awake nights—longing for your—

KITTEN: He storms around.

BEAU: Your soft, soft skin.

KITTEN: Under that big black umbrella.

BEAU: You don't even sleep with Quint.

KITTEN: I'm pregnant. Quint's baby.

(We hear a lightning bolt hit the train.)

KITTEN: *(Continued)* What's that?

BEAU: A lightning bolt hit the train.

KITTEN: I must find my son.

BEAU: A baby?

KITTEN: I slipped. Three months ago. *(Exiting)*

BEAU: You said the relationship was shot.

(HETTY enters fighting off BUNKY with a stick. BUNKY flails back with the sword.)

BUNKY: A trick sword in an umbrella. Ta DAH.

HETTY: Set it down.

BUNKY: En garde.

HETTY: Don't.

BUNKY: I'm here to save you.

KITTEN: Don't hurt him.

BEAU: You like torturing your mother?

BUNKY: Shut up, prince.

HETTY: You going to jail.

BUNKY: Quiet, bitch.

(BEAU pins BUNKY down. HETTY ties his arms and wrists.)

KITTEN: Why are you tying him up?

HETTY: He hurt my leg—

KITTEN: I'll get my first aid kit.

BUNKY: *(Screams)* Stop. I'd rather be a dog or cat. Or the meanest kind of ugly rat.

HETTY: I gag him.

BUNKY: Than a great big man with a dog and a gun.

HETTY: *(Twists kerchief as if to gag him)* He shut up good.

BUNKY: That shoots the birdies just for fun.

KITTEN: Heavens.

BUNKY: Back off, whore.

BEAU: Watch your mouth.

BUNKY: Arrest me. Mother—Mother—

KITTEN: H-h-he didn't mean that.

BUNKY: Kill me. Yeah!

KITTEN: You'll choke him.

HETTY: *(Stuffs away kerchief. Pulls out a pad and pencil.)* Cops can lock you up. Name, age, and address.

BUNKY: Bunky Legere. Seventeen. 2626 Saint Charles Avenue.

BEAU: I'm sure the boy made some mistake.

BUNKY: Keep out.

HETTY: You got papers to prove you Bunky?

BUNKY: A license.

HETTY: *(Squints at the license, as if it's hard to read.)* Probably stolen.

BUNKY: I can't apply for another license.

KITTEN: If it's a matter of a fine, I have money.

HETTY: Next of kin? Your mamma or daddy.

BUNKY: Quint, no, Kitten, no. Hey, Mamma, who's my next of kin? Quint Legere.

HETTY: Occupation?

BUNKY: Con artist.

KITTEN: Lord. I feel dizzy. My stomach's…

BEAU: You shouldn't get excited in your condition. Let me help you. I'll be outside.

(KITTEN exits to the bathroom and BEAU exits to the tracks.)

BUNKY: That's right, go. Hide. Pump some chemicals from your fucking shrink.

HETTY: Rains in February. Floods in May. *(HETTY slams the sword down.)* Amtrak don't allow no swords. Now, I could stick it in your neck and say you hit me first. Or jab it in your back.

BUNKY: It was a joke. . . *(HE puts on Walkman and hums along.)* Da. Da.

HETTY: Some jokes put you in jail. *(HETTY puts the sword under BUNKY'S throat.)*

HETTY: *(Continued)* Why you make trouble, bad ass?

BUNKY: Ask my therapist.

HETTY: Mind doctorin' is witches' work.

BUNKY: *(Hums)* Hmm. Hmm. Hmm.

HETTY: You listen when I talk, boy. *(SHE grabs the head phones)*

BUNKY: Oh no.

HETTY: You ain't never going to bully me. *(SHE takes rope and leads BUNKY out.)*

HETTY: One yard. No closer.

(THEY exit as KITTEN and BEAU enter.)

ANNOUNCER: BILLYBOP WITH YOUR HURRICANE UPDATE.

BEAU: That redneck again.

ANNOUNCER: AMTRAK TRAIN BROKE DOWN IN THE PEARL RIVER SWAMP.

BEAU: How accurate is this?

ANNOUNCER: ROADS ROUND THAT SWAMP ARE UNDER WATER.

KITTEN: Where's Bunky?

ANNOUNCER: BUT STATE POLICE BEEN NOTIFIED.

KITTEN: How will I talk to the Mississippi police? I don't want to be strong.

BEAU: Why be strong, when you're not in charge? Rain's starting.

KITTEN: *(SHE dials her phone.)* I'm phoning Quint.

BEAU: Don't you want to work on my paper?

KITTEN: I can't talk now. I've got to reach my husband. He's got a law degree and a lot of clout. I put him through law school. Lord, the line's busy.

BEAU: You see yourself as the source of Quint's success? Are you also causing your son's tragedy? *(Holds up BUNKY'S paper)* I found Bunky's F paper under my lecture.

KITTEN: Give that here.

BEAU: Bunky suspects you don't love Quint.

KITTEN: It's not that I don't love…don't…God, the depot's shaking.

BEAU: I wasn't ga ga for Elsa. But I screwed her.

KITTEN: Making up for it.

BEAU: I didn't get her pregnant.

KITTEN: *(Dials again)* When I talk to Quint, we fight. Bunky referees. Quint treats me like you treat Hetty.

BEAU: The porter?

KITTEN: Always ordering her about. Yeek. The phone's still busy.

BEAU: You feel guilty 'cause your relationship with your husband is destroying your son?

KITTEN: Not particularly.

BEAU: Your son breaks the law?

KITTEN: Quint insults me in front of B-B-Bunky. Does he feel guilty?

BEAU: Quint rakes in a half million a year. Why should he respect your opinion?

KITTEN: Because there are two parts to reality, a male and a female. Unless they work together there's no happiness. Lord. Rain's pouring. *(Slams*

14

down the phone.) Did you see a shadow pass the window? *(Calls)* Bunky.

BEAU: Just black birds. A raven's throwing herself against the pane. I hate to say this, sugar, but your son's super spoilt. When solving a problem, never overlook the obvious.

KITTEN: Quint gives Bunky anything he wants. Knives, swords, guns. He's trying to push, when the door reads, "pull." Don't look at me that soft way.

BEAU: You put Bunky in boarding school, he'll blossom.

KITTEN: Boarding school won't take him. When I tell Bunky to study, he screeches, "Screw you, friggin bitch." The school counselor advises counseling for my mother, biofeedback for Quint, and group therapy for me. He says they will expel B-B-Bunky if he doesn't learn limits. Beau, I'm not to react when he tells me "to fuck myself" or when he farts in public?

BEAU: My daughter's behavior isn't exemplary.

KITTEN: Yes, but she doesn't leave you a message at the office. "Bring a head of lettuce and a sharp knife." *(KITTEN passes BEAU the phone.)* Try Quint's phone number. My fingers are shaking so, I can't dial. It's 835-4040. Don't touch my hand.

BEAU: Does Bunky like Quint?

KITTEN: No. Quint used to go in B-B-Bunky's room at night for these d-d-discussions about his future.

BEAU: Line's busy.

KITTEN: Sometimes I would get jealous, Beau, especially on a Saturday night after we had been out drinking together, and I was feeling amorous. Then he had to first slip up to B-B-B-Bunky's room, while I fell asleep on the couch. Now Bunky's like a monster. I don't know what to do.

BEAU: Manic depression is a genetic imbalance. You don't have self-control. There are defects.

KITTEN: Why are you trying to rile me up? Bunky's psychiatrist, whom I recommended, tried to pick up on him. This adolescent psychiatrist is a pedophile. He strips all the Country Park boys when they have colds.

BEAU: Stay clear of the window.

KITTEN: I wanted to ask the D.A. to press charges, but Quint doesn't want the firm to know we need psychiatric help.

BEAU: Let me massage your shoulders.

KITTEN: Find my son for me, Beau; I can't take it.

BEAU: If I go, then will you sleep with me?

KITTEN: You're cackling for sex like an old rooster clucking and scratching.

BEAU: Well?

KITTEN: I've got to nap. If you've been through one Louisiana hurricane, you don't want to go through another. One reporter said, "Confusing advice comes because there are no answers. Any hurricane, even a flash flood, could kill you. And the newsmen are guessing as much as the listeners." If we drown, I'd just as soon be unconscious. Wake me when Bunky gets here.

(KITTEN closes her eyes. BEAU kisses HER and exits. HE does not hear the depot P.A. blare on)

ANNOUNCER: THE MAYOR OF PEARL RIVER HAS ISSUED A MANDATORY EVACUATION ORDER. EVERYBODY MUST EVACUATE. (P.A. fades in and out) MASSIVE FLOODING...WINDS OVER ONE HUNDRED MILES...IF THOSE RAINS KEEP ON COMING...

(Wind blows through the door. We hear MATILDA, the blind sheepdog, howling from the train)

KITTEN: (Cries out) Somebody help that dog. That sheepdog shouldn't have traveled without her owner. Dogs have feelings too. She howls like a baby. Little kids cling to you. Old ones disappear. I'm getting a Doberman Pinscher to toughen up. They have more teeth for attacking than any other dog. But you've got to shower them with attention, or they'll bite your hand off. The question is, "What influence do I have over Bunky?" That's a hard question to ask, if you're a mother.

(BEAU enters. KITTEN yawns and starts falling asleep.)

BEAU: Sorry, I couldn't find your son.

KITTEN: Aaaah. My panic level goes up when I talk about him.

BEAU: Does he know you're pregnant?

KITTEN: Maybe he's soothed Hetty. Bunky likes strangers. He was homeless once—for three days. 92% of street people are mental defectives. He's part of the 8% that wasn't. Don't look at me that way.

BEAU: Bunky's terrible but effective.

KITTEN: I know. It's nice to have a partner. Someone to talk to about the horrors—

BEAU: This isn't a teenager experimenting in the backyard—

KITTEN: But I've got a husband, and you've got a wife—

BEAU: This is a young man in public with a weapon.

KITTEN: Stay by the wall. I've two statues on my mantel. St. Anthony and St. Jude. I pray to St. Anthony when I'm confused and to St. Jude when I'm—. But you, you stick your daughter in reform school.

BEAU: Boarding school. After my first wife died, the girl charged about like a tigress in heat. I toss her some money, but we keep our distance. Marcelle always yells when she leaves for boarding school—"Go ahead," I say, "Go to it." God made teenagers obnoxious, so it's easier to let them go. The older they get, the nastier they are.

KITTEN: Bunky's my only accomplishment. I gave all my youth to that... that—You see him, ripped jeans, vile shirt. Who is he? What is he?

BEAU: It's not worth getting sick to your soul.

KITTEN: Don't touch me. Bunky was first in his class—Now I can't reach the child I knew. If I complain, he opens the car door when I'm driving and tries to jump out. Joins me at Antoine's for dinner wearing only one shoe. Yesterday someone spotted him walking down Saint Charles Avenue flailing a sword. Now he's swinging it at people. It's my fault. I'm a bad m-m-m-mother—

BEAU: Aw, sugar.

KITTEN: Stop. (*Holds up a pill bottle*) Vitamin C. It's one of my fragile days. Touch me, I cry. I'm so brittle. I'm living for the moment I can relax.

BEAU: Vitamin C? They're tranquilizers.

17

KITTEN: It's a prescription.

BEAU: You've been popping downers like peanuts.

KITTEN: If any of these predictions about the doom of my family are true, I want to be knocked out when my son-

BEAU: Most women are holding out for the perfect son, and they're waiting for a trap.

KITTEN: Don't blame it on women.

BEAU: I don't blame it on the fire that my hand gets burned. I shouldn't have stuck it in there.

KITTEN: I'm looking for... a place where I can feel safe... without intimidation.

BEAU: Growing up in my family wasn't exactly the hotbed of affection. When I put Marcelle in boarding school, I felt like I'd severed an artery. She was all I had after Mary Rose died.

KITTEN: What about for Marcelle?

BEAU: Huh?

KITTEN: The boarding school. You said she kept phoning you to come home.

BEAU: Yes, they sent her home because she was disturbing the girls with those nightmares about her mother. But the dreams subsided, and I sent her back. Now every time she returns to that school, I feel like I'm getting a transfusion from God. Everything that goes on, goes on there. It's like the world explodes inside that school, but at least I'm not in charge.

KITTEN: I'm working on letting go, trying to be happy—

BEAU: I understand what you're going through.

KITTEN: When I'm not in control.

BEAU: God, I wish I didn't.

KITTEN: And it's been so brutally hot—it has upset my sleep patterns.

(Sound of bull horns)

ANNOUNCER: EVERYBODY EVACUATE.

BEAU: Billybop again.

ANNOUNCER: OR YOU BE ARRESTED.

BEAU: That grating twang.

ANNOUNCER: THIS IS A MANDATORY EVACUATION. CITY OFFICIALS, SOUTHWEST LOUISIANA REQUIRING— *(P.A. fades to static)*

BEAU: Mind if I use your phone? *(HE picks up the phone and dials. SHE slips a pill.)*

BEAU: *(Continued)* Last Friday, my daughter Marcelle vanished from boarding school. Fifty phone calls later, I tracked her down to this ritzy new subdivision "Chateau Estates." They'd bullied her friend's mother into renting them six porno movies. Phone's busy.

KITTEN: *(Falling asleep)* How f-f-f-far away is the school?

BEAU: Two hours away if you drive ninety miles an hour… that's what they do. Relationships are like cars— now and then, you need a tune up. I need a jiffy lube. Marcelle needs a brake job. *(Clicks phone)* Aaah. I wonder if I'm dialing right. Oh, hello. I'm calling for my daughter, Marcelle Ellis. What? The school's evacuated. *(Dials again)* I'll try Elsa. I'm afraid next time Marcelle comes home, Elsa won't let her in. Last week-end, she dragged in drunk at one a.m. Elsa barred the doors—triple locks and a chain. The girl snuck back out at one thirty, then busted the door frame breaking in at four-fifteen. "She's not my daughter," Elsa shrieks. "Damaged goods from your first wife. Next time, I'm throwing her out." Elsa. The woman has about as much motherly spirit as King Kong. Phone's fading in and out. *(Dials again)* Hello. God, almost had something there. Don't hang up? I told Elsa, "Let's talk. I'd like to get to know you."
(Dials again) She left to scrub the German Shepherd in the bathtub. When I speak, she thinks I'm complaining. Elsa's a fiddler. She's always attaching or dismantling something. You have to make two phone calls to reach her. Machiavellian. *(Picks up phone)* Hello? Is this Elsa. I can't hear you. Has Marcelle arrived yet? *(Shakes the phone)* She hates the girl. Kitten don't go to sleep on me. *(Slams down the phone)* My wife's over-eating again. Blowing up like a poisoned dog in the sun. The only way she can dress up is by wearing these gargantuan muumuus and massive jewelry. She hits the

19

kitchen like a wild animal. She gobbles everything in sight. *(Picks up an empty pill bottle. Shakes it)* Gosh. They're only two pills left. Kitten. Wake up. Kitten. *(Calls out)* Hetty, Bunky. Kitten, talk to me. *(Sits her up and pinches her cheeks)* Don't check out on me. My first wife died when Marcelle was seven. I thought Mary Rose was happy, until I discovered she was an alcoholic. *(Stands her up)* Start walking. *(KITTEN collapses)* Look, I loved my first wife. We discovered our bodies together, and still she went and died on me. Bad things happen, but don't give away your life. That's right, open your eyes. God, wake up. Kitten. Wake up!

END OF SCENE 1

SCENE 2

(AT RISE: Short lapse of time. BEAU sits and plays Wishing Aces, flipping every third card.)

ANNOUNCER: BILLYBOP REPORTING BROKEN TRACK UP AND DOWN THE SWAMP.

BEAU: Abrasive man.

ANNOUNCER: EVACUATE, DON'T COUNT ON NO TRAIN.

BEAU: Awful grammar.

ANNOUNCER: NOBODY CAN FIX NO TRACK 'FORE THE STORM GO. *(Fades to static)*

BEAU: Double negatives.

BUNKY: *(Enters hands tied)* How's Mamma?

BEAU: Impending disaster. She just vomited up her breakfast, and all those pills you got her taking. Thank God she's revived to her usual state of acute embarrassment.

(BUNKY kicks BEAU'S briefcase)

BEAU: How do you describe one delusional person trying to help another?

BUNKY: Shut up, prince.

BEAU: Nice. We ought to call you Bunky Bright Eye, not Bunky. You never open your mouth without subtracting from the quality of life.

BUNKY: Untie me, and I'll talk?

BEAU: If I want to talk, I'll talk to my own kid. Not someone else's or an animal.

BUNKY: Awol.

BEAU: You sick?

BUNKY: No, I don't get ulcers. I give them. Ha, ha.

BEAU: Humor is your strong suit.

BUNKY: Huge roach. Ran over my foot.

BEAU: You're not scared of that? Ha. Ha. Maybe I'll put it in your hair.

BUNKY: Undo me...

BEAU: Just for a minute—(*Unties BUNKY*) Water leaking through the ceiling. Roaches scuttling about. My dog's probably squealing with terror. They don't allow pets in the evacuation shelters. I may never see my daughter again. I just gave her hell for changing the message on my answering machine. (*Picks up the phone*) Elsa? Is Marcelle there? (*Dials again*) Lousy phone fades off. Time for cards. Em' the Queen of Hearts. She peers to the side because she needs the King's money. There wasn't a moonlit night my Grandma didn't play Wishing Aces. You go through the deck once, flip every third card. If an Ace appears, your wish comes true. My first wife used to play it. After she'd an attack of delirium tremors, or a spell as we'd call it, she'd reach for a deck by the bed and wish for a new face.

BUNKY: (*Takes drum sticks from his backpack, hits them*) Pow.

BEAU: Died at twenty-nine. The sunny side of thirty. "Sunny's the young side of a number, shady's the old."

BUNKY: Pow. Pow.

BEAU: (*Looks at the cards*) Oh, the Suicide King. He's got a sword in his head.

21

BUNKY: Pow. Pow.

BEAU: Can't snap out of his depression.

BUNKY: Pooh! Spsh!

BEAU: He's got a decision to make between two people who are both lying.

BUNKY: Pow! Spsh! Spsh!

BUNKY: You give advice to students?

BEAU: The last one I talked to transferred to Alaska.

BUNKY: They say your daughter—

BEAU: I don't have a daughter, my daughter has me. She's locked up in boarding school... which is where you ought to be. What is it about teenagers? You screw up your own family, and you can't wait to screw up someone else's?

BUNKY: You lost.

BEAU: I didn't say I was good at this game. I said I know how to play it.

BUNKY: So what about you and super mom?

BEAU: Your mother is always in my prayers.

BUNKY: I should have known. There is no— *(Beats his drum sticks)* Pow! Spsh! Spsh!

BEAU: This behavior is more esoteric than I'm ready for.

BUNKY: Want to see me get all worked up? Blow out the stops. Pay back the wood. Ring out the sound. Break the skin to find the heart beneath. Pow. This morning I cut myself on that sword, and the blood felt so good. Ha. Ha. Maybe I'll sever an artery—

BEAU: Don't do that.

BUNKY: Make me stop. You can't. Feels real. *(Screams)* Ain't that right, Matilda?

BEAU: Who?

BUNKY: Blind sheepdog's got a bloody nose from beating against the cage. Anybody care? Crush her to a pulp, she don't scream. Swoosh!

BEAU: My responsibility as a man is to control my temper.

BUNKY: Sissy.

BEAU: And to tell the truth as I see it.

BUNKY: Spsh. Homewrecker.

BEAU: Don't spit. … I know this is tough. I'm in love with your mother.

BUNKY: Hmm. Hmm.

BEAU: I don't like this addiction. I worry about her.

BUNKY: Stop!

BEAU: She's not counting her pills.

BUNKY: I'll scream till you stop. Aaah!

(HETTY enters.)

BEAU: You won't listen. Fine. I'll tie you to the chair and leave you ranting to the moon.

(BUNKY screams till BEAU is gone.)

ANNOUNCER: BILLYBOP ANNOUNCING TRAIN TRAVEL SUS-PENDED. PATROL BOAT BE RETURNING FROM THEM SWAMP. TO EVACUATE, USE YOUR OWN TRANSPORTATION.

BUNKY: Great.

HETTY: Swamp rising. Alligators swishing about.

BUNKY: Untie me.

HETTY: I can't. Less you want some time alone with your mamma.

BUNKY: Mamma's an idiot.

HETTY: You chicken. Chick. Chick. Chick. Ha. You could never hunt alligators. Chick. Chick.

BUNKY: Yeah, I could.

HETTY: Hunting 'gators same as talking to your mamma. You noose that gator. Set your mamma down, and beat the head with a stick. You speak to her straight. Nothing you say can kill your mamma. Gator meat taste good.

BUNKY: You eat that?

HETTY: They eat us, don't they? *(Slashing noises)* Hurricane coming. Look, I leave you untied, if you talk to your mamma, I make a square of tape around you. *(HETTY tapes out a square and has BUNKY flatten down the corners)* You do all you want in it, but step out that line, and I tie you again.

(A crashing sound. KITTEN enters from the bathroom)

KITTEN: That bathroom is so disgusting.

BUNKY: We're swaying.

HETTY: Anything high up has to give.

KITTEN: Bunky, you're untied.

BUNKY : Mamma, I've got to talk to you.

KITTEN: *(Spots BEAU out the window)* Beau. Don't get on that train.

BUNKY: Ma, come here.

HETTY: Freeze that gator.

BUNKY: We used to speak nicely to each other.

KITTEN: I spoke, you listened. *(Calls)* Beau. Come on out.

HETTY: Noose it, now.

BUNKY: *(Takes out a photo pack)* See this picture. This friend took an overdose of alcohol and sleeping pills. Tied his head inside a garbage bag.

KITTEN: Heavens.

BUNKY: Asphyxiated himself. Another photo.

24

KITTEN: Our swimming pool?

BUNKY: I was going to drain it, do a swan dive inside. Dad would find me in this sea of blood.

KITTEN: I know it's my fault. *(Calls)* Beau, come off the train. What's that hitting down below?

HETTY: Alligators.

BUNKY: Don't go.

BUNKY: You know Dad's in the French Quarter with—

KITTEN: We're working it out separately.

BUNKY: Does tension excuse him from being nice?

KITTEN: Your dad calls me three times a day when we're apart. Something's just damaged the way we speak to each other in person. *(Runs over to the phone)*

BUNKY: Read this—

KITTEN: I don't want——

HETTY: She'll lie there. Like stone.

KITTEN: *(Reads)* From Quint to? I can't make out the name. J-j-j-jane. His secretary is moving in with him?

BUNKY: You didn't know?

KITTEN: I kept pretending my thoughts would go away.

BEAU: They've been "doing it" for about two years.

KITTEN: Sometimes, if you ignore a crisis long enough, it disappears. Get rid of this.

BUNKY: Jane's a whore. . . She wears spiked heels, red nails.

KITTEN: Tacky.

BUNKY: When Dad took me to see colleges, Jane arrives accidentally.

25

KITTEN: Sleazy.

BUNKY: Talks in spurts, like a geyser. "How wonderful." Spsh. "Spectacular." Spsh.

KITTEN: Dumb, too.

BUNKY: *(Removes photo album)* See this photo. Talking about money turns Dad on. Didn't you know he was bored?

KITTEN: No, I knew I was bored. Quint never expressed an emotion like, "I'm so happy or miserable." There is no marriage that is secretary-proof.

BUNKY: You even invited Jane to our Christmas party.

KITTEN: Quint asked me to.

BUNKY: *(Takes out a photo)* She's in the family portrait. In the same white mink like yours.

KITTEN: It wasn't like mine. Hers is mink, mine is fox.

BUNKY: I said to Grandma, "What do you make of the fact that Jane and Mamma are wearing the same coat?" Grandma snaps, "I don't read anything into it."

KITTEN: She puts on blindfolds for Quint, and he's not even her son.

BUNKY: Yeah! Grandma scolds me, "Even if it's true about Jane, you shouldn't mention it. The easiest and most honorable way out is to lie."

KITTEN: Mamma's not into justice; she's into appeasement. "Peace at any price."

BUNKY: And Dad doesn't want an adultery rap before the divorce.

KITTEN: The divorce?

BUNKY: Men don't appreciate low-maintenance women. As long as Daddy says, "Good girl," once a month you're happy. Jane drives the—

KITTEN: Company Mercedes.

BUNKY: Life's a bitch, then you marry one.

ROSARY HARTEL O'NEILL

KITTEN: Don't laugh. Before you were born, we used to talk all night. Now, nothing. It's as quiet as it can be before it becomes silence.

BUNKY: You been cheating too.

KITTEN: Just once.

BUNKY: How much does it take? Still— Beau is nicer to you than Dad.

KITTEN: What can Beau do? He's broke. He's had two wives. And that lunatic daughter at boarding school.

BUNKY: Start fighting for yourself, Ma. Remember, the first fencing lesson, say. "Yes I can."

KITTEN: The war's over. Let's bandage our wounds, limp home, and pray for amnesia. Thanks for telling me. .even though…I feel like someone dunked me in a bucket of ice.

HETTY: Leave her. Follow me. One yard. No closer.

(BUNKY and HETTY exit for the train. As KITTEN dials, BEAU enters, a kerchief binds his hand.)

ANNOUNCER: WIND UP TO HUNDRED AND FORTY MILE AN HOUR. JOSÉ A NUMBER FOUR STORM. BIG AS THEY GET.

KITTEN : Don't tell me! *(Into the phone)* Hello? Quint. J-j-j-jane?

BEAU: The blind dog bit me. She's gone mad from being caged. Some fool let her out for a run.

KITTEN: First aid kit's in the basket.

BEAU: Let me kiss you.

KITTEN: You're not worried about… the hurricane.

BEAU: I've heard said, "There is great danger in the body." Yeats.

(The sound of crashing trees. Wind. HETTY hurries into the room, carrying some jugs.)

HETTY: José's breaking through.

KITTEN: Where's my son?

BEAU: Will the roof hold?

HETTY: Probably not. After hurricane Camille, they couldn't find houses. Water—wash everything 'hind the tracks and out to sea. One wave carry a man in his house to another county. He so drunk, he sleep all the way. Coast guard pull dead bodies from cars, trees. Found an arm under some dirt.

KITTEN: *(Looking up)* What's that?

HETTY: Most folks don't die from drowning.

BEAU: Roaches like sparrows—

HETTY: They die from the wind.

BEAU: Soaring for the roof.

HETTY: Houses bust open like match boxes.

KITTEN: I've got to find my s-s-s son.

(KITTEN exits with BEAU following.)

ANNOUNCER: EMERGENCY BULLETIN. JOSÉ TO HIT THE PEARL RIVER SWAMP. WAIT AT THE HIGHEST SPOT.

(BUNKY enters with a lantern.)

HETTY: Fill these jugs 'fore the water stop.

BUNKY: How is Mamma?

HETTY: Spooked. Remind me of that crazy rich woman. Found her body—back in the woods—still holding a sack of silver. She was—

BUNKY: I can't see through the sheets of rain.

HETTY: She was packing to leave when the hurricane hit.

BUNKY: What happens then?

HETTY: It quiet. Everything turn green like it over.

28

ROSARY HARTEL O'NEILL

BUNKY: What's that thrashing?

HETTY: Alligators.

BUNKY: I've got to find Mama.

(BUNKY goes out. Moments later, BEAU and KITTEN enter with blankets, raincoats.)

KITTEN: What would your grandma do now?

BEAU: Ha! She would probably bawl out the porter. Threaten to sue the Panama Limited. Then tell us a story.

KITTEN: Can't catch my breath.

HETTY: Well, tell us a story.

BEAU: Now? I'm not the parlor entertainer. All right. I'll tell you Grandma's favorite story, "It's All Mine." Once, there was an old man with a beard so long it hung below his waist. Every afternoon, he would take this beautiful young girl for a ride in his buggy, and ask her to be his bride. On the drive, he'd point out these magnificent plantations and say, "You see that field of cotton, those herds of cattle, that lake, those mansions," then twisting his beard from top to bottom, he'd say, "It's all mine. All mine." The young girl married the old man. And on their wedding day, he drove past the fields of cotton, the herds of cattle, the mansions to a shack overgrown with weeds. "Get down," the old man whispered. "We're home." What happened to those plantations, the cattle, all that land you claimed was yours?" the girl cried. The old man twisted his beard and wheezed. "I never said those were mine. I said, my beard was mine. And it is. It's all mine."

(A crash. BLACKOUT.)

KITTEN: (Screams) Bunky!

HETTY: There go the lights.

BEAU: I'll get the lantern.

HETTY: Talk, Beau.

BEAU: Grandma passed through the hurricane of forty-seven with her old maid sisters. They closed the shutters, stacked the family portraits in a

29

heap, sat around them. Then they scared each other with ghost stories or prayed—

KITTEN: *(Takes out a Rosary.)* Here's my rosary.

BEAU: I've never been religious, and I'm not going to start.

KITTEN: I'm going outside.

BEAU: No. You won't do Bunky any good.

HETTY: He smart.

(Lights come up.)

BEAU: The lights are back.

KITTEN: "Hail Mary, full of grace, the Lord is with thee."

HETTY: Keep going, Beau.

BEAU: Grandma would say, "This true story was confided to me by a priest."

HETTY: A holy man.

KITTEN: "Blessed art thou among women—"

BEAU: Father Fannen is dead and gone. And Father Fannen would never lie.

KITTEN: God, forgive me. But I want to live to tell Quint off.

BEAU: I'll say something I've never told anyone, honey. I need a night light to fall asleep. Ha.

KITTEN: I can't laugh. *(At the window)* I can't see my son. We're going to die in this lousy hurricane. We'll be trapped, like the—the—-

BEAU: Bride that was buried alive because they thought she was dead.

KITTEN: What's keeping Bunky?

HETTY: Don't go out.

BEAU: You'll frighten him and make things worse. Hold my hand. "The red satin casket story." When they opened the casket to take the diamond off her finger, the woman had clawed away all the silk lining. I want to be embalmed. Then buried in the family tomb. I can't believe I won't live to inherit a—Wait. You can't go out.

KITTEN: I can't worry about a flood; I'm so upset about my s-s-son.

HETTY: I hold the lantern up for Bunky to see.

KITTEN: Something's ramming the floor.

HETTY: You got a good love story?

BEAU: The story of John Darling.

KITTEN: Hear that screaming? *(Yells)* Bunky.

BEAU: My grandma had a cousin, named John Darling. When she was little, grandma thought people were calling him darling to be affectionate. Darling was his last name, see.

KITTEN: I'm going out.

BEAU: *(Holding her down)* John Darling was unhappy in love. No one was good enough for John. And at forty, he was alone and miserable.

HETTY: There she blows.

BEAU: One day John took a schoolteacher home to his mamma's for dinner.

KITTEN: Where's Bunky?

BEAU: And John began bragging about what he wanted in a wife.

HETTY: Something's knocking the pilings.

BEAU: Stay with me. "My wife will have to be beautiful, charming, educated," John said. "She must be well-bred, cultured, intelligent..."

KITTEN: I'm so upset about Bunky.

BEAU: John went on and on as the old maid sliced her peas and carrots and stared into her plate. "My wife must be a good cook, a wonderful mother. She'll have to be well-traveled, exquisitely dressed, with an independent income."

31

HETTY: We heaving.

BEAU: Finally, the spinster put down her napkin, and said, "And when you find her, John Darling, she'll never want you." Ha. Ha. Isn't that funny, Kitten? I don't know why that story makes me sad.

HETTY: Tell us 'bout the future, Beau.

BEAU: I didn't get tenure.

KITTEN: You lost your job.

BEAU: My life doesn't add up to zip. It's the absolute simplicity that makes it so difficult. I've no backup plan, Kitten. No reserves. I thought if I achieved something, it would excuse my history, plug up the holes, ring up the checking account. Boy orator goes blank.

KITTEN: What does your wife say about that?

BEAU: Ex-wife.

HETTY: We swaying again.

BEAU: I got kicked out of my house.

HETTY: Two strikes. Three you're out.

BEAU: Oh. What the hell. I'll go find Bunky. I'm no longer scared of things through loving you, but I wouldn't say I'm sane.

(Exits. LOUD CRASH. LIGHTS blink off.)

ANNOUNCER: BILLYBOP. EVERYTHING'S GONE UNDER THE SWAMP.

(BUNKY enters, runs to KITTEN. Lights flutter on.)

HETTY: Bunky.

KITTEN: Son, are you all right?

BUNKY: I clung to a post. Because of that I'm alive. Better party.
(Takes a huge swallow from BEAU'S flask) I've got to have gratification now. I can't wait until I'm 21.

KITTEN: *(Calls to train)* Beau. Bunky's back.

HETTY: Everybody put your things up.

BEAU: *(Entering)* It's green outside. Smells like wet leaves.... the insides of leaves.

BUNKY: We're shaking. You feel that wind.

BEAU: Something's pounding against the wall.

HETTY: Everybody get on the floor.

BUNKY: *(Drinks)* I hope I can pass out so I don't cry.

HETTY: Crying's another word for praying. We come in screaming, alive with the spirit, and we go out a-screaming. . .

(LIGHTS flash on and off.)

KITTEN: What is that?

HETTY: On the battlefield, grown men cry out. "Jesus Christ."

KITTEN: Lantern's dead.

HETTY: "Protect my brother. Save my friend. God help me." Soldiers sing going into battle to lift themselves up. Being scared ain't nothing. Many scared souls devote their lives to saving others. You got to be willing to let go.

BUNKY: Awoo!

HETTY: To move on when your gig is up.

BEAU: Hetty, I apologize.

HETTY: For what?

BEAU: Being a wise guy. You help others. I'm sorry.

HETTY: Hold on to yourself, and you find the strength. You got the voice, the look, and the drive of a good fighter.

ANNOUNCER: HURRICANE JOSE BE TWISTING TOWARD PEARL RIVER. THIS IT, Y'ALL. HERE A LOVE SONG...

BEAU: Want to dance? It's a good song.

KITTEN: So?

BEAU: Have you noticed when most men get married, they never dance? Kitten, I only have one regret, I never married....

KITTEN: Ssh! Bunky's looking.

BEAU: I always wanted to, but there were so—

KITTEN: You've got a rip in your T shirt. I wish I had the right needle.

HETTY: Bunky, come back here and teach me real slow how to swim.

(THEY move to the side.)

BEAU: Every time I look at you, I think, would you marry me?

KITTEN: You're insane.

BEAU: Put on my ring, Kitten.

KITTEN: Kaitlin's my real name. The only reason you want to marry me is because we're about to drown.

BEAU: Admit you love me.

KITTEN: When Quint touched me, I imagined he was you. Your strong shoulders on top of me.

BEAU: And what else? We'll make up our own ceremony.

KITTEN: With the depot shaking and alligators slashing about.

BUNKY: Do what you need to do, Ma. We only got a little time.

HETTY: I've witnessed a lot worse.

KITTEN: You don't want to get married, Beau.

BEAU: God, yes.

KITTEN: You can't handle another wife.

HETTY: Would you give up your life for her?

BUNKY: Raise her children?

KITTEN: Put yourself second?

BUNKY: *(The floor shifts)* Ooh. My stomach's doing a free fall. You know that ride in a bucket when you drop off a side of a building?

BEAU: Bunky, be my best man.

HETTY: Marry her, quick.

BUNKY: Remember the first fencing lesson, Ma. Say, "Yes, I can."

BEAU: Repeat after me. I, Beau.

BEAU and KITTEN: I, Beau, I mean, I, Kaitlin, take you as my lawfully wedded spouse. For better for worse, in sickness and in health, till death do us part.

HETTY: I now pronounce you Husband and Wife.

(THEY kiss. Tranquility descends. HETTY and BUNKY clap wildly.)

BEAU: Oh, my God. We just got married. And you're pregnant.

BUNKY: What?

KITTEN: No. I'm not. I… said that…so you'd keep away.

BEAU: You're not having a—

KITTEN: I wouldn't take pills if I was.

BEAU: For a moment, Mrs. Ellis, let me feel your lips on mine.

(BUNKY and HETTY chuckle and stomp off.)

BUNKY: We're moving, and nothing's shaking.

HETTY: It ain't green no more.

KITTEN: Everything is so quiet.

BEAU: There's this softness in the air.

KITTEN: The sky's lightened to a pale blue.

ANNOUNCER: THIS JUST IN FOLKS...JOSE'S TWISTED PAST THE PEARL RIVER SWAMP AND IS HEADED FOR THE GULF.

BUNKY: That's it?

ANNOUNCER: DAMAGES COMING IN. ONE HUNDRED FIFTY-THREE PEOPLE DEAD.

(An awkward moment of silence. Lights down. Sometime later. Lights up. They hear a motor boat. HETTY and BUNKY cross to the window.)

HETTY: Mississippi police come when things over.

BEAU: I don't want to act rhapsodic, but I thought this was our swansong.

BUNKY: Swansong?

BEAU: "The hour, when the swan must fix his eye, upon a fading gleam, float out upon a long, last reach of glittering stream, and there sing his last song." Yeats. Going to leave academia, write a Southern Gothic novel set in Pearl River, Louisiana.

SOUND: *They hear a fog horn, the excited whistle and clamor of an approaching boat.*

KITTEN: Let's flag that boat.

HETTY: Look at those cards.

KITTEN: Blown every which way.

BUNKY: Hey Beau, an ace is flipped up.

(All exit except BEAU who crosses back for his recorder and speaks into it.)

BEAU: For several hours, in the Pearl River Swamp, we lived on the edge of hope—in a state of wishing. Wishing for one more minute, one more hour, one more day. Astonished that the expected act of breathing could be jeopardized. And those who have wished for life and won are blessed with a reprieve. A haunted legacy in which we savor our joy at being alive, grateful for a day that is simple once again, for familiar faces and the predictable routine. Aware that failure no longer matters because each moment lived is the winning ace.

CURTAIN

Photo: Christian Raby
Pictured: Linda Dileo, Michael Simpson

37

NEW ORLEANS COMEDIES

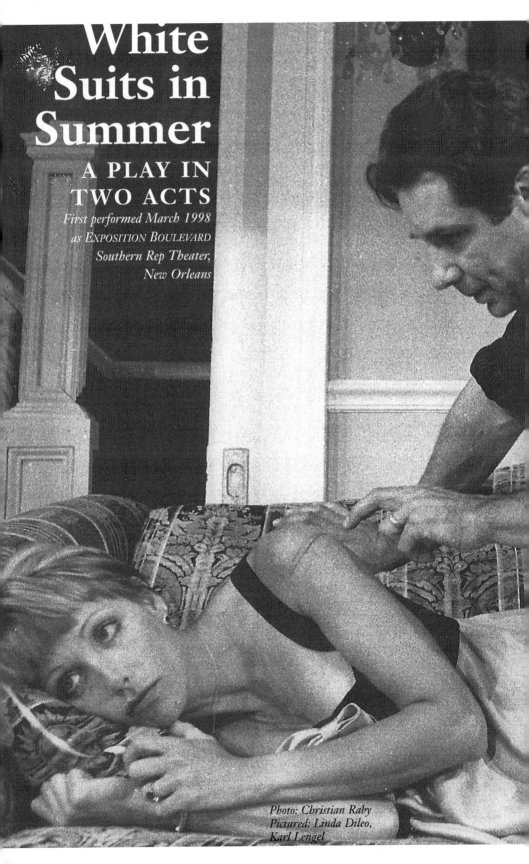

White Suits in Summer

A PLAY IN TWO ACTS

*First performed March 1998
as EXPOSITION BOULEVARD
Southern Rep Theater,
New Orleans*

*Photo: Christian Raby
Pictured: Linda Dileo,
Karl Lengel*

CAST OF CHARACTERS

BLAISE SALATICH, a handsome, out-of-work actor, 28

LUCILLE, his serious wife, an art critic, 38

SUSANNE DUPRÉ, his ex-lover, a famous painter, 28

TED CLAPPER, her frustrated manager, 26

OFFSTAGE VOICES of priests, nurse, and a cop

SETTING

A mansion on Exposition Boulevard, New Orleans. We are in a big, finely-proportioned parlor with a high ceiling, Orientals, a crystal chandelier. The atmosphere is that of a grand sanctuary, where the landowner can view Audubon Park as a superior. Floor-to-ceiling windows, sometimes used as entrances, open onto a gallery overlooking a wide lawn, which tumbles onto Audubon Park. During the daytime one has the feeling of a semi-tropical park, and at night of an oak garden, which climbs into the stars.

TIME

The present. Sunshine, already hard on the windows, fills the room with a sharp light.

ACT I
SCENE 1

(A summer day. Noon. The present. Several suitcases line the stage. LUCILLE, 38, runs onstage. SHE's very healthy with a mass of hair and deep-set hazel eyes. There is a curious blend of country carelessness and intelligence. Her husband, BLAISE, enters, buttoning his shirt. HE is handsome, about 28, but his carriage makes him appear older. HE is tall, long-limbed with a wide forehead, thick brown hair, and fine sensitive eyes. HE wears conservative dark clothes, obviously expensive, and HE wears them well. Harsh sunlight falls over the gallery as TED CLAPPER, in a rumpled white suit, approaches. HE checks back for fear his car will be towed. An effusive businessman, HE'S in his twenties, but his face looks older.)

TED: Anybody home? *(Crosses to BLAISE)* Teddy Clapper.

LUCILLE: Who?

TED: New Orleans Country Club? Southern Yacht Club? Now I'm managing Susanne Dupré.

LUCILLE: Susanne Dupré. *(Screams in delight)* Oh my. Oh God. Oh, no.

TED: *(Searches about)* My glasses broke. I've a second pair.

LUCILLE: I'll fix them. You know my husband. *(To herself)* Oh my God. Susanne Dupré.

BLAISE: Can I help you with something?

TED: Mom and I want you to host an exposition of Susanne Dupré.

LUCILLE: *(To BLAISE)* This is the miracle we've been waiting for.

TED: *(Looks out)* They're not giving me a ticket? I double-parked by a fire hydrant, then barged into the curb...

BLAISE: You should move your car.

TED: Like I said, we're looking for patrons to do an exposition of...

(Phone rings. TED searches for phone, gives up when ringing stops.)

TED: *(Cont.)* Mom might phone. I've rough car trips calling her. She fired the night watchman and bought me a phone. My mother is the sweetest, panicked person on earth. I advanced up to escort when Dad departed this world...

LUCILLE: I saw it in the obituaries.

TED: A show on Exposition Boulevard could be an important event. Susanne's a young legend.

LUCILLE: A practitioner of the—

TED: Nobler forms.

LUCILLE: Her show in Berlin left me—

TED: Ecstatic as did her show at the—

LUCILLE and TED together: Guggenheim in New York.

(TED'S cell phone rings. HE waves it off.)

TED: We'll ignore that. All Mom's friends are dying, so it's not great for her. Her two best friends died within weeks. What with her heart surgery and the cataracts...

(Phone stops ringing. HE searches for the scrapbook and pictures.)

TED: *(Cont.)* Mom made a scrapbook of your wedding. She keeps saying, "Why couldn't you've married Lucille?" *(To LUCILLE)* Every boy at Jesuit High School was in love with you.

BLAISE: *(To TED)* Thanks for the gift.

LUCILLE: *(to TED)* Your glasses fixed.

TED: Amazing. *(Phone rings, TED answers it)* Hello there. *(To BLAISE)* If I don't respond instantly, Mom calls the cops. *(Talks into the phone)* Yeah, Mom. I gave Lucille the clippings and the...no. *(To himself)* Where are those grapefruit spoons? *(Checks about; to LUCILLE)* Mom had them replated. *(To BLAISE)* My family's in fine jewelry and heirlooms. *(Into the phone)* I got them. *(Hangs up)*

LUCILLE: *(Peeking in the box)* Another priceless treasure from Uncle.

TED: Mom says ya'll have the finest art collection.

BLAISE: He gave it to the museum.

(Phone rings, but TED ignores it, looking for an outlet to recharge it.)

TED: If I'm gone long, she'll find me—hunt me down. My sister came for a month with her kids—wild, exhausting six, seven, and twelve-year-olds. After she left, it required weeks of down time to revive Mother.

LUCILLE: Wouldn't it be wonderful to have kids 'round the house?

TED: Little Lucilles and—

BLAISE: We're not having children yet.

LUCILLE: I didn't mean today.

TED: Where's that outlet?

BLAISE: With Uncle Gene's illness and—

LUCILLE: Blaise's goal is to become a great actor, get fame, start his own production company.

TED: *(Interrupting, to BLAISE)* Say, weren't you and Susanne schoolmates at—?

BLAISE: Berkeley.

TED: Right. I told Susanne a political edge would move her ahead faster. She started her triangle series in Berlin.

(BLAISE guides him to an outlet.)

LUCILLE: Splendid.

TED: I organized this smashing opening at the Mary Boon in New York. She constructed and deconstructed Naughty Marietta and the Casket Girls at the Whitney. *(TED'S phone rings)* Mom gets foggy and keeps calling. *(Speaks into the phone)* I'll pick you up for dinner.

(HE hangs up. The phone rings again. TED throws up his hands.)

TED: *(Cont.)* Each time, it's an earnest pitch—when can I expect you? Mom's got a housekeeper, a chauffeur, and a cook, but she's essentially alone. Eating out and her poodle, "Bootsy," are all that keep her going. Pardon me. *(Picks up the phone and talks to his Mom)* Yes, I gave them the— no, no. I'll do it. More gifts—certificates for silver frames for your wedding portrait and invitation, and for baby rattles, cups, brushes, diaper pins, cutlery, and dishes. All to be engraved later.

LUCILLE: How extravagant.

TED: We've tons of wedding and baby gifts—never bought or returned— and Mom wants you to have them all—in case something... She should never have had heart surgery of that magnitude. *(Into the phone)* Yes. She's got it. Goodbye, Mom. *(Hangs up the phone)* I handle Mom's expenses, the understatement of the year. Time's coming when I'll have to move in—

BLAISE: *(Checks his watch)* Excuse me.

TED: Wait. About the show—

LUCILLE: 'Course we'll sponsor it. We'll use the side gallery.

TED: Excellent.

LUCILLE: Uncle will contribute. I've got great ambitions for Blaise.

TED: Is that a meter maid out there? What?

LUCILLE: Don't leave.

TED: No, I thought you said... Three shapes of them are ticketing my car. Bat women from hell. *(To LUCILLE)* I'll be right back.

43

BLAISE: Take your time. I'm going for a smoke. (*Exits*)

(*Moments later. LUCILLE, high-strung, turns up a baby-minder, a ritual SHE deals with continually.*)

SOUND: UNCLE GENE, *moaning upstairs. LUCILLE speaks into the machine.*)

LUCILLE: Nurse? Can't you ease Uncle's pain?

NURSE. (*OFFSTAGE*): I've got a call in to the doctor.

(*SUSANNE, 28, enters quietly with her portfolio and paint box. SHE is dressed casually in seductive clothes. Hollows shadow her cheeks and her slender neck. There is a quality of nervous tension, the mental strain of an artist who puts unrelieved pressure on herself.*)

SUSANNE: Hi. I'm Susanne Dupré.

LUCILLE: Oh my. Oh my Lord. You're an absolutely brilliant artist. I'm Lucille, Blaise's wife.

SUSANNE: Hello. Ted sent me in.

LUCILLE: Anyone in love with painting admires your work. (*Looks about*) Where's Ted?

SUSANNE: Parking the car. Is this a bad time?

LUCILLE: Sorry—I'm in such a tether.

SUSANNE: I understand. My challenge is to discern reality.

LUCILLE: Ah. To paint things the way they truly are—

SUSANNE: Not through false glasses.

LUCILLE: New Orleans must be quite an interesting study when—

SUSANNE: Viewed as an outsider. (*Stares at her*) You're lovely. (*Overcome with disappointment*) I don't think I can exhibit here. It's too—fussy.

(*SUSANNE looks out, her face hot and sweating. Music floats in from the Cathedral. Isaiah 6: "Here I am, Lord. It is I, Lord? I have heard you calling in the night. I will go, Lord, if you lead me. I will hold your people in my heart."*)

LUCILLE: Choir practice from Holy Name Church. I can hear them even better from my classroom at Tulane.

SUSANNE: (*Avoiding LUCILLE'S face*) You teach?

LUCILLE: Art history. At Tulane.

SUSANNE: What a view. The sun sifting through Spanish moss. And the park dancing all around. I feel like I'm being reborn, nourished by Utopia. People would be calmer if they lived in beauty. Marvelous house.

LUCILLE: It's been in my family for generations.

SUSANNE: And will stay there.

LUCILLE: These houses are great 'cause they keep memory alive. (*Moaning through the baby-minder*) My uncle has cancer.

SUSANNE: Sorry.

LUCILLE: I use a baby-minder. It's sad.

SUSANNE: With a certain—

LUCILLE: If you need to buffer entropy, this is a good training ground.

SUSANNE: My presence feels inappropriate.

LUCILLE: I adored your Berlin exhibit. "How the Feminist and the Archetype Intersect."

SUSANNE: What did your husband think?

LUCILLE: Right. You met Blaise.

SUSANNE: Well?

LUCILLE: He framed my article comparing your painting to Beckett's drama. *(Hands SUSANNE the article.)*

SUSANNE: "Apocalyptic Isolation." Some title.

LUCILLE: You're a prodigy.

SUSANNE: People get noticed if they do something unusual and live in New York in their twenties.

LUCILLE: You're welcome to stay—

SUSANNE: There is motion here, but again—it's not the house I was hoping for.

LUCILLE: We could paint the walls, redo some lights.

SUSANNE: *(Shaking her head)* No.

LUCILLE: Blaise needs to meet people in the arts.

SUSANNE: It won't work.

LUCILLE: He wants to do leads in film and theater, the whole panoramic portrait.

SUSANNE: Not tiny parts, shards in the mosaic.

LUCILLE: We can create projects for you both from here.

SUSANNE: *(Picks up a large white album)* Your wedding album.

LUCILLE: There's Blaise kissing me at the altar, feeding me cake.

SUSANNE: You're still newlyweds. Love hasn't changed to respect.

(SUSANNE fidgets with a cigarette. TED enters.)

TED: I can't stay. I promised to take Mom to Antoine's.

LUCILLE: Don't worry. Susanne and I can discuss the exposition.

SUSANNE: If we have one.

TED: Don't mind her. *(Whispers to SUSANNE)* You'll do what I say.

SUSANNE: I don't know. *(To herself)* Change carries consequence.

TED: I'm off.

(LUCILLE ushers TED to the door. BLAISE enters from the park, brushes past SUSANNE, walks to get liquor.)

BLAISE: Oh, Susanne.

LUCILLE: Right. You knew each other. Kiss me, dear. *(He kisses her)* We're still honeymooning.

BLAISE: Excuse me. *(Leaving)*

LUCILLE: Don't be rude, darling. I need your input on the exposition.

SUSANNE: Maybe you shouldn't have it, just enjoy the park, and—

BLAISE: Can I get you a drink? Every Southern home has a recovery shelf. *(To SUSANNE)* A Bloody Mary?

SUSANNE: Perrier. Might as well drink water with class.

LUCILLE: You'll let us host you?

SUSANNE: Not sure. I feel mostly good about what Ted and I are doing— It's simply a desire for a real home—that the other galleries can't fulfill.

BLAISE: Maybe this need is invalid.

SUSANNE: I think not—

(BLAISE wipes his forehead, which has broken out in a sweat. LUCILLE chuckles in the embarrassed silence and passes condiments.)

LUCILLE: *(To SUSANNE)* Your use of triangles intrigues me. We must include "Shakti's Heart"—your triangle symbolizing the Hindu Goddess.

BLAISE: It's too Gauguin for me. Actually, that piece depresses me the least.

LUCILLE: Blaise!

BLAISE: *(To SUSANNE)* Weren't you supposed to search out dark, lugubrious triangles?

SUSANNE: The easy expositions are over, and the tough ones just begun.

LUCILLE: Showing here will not be as difficult as you think.

(BLAISE starts to exit.)

LUCILLE: *(Cont.)* You're not leaving? Relax, dear. This is for you.

BLAISE: I like to pace. If I sit, I might miss something.

LUCILLE: *(Clears her throat)* Tell us about your recent work.

SUSANNE: I've been correcting energy-draining behaviors.

LUCILLE: That affects your painting.

SUSANNE: And life.

LUCILLE: Your paintings are sharper.

SUSANNE: Painting is about paying attention in a Buddhist way.

BLAISE: That's hard to do.

SUSANNE: I slip into the skin of people I see—even if it hurts.

LUCILLE: You paint "fruitful blank spaces" which life fills in.

SUSANNE: When I smile...I'm thinking of something enticing.

LUCILLE: You're smiling now? Isn't she, honey?

SUSANNE: You can use art to heal, to face a part of yourself you hate.

LUCILLE: Go on!

SUSANNE: In my last triangle series, I saw myself in the colors and mended my ways.

LUCILLE: *(To SUSANNE)* How do you know when a painting is finished?

SUSANNE: *(To BLAISE)* When you love it.

(A moan through the baby-minder. A bell rings. LUCILLE rises to leave.)

LUCILLE: Uncle calls every five minutes.

BLAISE: Nurse is there.

LUCILLE: Yes, but he waits for me. *(To BLAISE)* Darling, get Susanne's press agent, mailing lists. Talk strategy.

SUSANNE: I don't know.

LUCILLE: We'll give you two an outrageous reception: jazz band, oysters etoufées, mint juleps.

SUSANNE: But does the world need another show?

LUCILLE: 'Course. Artists make dreams. *(To BLAISE)* Kiss, kiss, love bug.

(LUCILLE adjusts the baby-minder and flutters off. BLAISE gives SUSANNE a hard look.)

SUSANNE: Love bug.

BLAISE: When did you move to New Orleans?

SUSANNE: Before your wedding.

BLAISE: You came to our wedding?

SUSANNE: *(Removes a newspaper notice)* I sat in back of the church. Didn't make the reception.

SOUND: Doorbell rings.

MAID: (OFFSTAGE) The prescription. I've got it, Miss Lucille.
(BLAISE turns down the baby-minder.)

SUSANNE: Lucille is, like a mother... You think about California?

BLAISE: I recall lots of dead things. *(Starts to leave)*

SUSANNE: After your wedding, I slept all day. I felt like a part of me was melting—

BLAISE: Now you've seen me and I've seen you.

SUSANNE: Why did you move here? For the?

BLAISE: Restaurants—You can be a starving artist in your teens, but in your twenties you like to dine out occasionally.

SUSANNE: When I started painting, I didn't worry about sales.

BLAISE: As long as you work for your soul, it's great.

SUSANNE: Sometimes I can't—sleep.

BLAISE: You need to—

SUSANNE: I'm not taking pills or fooling around.

(LUCILLE enters with mail to get a bottle of gin.)

LUCILLE: The mail came.

BLAISE: My headshots!

LUCILLE: Why send them? Soon, we'll produce you here. Money's the crucial factor.

SUSANNE: And talent.

LUCILLE: Persistence. I won't let Blaise fail. *(Pause)* Uncle wants a Ramos

Gin Fizz made of orange flower, water, and gin.

BLAISE: I'll get it.

LUCILLE: *(Checks the baby-minder)* You plan which paintings to hang. *(Moaning through the baby-minder; she starts to go)* Everything's an argument with Uncle. Is there any nutritional value in gin?

SUSANNE: *(To BLAISE)* Joy and celebration.

LUCILLE: Mm. I can hardly get one job done when something hits me. *(Kisses him boldly)*

BLAISE: I should help you.

LUCILLE: Give me a kiss, pumpkin. A bear kiss. *(Pause—Exits)*

(A breeze rises. BLAISE gazes at SUSANNE so the light from the great porch lanterns catches her face with streaks of brightness. Distant thunder. The gallery is blanketed with a golden coppery light. A hymn floats from the Cathedral: "On Eagle's Wings." "And he will raise you up on eagle's wings. And hold you in the palm of his hand.")

SUSANNE: *(Sings)* "And he will raise you up. And he will raise you up. And he will raise you up...on the last day." I love rain on an unexpected day. Every pore opens to the wind.

BLAISE: Nice.

SUSANNE: That's what I remember about New Orleans. The music—and the rain.

BLAISE: I don't have time for this.

SOUND: Thunder.

SUSANNE: There's a sense of romance about the rain. The sun is around us, but the rain is within us. *(Removes her sketchbook, draws)* When I got here, the rain seized me. Mind if I draw you?

(SHE moves closer, drawing him. Footsteps inside. BLAISE calls out.)

BLAISE: Who's there?

SUSANNE: I'm putting you in a triangle—

BLAISE: Lucille? (Picks up a book.)

SUSANNE: Using weightlessness to let your image soar.

BLAISE: Five minutes is all.

SUSANNE: You've a wonderful body.

(With a flickering smile, BLAISE clutches his book like a Bible.)

BLAISE: I read one self-help book a week—

SUSANNE: Dressed or undressed—

BLAISE: The Greatest Salesman Alive, takes a year to finish 'cause it's—

SUSANNE: Self-hypnosis.

BLAISE: You read one chapter three times a day for a month.

SUSANNE: What contacts do you have here?

BLAISE: None. I'm competitive with people.

SUSANNE: Hold that pose.

BLAISE: I forget how I'm supposed to behave.

(BLAISE gives SUSANNE a hard, silencing look.)

SUSANNE: When I saw you in "Hamlet", you defined the word, star.

(SHE takes out his picture as Hamlet. LUCILLE hurries onstage.)

LUCILLE: We've lovely watercress sandwiches and crab soup. Give me a kiss. (LUCILLE kisses him) Oh Lord. She's painting here.

ROSARY HARTEL O'NEILL

BLAISE: Stay and watch.

LUCILLE: Ooh. Uncle won't eat 'less I join him.

BLAISE: *(To LUCILLE)* I'm tired. Let's go nap.

SUSANNE: I should let you two alone.

LUCILLE: Don't be silly. Uncle cries out for attention. His paper is damp. His milk is warm. There's dust on the floor. The new maid is lazy. She barely came in the month we were gone. Then I've got to prepare the shopping list.

BLAISE: Let me help you.

LUCILLE: No. Sit for Susanne. You know how Uncle treats the maid when I'm not there.

(LUCILLE buzzes off. BLAISE follows uneasily, stands in the doorway as the night turns black. SUSANNE toys with a palette knife. Seeing it, BLAISE trembles. SUSANNE speaks maliciously.)

SUSANNE: You've broken out in a sweat.

BLAISE: New Orleans is melting me.

SUSANNE: How long have you been unemployed? Eight months?

BLAISE: Warm.

SUSANNE: Nine?

BLAISE: Warmer.

SUSANNE: A year? Two?

BLAISE: "Regret not the glitter of any lost day." Tennessee Williams.

SUSANNE: What happened in Hollywood?

BLAISE: Nothing.

SUSANNE: You told Lucille you'd talk—

BLAISE: I thought I'd make a bundle.

SUSANNE: Doing what?

BLAISE: Selling chunks of my soul at varying intervals.

SUSANNE: Did you?

BLAISE: I auditioned weekly for months.

SUSANNE: That's a lot of no's.

BLAISE: I was holding on for the word, yes—

SUSANNE: *(Slyly)* To lose yourself in the play?

BLAISE: Right.

SUSANNE: You went to interviews with producers?

BLAISE: Yes.

SUSANNE: Casting directors?

BLAISE: So.

SUSANNE: Ah, Blaise Salatich. You've played all these parts blah-blah-blah.

BLAISE: Exactly.

SUSANNE: Finally, a director of a major picture hires you and he gets fired!

BLAISE: Who told you that?

SUSANNE: Did you go back to the old ways?

BLAISE: No.

ROSARY HARTEL O'NEILL

SUSANNE: Numbing yourself with—?

BLAISE: No. I wanted to, by God.

SUSANNE: But you didn't.

BLAISE: I kept busy, worked out. Ran.

(HE feels for a cigarette. SHE takes it out for him.)

SUSANNE: You didn't slip once after so many months?

BLAISE: Never.

SUSANNE: So you auditioned for special parts.

BLAISE: Right.

SUSANNE: You were a hand model? A parts model? What?

BLAISE: Soft porn is what they call it. So.

SUSANNE: What happened on your last audition?

BLAISE: Producer arrives in this enormous barrel-like hat.

SUSANNE: He asked you to his hotel room.

BLAISE: Devouring pistachio nuts, telling me his tale of woe.

(SHE hands him a drink.)

BLAISE: *(cont.)* Asks me to sit on the bed and unbutton my shirt... This can't be happening, I thought. I was anxious, but it was a lead. "I'd like to cast you," he said. So, I took off my shirt. He stared till my ears got hot. This can't be happening, I thought. He made me lie on the bed. Then he undid my belt and unzipped my pants. This can't be happening. I backed off. There was this screaming, this hotness. He came at me with a knife. Blood everywhere, drenching his shirt, pants, the floor. Looked like he was coming at himself with the knife.

SUSANNE: He died.

BLAISE: I'm trashed in California.

(*SUSANNE adds ice to his drink.*)

SOUND: *The song, "Here I am, Lord" is heard from the church.*

LUCILLE: (*Entering*) Uncle wants ice chips for his drink. Your sketch is rapturous. (*Looking at SUSANNE'S drawing*)

BLAISE: (*to LUCILLE*) Stay, sweetheart.

LUCILLE: Did Susanne agree to—

SUSANNE: I do!

LUCILLE: Glorious.

(*LUCILLE exits.*)

SUSANNE: You have an agent here?

BLAISE: She calls herself one. The only help I ever got was from other artists. They taught me how to face guerilla warfare, to be outspoken, aggressive.

SUSANNE: You can't be an artist unless you plunge ahead. Courage brings peace. Dream big. Fight back. Nirvana awaits. When you march forward, you stand up for the weak, the old, the silenced poets of the world.

SOUND: *A car horn toots.*

(*SUSANNE starts, and crosses to BLAISE.*)

SUSANNE: (*Cont.*) I have to go. Ted gets impatient.

BLAISE: I've missed you.

(*BLAISE smiles sadly. The car toots again. SUSANNE hurries out. LUCILLE enters with a folder.*)

LUCILLE: Good news. Uncle's financing the exposition.

BLAISE: *(Sarcastically)* Victory is ours.

LUCILLE: Ours? Did you drink all this gin?

BLAISE: It's a negotiable indulgence. *(Hands her an envelope)*

LUCILLE: Oh dear.

BLAISE: Why does Uncle send us business letters? You talk all day.

LUCILLE: He's a Soniat. Soon as they have an opinion, it becomes a legal document.

BLAISE: Throw it away.

LUCILLE: Wait, it's a lien on this house. He didn't mention—

BLAISE: He was annoyed, you said—

LUCILLE: With your career and our stay abroad.

BLAISE: But he gave us the house.

LUCILLE: Before he did—he took out a mortgage—

BLAISE: "You don't have to be rich," he said, "when your relatives are rich."

LUCILLE: To pay some of his insurance.

SOUND: Doorbell rings.

NURSE: *(OFFSTAGE)* Good evening.

MALE VOICE #1: *(OFFSTAGE)* Patient's sleeping.

LUCILLE: Dominicans slinking about...badmouthing you to Uncle.

(LUCILLE fixes the baby-minder.)

MALE VOICE #2: *(OFFSTAGE)* We brought pictures of the baptistery.

LUCILLE: They snuck this folder by his foodtray.

(LUCILLE hands a folder to BLAISE.)

BLAISE: A last will and testament—

LUCILLE: They're promising Uncle Heaven.

BLAISE: He believes these hypocrites.

LUCILLE: He keeps asking for you.

BLAISE: You swore when I said he could live upstairs—

LUCILLE: Would it hurt to have a conversation?

BLAISE: I'm not going to be two-faced.

LUCILLE: Uncle's slipping.

BLAISE: Live in tight-assed denial.

LUCILLE: He says you married me for money, that acting is a profession for—

BLAISE: For parasites? He thinks if I can't get a TV show, I should quit. Everyone wants to see a play for nothing. They expect you to rehearse on your own time, at midnight, when you're depleted, or at 4:00 a.m. before you go to your real job. Find some way an institution can make money off you. Then we have crappy actors, working for free and alienating a dwindling public.

LUCILLE: Can't you say you're also interested in sales?

BLAISE: I'm not getting in that pot. The last man who got in there got eaten.

(Laughs, but SHE doesn't join in. HIS phone rings. HE doesn't answer.)

LUCILLE: Uncle thinks you're narcissistic. Well, you do, do for yourself.

BLAISE: What in God's name are you talking about!

LUCILLE: I'm just asking you to visit.

BLAISE: He doesn't respect me.

LUCILLE: You know he...he's...sick. That's why he's irritable, and can't be with you more than five minutes. I love him. I remember how he was when I was a little girl. I can't think of life without— He's not himself, now he's dying.

BLAISE: Are we sure? God!

LUCILLE: The doctor phoned about the living will. Lord, I can't take it. Poke your head in the door.

(SHE exits. BLAISE gazes after HER, breathes deeply. We hear wind from a summer rainstorm, sweeping over the park. HE picks up the book, and goes inside. Lights fade.)

ACT I
SCENE 2

(The gallery gleams with wetness from a rain. Pink, purple, and blue colors shadow the decor. Dance-hall music plays from the stereo. BLAISE is rehearsing a dance sequence for an audition and talking on the phone. SUSANNE appears, dressed in an exotic gown. HE hangs up.)

BLAISE: My wife's not home. *(She smiles)* Don't you have an opening?

(He wipes his face, swallows water. SUSANNE strolls over and drinks from his glass.)

SUSANNE: How are you newlyweds making out?

BLAISE: *(Walks out on the veranda)* Most of the guys I grew up with are still here. Sundays you'll see them running behind baby carriages in the park. Weekdays the wives race-walk and—

SUSANNE: Recount their husbands' infidelities?

BLAISE: *(Observes her with a flickering smile)* My therapy is not to pursue a sexy woman one day at a time, and to spend time with other recovering husbands and not talk about it. Ha.

(HE resumes practicing a step. SHE watches him, her eyes moist.)

SUSANNE: Your hair's fallen over your face. Let me get it.

BLAISE: Don't. Moses came from the mountain and said, "I bear good news and bad news. The good news is I got him down to ten. The bad news is adultery is still in."

SUSANNE: That's in the Far East. If you accept a second-rate provincial marriage in the South, it's a sort of burial.

SOUND: *Dance music swells from the stereo.*

SUSANNE: *(Cont.)* Dance with me. Please. The assumption we'll start with is we're not finished.

BLAISE: My wife will be here—

SUSANNE: Let me enjoy you for a moment—arm's length at a safe distance. *(Her eyes dart up and down his body. SHE lifts his arms, laughing, stretches them around her, her head near his. SHE cradles his face. HE freezes momentarily, like a deer sensing hunters.)*

BLAISE: Shame upon you, Susanne.

SUSANNE: Undo that button.

BLAISE: Remove your hand.

SUSANNE: I love this shirt. Before you, I knew a kiss was something you did with your mouth, but I didn't know what it was.

BLAISE: Stop.

SUSANNE: Lucille couldn't be a good lay—her housecoat is so aesthetically offensive.

BLAISE: Quiet!

SUSANNE: Don't walk away. If you're going to say something, say it to my face.

BLAISE: I've changed.

SUSANNE: You haven't.

BLAISE: I don't require madness, any serious addiction.

SUSANNE: I've been dreaming of you—

BLAISE: The best way to remember something is to forget it.

SUSANNE: You're teasing me.

BLAISE: You know me better.

SUSANNE: I know how you felt me in the dark. I saw your face when you walked down the aisle. You loved me then and you do now.

BLAISE: That's a strange thing to say—

SUSANNE: I've dreamt of you since you married. I have a sixth sense and your thoughts have flown to me.

BLAISE: Get away.

SUSANNE: I can't wait for dreaming. Now you tell me to tear your memory from my eyes? I can't.

LIGHTS: *The veranda lights blink on.*

Suddenly SUSANNE is all nerves and sobs. SHE buries her head in his shoulder.

BLAISE: Shh, go over there.

SUSANNE: Terrible night. Dark, moon yellow and slippery.

(LUCILLE pounds on the door.)

LUCILLE: *(OFFSTAGE)* Blaise! Honey? Help me with these bags!

(SUSANNE rushes off. LUCILLE stumbles in, puts down the laundry.)

BLAISE: That was Susanne. Inviting us for champagne after her show.

LUCILLE: I don't think I can make it.

BLAISE: You look exhausted.

LUCILLE: Uncle's no use for these clothes since he's never—

BLAISE: *(Rubbing her shoulders)* Don't exaggerate.

LUCILLE: Getting out of bed. Still he insists I run by the cleaners…Uncle wants me to pick out his burial suit and store it in a plastic box.

BLAISE: Close your eyes.

LUCILLE: All his shirts are yellowed—

BLAISE: Wearing you out with errands—

LUCILLE: He demands we fire Nurse.

BLAISE: When he could hire a driver. Has he mentioned the mortgage?

LUCILLE: He makes me read him the headlines, check his stocks.

BLAISE: Explain why we're paying off his personal loan.

LUCILLE: I can't bring the subject up.

BLAISE: You shouldn't have to.

LUCILLE: We'll have to economize while I get him to replenish my accounts. It's scary watching him fail. He gets mad when I say you're unemployed. And when I say Aunt's dead, he screams, "Nobody told me."

BLAISE: His body is shutting down, for God's sake.

LUCILLE: I know he's dying. Lord, I saw the diapers. Go see him.

BLAISE: I can't tell him what he wants to hear.

LUCILLE: He'll be ruthless if you don't comply.

BLAISE: Here's money for the note.

LUCILLE: You pawned your wedding ring? You said you would never!

BLAISE: I'll get it back... Summer stock theaters are auditioning. I've been getting calls.

LUCILLE: You promised we could live here. I can't go off to God knows where. Leave Uncle. Don't be selfish. Next spring is time enough to start all that.

(BLAISE storms out. LUCILLE follows.)

(The coach lights on the gallery cast a weird glow. SUSANNE returns, disheveled. TED, in a smart white suit, follows, calling "Susanne.")

TED: Some Latino festival's in the Quarter. I could barely get uptown.

SUSANNE: We don't need the obligatory traffic update.

TED: You look like a leftover from Saturday night. Fix up.

SUSANNE: I'm dressed.

TED: You been drinking again?

SUSANNE: I deal with sponsors best when I'm manic.

TED: I leave you, and you have to get drunk. Sixteen hundred is a lot to sink into a one-time dress.

SUSANNE: I'm trying to figure out—

TED: Comb your hair.

SUSANNE: If I've ever made a fool of myself—

TED: Change that lipstick.

SUSANNE: With these people in the past.

TED: Here's your makeup and purse.

SUSANNE: I'm not carrying this "going to the dance" bag.

TED: Stuart's coming. You needn't cultivate him if he's cold. *(TED'S cell phone rings)* But whatever's nice about him, I want you to find it. He never risks sweating. Soon as May ends, he's off to Newport.

(SUSANNE exits.)

TED: *(Answers phone)* Ma. I know about the festival. Don't mention that horror again. Susanne goes out of her way to make things difficult...she's not a nymphomaniac. *(Hangs up, paces; we hear a crash offstage)* Susanne!

SUSANNE: *(OFFSTAGE)* I'm okay.

TED: *(Calls to SUSANNE)* Hurry up. It's your big show!

(BLAISE enters in a white jacket with drinks. TED confronts him.)

TED: *(Cont.)* It might be bearable if someone wasn't screwing up her mind. Mother heard you were… I'm beginning to understand those red-eye bus trips. The nights Susanne would cry all the way till morning.

BLAISE: Have a martini.

TED: *(Slaps it off)* What! No! I don't want a shitty drink. I helped her break through her perfectionism… I got her to paint even when she was drinking and walking the floor… And she would still be painting if…

(LUCILLE enters, dressed in a long gown and carrying a soup tureen.)

LUCILLE: Turtle soup from the country club.

BLAISE: We're famished.

LUCILLE: Oh Lord. I'm so thrilled about seeing Susanne's show with Susanne.

TED: Y'all go eat. *(Calls)* Susanne! Soup's hot. *(To LUCILLE)* That's what I've been missing—

LUCILLE: Indulgence.

(SUSANNE enters. BLAISE looks at her with entrancement. TED inspects her to make sure she's dressed properly.)

SUSANNE: I can't eat. Thinking of those turtles without their shells—

BLAISE: You look like you just arrived from New York.

TED: Is that's a compliment?

SUSANNE: I like to dress up fancy. Leave the Poor Clare nun for the designer dress. *(To BLAISE)* Ted's my motivation.

BLAISE: I wouldn't have thought you needed motivation.

SUSANNE: You've an air of heightened Edwardian elegance.

BLAISE: It's my look.

SUSANNE: Well, it's working.

TED: Honey, put this napkin on. Last time you spilled—

SUSANNE: I'm not wearing a bib.

BLAISE: Please.

SUSANNE: *(To BLAISE)* You must be thirsty?

BLAISE: Especially for a good sherry.

(BLAISE pours sherry in his soup.)

TED: Water for me.

SUSANNE: I'll have a drink of water with my two friends.

TED: You only have two friends?

BLAISE: Some people don't have any.

SUSANNE: Blaise likes my humor when I'm half-crazed with exhaustion.

BLAISE: Ted. You needn't have worried about Susanne's drinking.

(SUSANNE drops her eyes onto the sherry as if she'll drink it, but SHE only sniffs it with distaste.)

SUSANNE: I can't believe you didn't trust me.

TED: Well, your mind was wandering, and you were brushing your teeth a lot.

SUSANNE: You imagined I...

ROSARY HARTEL O'NEILL

TED: Was taking these big slugs before I could get to you.

SUSANNE: I'm going for a walk. Give me my cape.

TED: I'll accompany you.

SUSANNE: I don't need a Mother. I'm about to scream—

TED: You can't go in the park. All dolled up with that jewelry.

SUSANNE: Don't touch me.

TED: Someone will kill you. Leave your purse.

LUCILLE: Your show's in an hour!

(SUSANNE *leaves,* BLAISE *picks up a cigarette, follows her. Uneasy,* LUCILLE *arranges the table, watching* TED, *who eats nervously and glances out at the two.*)

LUCILLE: *(Cont.)* Pearl-handled spoons, smooth from years of eating pleasure. How could one be grumpy with such a spoon?

TED: I couldn't.

LUCILLE: My aunt had a service for sixty in this pattern. See?

TED: An acorn's chiseled at the neck.

LUCILLE: She used to count silver after every party...demitasse teaspoons, tablespoons, soup spoons, serving spoons, grapefruit spoons... You're not listening.

TED: I am. I'm just—of course I hear you.

LUCILLE: My aunt had a special drawer for her spoons...she took...

TED: Let me help. You shouldn't have to pick up alone.

LIGHT: *Lights fade.*

ACT I
SCENE 3

(7:00 the next morning. Steamy hot. The sun bathes the scene in gold light, intensified by the dampness. Blaise, in a crumpled white jacket, has been fitfully dozing. Looks at his watch. Grabs a journal, pen, writes.)

BLAISE: I must be vigilant. Stay honest. *(Writes some more)* Better to hammer stone in a quarry like Howard Roark than to sell my soul to the parasites. *(Phone rings, BLAISE answers it)* Hello...You want to buy a...No. Susanne has not come back.

(BLAISE hangs up. TED rushes in, his suit rumpled.)

TED: Is that...Susanne?

BLAISE: The phone is a terrible invention that allows people to enter your home without being invited. Your mother.

TED: How could Susanne run off?

BLAISE: I phoned the hospitals.

TED: She's a manic-depressive. Takes four pills a day.

BLAISE: I can't spend my day worrying.

TED: I'm not sure you worry about anyone but yourself... Susanne used to be an addict, smoking pot, sniffing coke; she was an alcoholic...

BLAISE: Coffee?

TED: I never drink coffee in the morning. It keeps me awake.

(BLAISE pours two jiggers. Hands one to TED.)

TED: *(Cont.)* I've no control over her.

BLAISE: You've more control than anyone else.

TED: I think it's going to come to me—how to deal with her—if I keep

ROSARY HARTEL O'NEILL

running my mouth. God knows what it's doing to my system. I'll probably give birth to six ulcers. *(Phone rings, TED answers it)* Hello, Ma. No, she's not back yet... No one's called. I'm not rude... Look, I can't talk. I said good-bye. Mom. *(Pretends he's talking to someone else)* I'm coming. *(Speaks into the phone)* I'll call you. *(Hangs up the phone, picks up Blaise's journal)* What's this? Private concerns—

BLAISE: *(Grabs the book)* How bad off was she?

TED: The others stopped drinking about eleven. They were drunk, and didn't want to get drunker. *(Checks his watch)* At one, she took her paintings and disappeared.

BLAISE: You can't handcuff yourself to her.

TED: Her life's blood's in that show, and the assassins are sharpening their knives.

BLAISE: I told her if you're going to invite critics, at least have ones who like you.

SOUND: *Cell phone rings.*

(TED answers and speaks into it.)

TED: Mom?... I can't talk. No. I can barely hear you... God, what! I'll call back when I get privacy.

(TED hangs up, exits. BLAISE crosses to the liquor tray, pours bourbon in his coffee. Picks up a cigarette and walks to the gallery, returns and sits by the phone. LUCILLE arrives, lugging a portfolio. SHE switches up the baby-minder. We hear a moaning. SHE turns, her eyes strange, unblinking, taking in BLAISE.)

LUCILLE: After church, the Holy Spirit inspired me. I drove by the Quarter. You won't believe it...I found Susanne's paintings.

BLAISE: Where?

LUCILLE: Literally on the pavement. The manager said Susanne drank herself into a stupor. He took her incapacitated body out of the bar— *(Lifts paintings)* Look. It's her new triangle series.

(UNCLE *moans through the baby-minder. LUCILLE looks up, nervous. BLAISE puts away the portfolio.*)

BLAISE: I'll take these till later.

NURSE: *(OFFSTAGE)* It's Nurse. Your uncle's having difficulty breathing. I've called an ambulance.

LUCILLE: Oh God. We can't take him to...

NURSE: *(OFFSTAGE)* Doctor wants him at the hospital.

LUCILLE: Yesterday he was his impish self. *(Laughs nervously)*

NURSE: *(OFFSTAGE)* He needs you.

LUCILLE: Where's the holy water? And those relics? I keep thinking if he doesn't go to the hospital, he won't die.

(*LUCILLE exits. Squad car sirens blare. BLAISE hides the paintings. Flashing lights brighten the gallery. There are scrambling sounds outside, car doors slamming.*)

LUCILLE: *(OFFSTAGE)* What's that?

BLAISE: A police car.

TED: *(Rushing on)* Was I parked in the wrong zone?

(*SUSANNE traipses in, barefoot, with a rumpled newspaper. Her sequined gown is ripped, her hair messed, her eyes glazed. A cape flung over her keeps falling off.*)

COP'S VOICE: *(BLARES OFFSTAGE)* I'm on a twenty-one flag-down with a nineteen. Took her from the VCD to the Second District.

TED: Who was that?

SUSANNE: The city's most prominent policeman. He teaches sailing at the Southern Yacht Club, where he and his family are members. He doesn't put the people he arrests in the police report; they go on the society page.

TED: Let me get that cape. There's blood in your hair. A cut on your shoulder.

SUSANNE: I always dress wrong.

TED: *(Exiting)* I'll get something to wash you up.

SUSANNE: *(Looks at her corsage)* My flowers are wilted. They were happy earlier, but now they're grieving. Throw them out. *(Yanks off petals and mumbles)* He loves me. He loves me not. He loves me—

BLAISE: Not.

SUSANNE: I don't listen to the words.

BLAISE: I'd like to start my day not talking to you. So the first hours aren't spoilt–

SUSANNE: Sorry. I was trying to be successful; partially to impress you and partially to get your sympathy if that didn't work out. I'm going to ask for what I want, as soon as I figure out what that is—

BLAISE: Cigarette, maybe?

(BLAISE passes one to her. SHE bursts out sobbing.)

SUSANNE: The trouble with past relationships is they're endless.

BLAISE: Have a smoke?

SUSANNE: I'm holding out for as long as I can. I've stopped, but I don't know if I've quit. *(Laughs, holds her forehead)* Oh, my head.

BLAISE: Let me close these blinds. You don't have to kill yourself. Sleep.

SOUND: *Choir practice from Holy Name Church resounds the hymn, "I danced in the morning when the world was begun, And I danced in the moon and the stars and the sun. And I came down from heaven and I danced on earth at Bethlehem."*

(SHE pulls him down on her. THEY kiss.)

END OF ACT I

ACT II
SCENE 1

(Parlor. BLAISE leans over and kisses SUSANNE, who looks bruised and delicate. TED enters. HE and BLAISE wear the same crumpled white suits from before.)

TED: *(To BLAISE)* You used to be lovers.

BLAISE: Says who?

TED: Mother. She did some research. You're tormenting Susanne.

BLAISE: Please!

TED: She can't be creative around you.

SUSANNE: It's okay, Ted.

TED: No, it's not. You were on the verge of greatness—. Now look at you. Walking around comatose. Remembering Blaise's comments, and saying your talent's lost. What's he doing to you?

BLAISE: Have you forgotten I'm married?

TED: I haven't forgotten your lovely wife, but evidently you have. *(Yelling offstage)* WHY DON'T YOU GO TO YOUR WIFE?

BLAISE: Fine.

(Exits. TED goes to the bar, seizes a drink.)

TED: What happened after you left the party?

SUSANNE: I was drinking in the Napoleon House. I think I was drinking there. I hope I was—there. Ha!

TED: And afterwards?

SUSANNE: They say I got in a brawl over some Mardi Gras beads, was beat up. There's this huge gash on my shoulder.

TED: What do you remember?

SUSANNE: Not much. I forgot my shoes.

TED: *(Alarmed)* And your paintings?

SUSANNE: I left them...someplace.

TED: Try to recall where.

SUSANNE: Wait...wait...no...nothing. It's over.

TED: Think now.

SUSANNE: The exposition of Susanne Dupré.

TED: Think hard!

SUSANNE: I don't want to—

TED: Why not?

SUSANNE: These aren't my people in the stiff suits and straight chairs.

TED: WHAT SHOULD I MAKE OF THAT CRACK?

SUSANNE: I thought I'd be happy seeing the...applause.

TED: AND YOU WERE!

SUSANNE: How do I hold on to reality? When can I paint?

TED: Let's find the paintings you lost.

SUSANNE: People say talk about yourself, paint later.

TED: I come from a line of Southerners with modest talent.

SUSANNE: Oh, please!

TED: I wanted to lift you to world class. You've ten shows this month.

SUSANNE: Cancel them.

TED: You've spent the money. You know the work it took to get those? You're going to drop your schedule? Become a floating artist? Why are you the talk of the art scene? Because you've got me pushing you and panting ten steps behind. God. I should have seen the narcissist you are. Always sending me to do one more thing. I'm disgusted. You want to cancel things? Fine. Where's my coat? Remember the revenue of the art business is the same as sausage.

SUSANNE: (Calls after) You don't mind what mediocrity I paint, long as you can sell it.

(TED exits. Doorbell rings. Offstage, we hear Nurse answer and priests enter, whispering and fawning.)

(BLAISE enters. SUSANNE undoes her blouse, exposing a shoulder wound. There is a startling change in BLAISE'S manner. HE crosses cautiously to her.)

SUSANNE: (Cont.) Would you...fix this...bandage?

BLAISE: You're scary.

SUSANNE: It looks more theatrical than it is. (Gestures to the newspaper) You saw the review in the Times?

BLAISE: You remember that book that says you have to pass through stages to evolve? That critic hasn't passed through stage one.

SUSANNE: Take a look.

(SHE hands him the paper. BLAISE turns on a silk lamp and reads. A flicker of light, narrow and intense, streams down. Church bells chime seven o'clock.)

BLAISE: Nasty.

SUSANNE: I'm so embarrassed.

BLAISE: Does he have some vendetta against you?

SUSANNE: I have to stop reading these notices.

ROSARY HARTEL O'NEILL

BLAISE: "The event was very organized," he says. "Thank God. I'd hate to think it meant something."

SUSANNE: My flesh crawls when I hear that voice coming through the pages.

BLAISE: Never listen to those who demean your gift.

SUSANNE: I felt the slaughter coming—

BLAISE: Their motive is envy always.

SUSANNE: It happens every now and then, but I was hoping for then and not now.

BLAISE: Art's a bleak world—

SUSANNE: I shouldn't let it hurt me.

BLAISE: You're human—

SUSANNE: Chaotic moments come but... Sometimes I just feel wounded.

BLAISE: Everyone has a broken heart. Everyone has suffered or will suffer incredible loss. Don't budge. Don't bow. You don't have to hide and lick your wounds like the youthful Cezanne.

SUSANNE: I hated those paintings. I had sessions with Ted, went away—

BLAISE: Monet refused to show his water lilies—

SUSANNE: And came back with something that'd deteriorated.

BLAISE: Faberge told his artists to dream of golden castles.

SUSANNE: I've been dreaming about you—of how hard these months have been—

BLAISE: (His voice drops) They were tough on everybody.

SUSANNE: Lucille's made a big splash in the papers.

(BLAISE takes out a cigarette, tosses it aside.)

BLAISE: You're not going to force me to do something, not in my best interest—

SUSANNE: You like it with her?

BLAISE: Lucille is kind, reliable. She won't run off with—

SUSANNE: You've anesthetized yourself?

BLAISE: I'm going to be working in my own theater business.

SUSANNE: Where?

BLAISE: Summer stock theaters are starting up.

SUSANNE: There's none here.

BLAISE: We'll open one. I'll do it slower than you'd want me to. Time line, one to two years to get running. In my later years I'd like to be back in New York.

SUSANNE: Where do we fit...together?

BLAISE: You're doing what you need to for your career, and you're making progress.

SUSANNE: Not true.

SOUND: The morning angelus chimes from Holy Name Church. Sunlight glows over the park.

BLAISE: I wish you well. I do, I mean it.

SUSANNE: You can't expect me to hang around—watching you two—

BLAISE: It's a marriage blanc—

SUSANNE: Night after night—

BLAISE: A sexless marriage— *(Retrieves the paintings and turns to her with pleading eyes)* Lucille found your sketches—slightly damaged.

SUSANNE: I don't care about the paintings, strangely—

BLAISE: You can repair them. Throw yourself into—

SUSANNE: Burn them. I don't want to paint now.

BLAISE: 'Course you do.

SUSANNE: Are you keeping them to torture me?

BLAISE: Calm down.

SUSANNE: No! Ted never could see why some art had to be destroyed. *(Lighting a match)*

BLAISE: They're not your best work. True.

SUSANNE: I spent seven months making paintings I despised. I created monsters, and I want them killed!

(SHE thrusts sketches into the fireplace.)

BLAISE: God. Don't do that.

SUSANNE: I didn't want to hang this. Ted tore it out my hands.

BLAISE: Stop shouting.

SUSANNE: The painting is a shroud, and nothing happens till—

BLAISE: Enough!

SUSANNE: The spirit returns, and the painter gets back inside. I hate them! Hate! Hate! *(Sobs)* Can't you...

BLAISE: Okay, Susanne.

SUSANNE: Burn the paintings for me?

(BLAISE downs liquor. Takes a match to the fireplace.)

BLAISE: There. I'm burning—

SUSANNE: We're burning them!

BLAISE: Right. We're doing it.

SUSANNE: Oh yes. Yes. Now people can remember me like I was.

(Ambulance sirens come louder and louder. SUSANNE runs out. TED rushes on stage, followed by LUCILLE.)

TED: That's the ambulance.

BLAISE: *(Crossing down and looking out)* It's here.

LUCILLE: Oh God, it's time.

NURSE: *(OFFSTAGE)* Make way, everyone.

MALE VOICE #1: *(OFFSTAGE)* We're coming through. COMING THROUGH.

ACT II
SCENE 2

(Later that day. The gallery glows in afternoon light. Blaise is reviewing a book. Lucille enters lugging a man's suitcase, bags, and canes. Blaise goes to embrace her, but she backs off.)

BLAISE: Your uncle died?

LUCILLE: Lord. Oh. Yes. During the Last Rites, Uncle couldn't breathe; I needed you.

BLAISE: Didn't you get my message?

LUCILLE: Don't. The Bible says honor your relatives—

BLAISE: It also says don't lie. *(Smiles vaguely)*

LUCILLE: Kindness is something your family either taught you or not. You needn't feel nice, but you should act nice—

BLAISE: Janus-faced.

LUCILLE: The service is Wednesday morning, for those interested. Uncle's last words were: "Where's Blaise?" He wanted me to have a real partner. *(Fumbles out a plastic bag)* The attorney gave me these trinkets: some spoons, Uncle's rings and his watch, and his will. *(Hands Blaise the will)*

BLAISE: You want me to read it?

LUCILLE: Sure.

(BLAISE reads. His face pales.)

LUCILLE: What's wrong?

BLAISE: I don't know how to—God—

LUCILLE: *(Grabbing the will)* The entire estate goes to the Dominicans except for... What's this? He's willing me—these pearl-handled spoons?

BLAISE: The bastard went through with it. Here I felt...

LUCILLE: I can't...believe it—

BLAISE: If I stayed away—He might leave you something—

LUCILLE: Oh, my Lord. Mercy. Oh, no.

BLAISE: You look weak.

LUCILLE: There hasn't been time to tell you with all the commotion...but I took a pregnancy test.

BLAISE: It's just...We've barely had sex.

LUCILLE: The doctor said it's unlikely. We'll have the results later today. Don't be depressed, I can't take it if you are. A woman always fears she'll miss out— Since we've been home you...neglect me to share confidences with Susanne.

BLAISE: God! Don't talk this way.

LUCILLE: Are you screwing her?

BLAISE: No. You're overwrought.

LUCILLE: I'm falling apart. Uncle tried to set things straight. He tried and tried to talk to you...

BLAISE: Don't punish me because your mean uncle—

LUCILLE: You dawdle with nowhere plans— Why do this to us?

BLAISE: I'm going out. (*Grabs a cigarette*)

LUCILLE: I needed you at the hospital and I need you now. Marriage means being there. (*LUCILLE looks around with dismay; BLAISE puts on his tennis shoes*) You can't just waste hours with some part you may never play. (*Picks up the empty portfolio*) Where are Susanne's paintings?

BLAISE: "Disparus," as the French would say... I—We burned them.

LUCILLE: (*Horrified*) Not possible.

BLAISE: Susanne couldn't bear seeing...art she hated.

LUCILLE: (*Stunned*) They were priceless.

SOUND: *The phone rings. BLAISE answers it.*

BLAISE: It's Blaise... Yeah...

LUCILLE: Artists must separate ego from art. Art claims its own life. You can't destroy it because the artist isn't—in the same place— (*Irritated*) Tell whoever's calling about Uncle.

BLAISE: *(Into the phone)* I love the part. They're paying that much? When? *(Hangs up; to LUCILLE)* Some friends are starting a summer theater. They've been calling me.

LUCILLE: Where? Why didn't you say something?

BLAISE: New York. I want US to go.

LUCILLE: Now?

BLAISE: I don't want to turn into all I've hated. I'd rather do everything bad and get caught.

LUCILLE: We have to clean out Uncle's place.

BLAISE: The Dominicans can do it. There's nothing holding us, sweetie. You can visit anytime, but I'm never coming back—ever... You said you'd support—

LUCILLE: Opportunity, at the right time—

BLAISE: Every day I do what I have to and you look sadder.

LUCILLE: Your talent won't take care of us.

BLAISE: I'm beginning to hate the sight of this house—with the big mortgage. Here, I'll assign you my interest.

LUCILLE: I won't live in some rattrap.

BLAISE: I never asked that—

LUCILLE: I can, could, and probably will leave Exposition Boulevard soon.

BLAISE: Good girl.

LUCILLE: But we don't have to leave it now.

BLAISE: I won't let property trap us. I'm an artist.

LUCILLE: Says who? Sorry.

BLAISE: I'm going. *(Haltingly)* You'll come?

LUCILLE: I need to hire a good lawyer. Uncle was out of his mind when he made this will. Undue influence is how it happened.

BLAISE: I'm heading back. Eventually something is going to hit. If I keep pushing, I'll keep finding. I've got the drive—

LUCILLE: You're crazy.

BLAISE: I'm not sure but I'll act in my best interest—

LUCILLE: Self-absorbed—

BLAISE: And from that strength.

LUCILLE: Reckless—

BLAISE: I won't be fooled!

(Exits)

(A bit later, the house phone rings and LUCILLE gets it. TED enters carrying a large box. LUCILLE gasps at his miserably timed appearance. SHE hangs up the phone.)

LUCILLE: Susanne's not here.

TED: What's wrong?

LUCILLE: Uncle died. Blaise's moving. I'm disinherited.

TED: All in one day?

LUCILLE: And I found out I'm not pregnant.

TED: Maybe that's a good thing.

LUCILLE: I'm by myself now.

TED: I need your help. *(Lifts one of SUSANNE'S drawings from the box)* Do you recognize this?

LUCILLE: My eyes are blurry.

TED: Discarded sketches. I've retrieved hundreds. Could you organize them? Take over her lectures?

LUCILLE: I'm starting to cry...

TED: You know her work better than anyone.

LUCILLE: First, I need to confront this letter. *(Hands it to TED)* Read it? After his will, I can't bear to.

TED: It's from your uncle.

LUCILLE: I'm his only heir and he gives all to the Church.

TED: *(Reads)* "Dear Lucille, You and Blaise need to start out on your own."

LUCILLE: Nasty!

TED: *(Reads)* "Still, your aunt and I wanted you alone to have this bag."

LUCILLE: Worthless heirlooms—

TED: *(Reads)* "Special spoons for a special heart." Uncle Gene.

LUCILLE: Rusted silver...

TED: A few dollars a spoon.

LUCILLE: *(Opens bag)* What's this? Oh!

TED: A paper?

LUCILLE: Heavenly mother! Oh, no?

TED: *(Takes the paper)* It's a life insurance policy for—

LUCILLE: Six, seven...

TED: Eight figures.

LUCILLE: Oh, no!

TED: You're the beneficiary.

LUCILLE: Good Lord! There must be some mistake.

TED: There's your name. The policy is paid in full.

LUCILLE: It's a miracle! Oh, my!

TED: Fabulous!

LUCILLE: I'll pay off the mortgage. I can live here like—

TED: You did before! Great.

LUCILLE: We'll start a tradition.

TED: A new artist a month at Exposition Boulevard.

LUCILLE: Oh, my God. Mercy. Yes.

TED: But can the heiress still do Susanne's lectures?

LUCILLE: You haven't canceled anything yet?

TED: No.

LUCILLE: We'll create a retrospective with Tulane.

TED: Mother will be delighted.

LUCILLE: We'll work upstairs, clear out Uncle's quarters.

TED: Wonderful!

(THEY continue to plan as they exit.)

ROSARY HARTEL O'NEILL

SOUND: *From the Cathedral we hear the hymn, "City of God." "Let us build the City of God, May our tears be turned into dancing, For the Lord, our Light and our Love, has turned the night into day."*

(Moments later BLAISE walks in to pack. SUSANNE enters nervously, looks at the park.)

SUSANNE: Beautiful night... Starry skies. Moon's coming up over the park. It rained earlier and we needed the rain... Oh...is that Ted with Lucille?

BLAISE: *(Looking out)* Who knows?...I'm leaving.

SUSANNE: You work on a short fuse.

BLAISE: The essence of flight is immediacy.

SUSANNE: You're leaving to do a play?

BLAISE: Something like that.

SUSANNE: I once ran off with a guy who promised me a string of pearls. I did what I was supposed to do, but—

BLAISE: People don't pay you well in the theater I work in.

SUSANNE: You owe me pearls.

BLAISE: It pays in the high two figures like an allowance. The smart actor—

SUSANNE: I'm dreaming of you—

BLAISE: Makes you buy a ticket to see him.

SUSANNE: Your touch—

BLAISE: I can't think of one successful actor with a—

SUSANNE: Your body—

BLAISE: Happy home life. One of my friends is in drug rehab—

SUSANNE: To me you are—the sound of leaves stirring—

BLAISE: Another jumped off the Mississippi River Bridge—

SUSANNE: Water over cool stones—

BLAISE: My most stable friend had a nervous breakdown—

SUSANNE: You arouse the dark side of my soul. Say I can come, Blaise. Just say—I can come.

(HE takes her in his arms, kisses her.)

BLAISE: Wouldn't it be wonderful if it were so?

SOUND: A melancholy refrain from "The City of God" is heard from the Cathedral. "Let us build the City of God, May our tears be turned into dancing, For the Lord, our Light and our Love, has turned the night into day.")

CURTAIN

Photo: *Christian Raby*
Pictured: *Karl Lengel*

A Louisiana Gentleman
A PLAY IN TWO ACTS

Performed at
Théâtre de Nesle, Paris, France
and Brotfabrik Theatre, Bonn, Germany

Photo: Christian Raby
Pictured: Shelley Poncy, Barret O'Brien

Cast of Characters

BLAINE ASHTON—A kind young man, 24, who is attempting to sculpt a happy life for himself, despite the women around him who are hungry for his strength.

GILLIAN PEDERSON-KRAG–A 36-year-old actress. Seductive, talented. Her beauty and style evoke jealousy in others. She pushes herself to extremes to gain acceptance from those she loves.

DALE ELLEN ASHTON—Blaine's 16-year-old sister. She has a haunted radiance that makes her fragility more precious. Like a butterfly, her short life is all the more beautiful. She has lost her father and is trying to tap into her psychic power.

SARA AIMÉE BIRDSONG—45-65, the aunt. Sara jealously guards her reputation as the most glamorous woman in New Orleans. She doesn't know how to survive without a man to take care of her.

Setting

BLAINE ASHTON'S apartment in Baroness Micaela de Pontalba's Buildings, the French Quarter, New Orleans. The apartment fronts the old heart of the city—Jackson Square, the Cabildo Museum, the Saint Louis Cathedral, and the Presbytere—shrines now molding in the humid air from the Mississippi River. With their high ceilings, tall windows, and brick, the apartments remind one of the Palais Royal, the Parisian buildings that inspired them. Giant furnishings bleached by the sun—a chaise lounge, an armoire, an oriental carpet of raspberry and cream—lend the room a mythic poignancy. The apartment seems to scream "If I had to do it over again, I would prioritize extravagance." And this selfishness is seen in the slightly empty feeling that surrounds the effigies to the past, the statues, the portraits of family members with their smiles of deceit. Over the mantle, a portrait of Dr. James Ashton lords over the marble busts of his children, Blaine and Dale, below.

The set contains an area for a balcony, a living area and a bedroom. The architecture is barely suggested. All three areas form a harmonious whole, like a complete scene rather than disparate ones. A dreamlike timeless present mood should result from an emphasis on motion and the expanse of lavender sky encircling the apartment. The sequence of scenes should have a whole, flowing feeling and changes of time should be accomplished by changes of lighting.

Time

The present. It is twilight, that uncertain time between the quiet of night and the noise of day when the apartments blend into the shadows. Lost characters drift out on the streets, joining the tourists with their throwaway cameras and the homeless musicians who play through the night. Melancholy pervades, a sense of time fleeting, a rose before the petals fall. Outside, the cafes, shops, and drinking houses blink on their lights. And since it is a damp Christmas Eve, an Irish coffee, cognac, or Miller on tap warms the sight. The French Quarter has always attracted the rich and poor to close the door on guilt and savor life.

ACT ONE
SCENE 1

(The present. The apartment is piled with medical books and a bare Christmas tree. BLAINE and GILLIAN are kissing heavily. Bells from the Saint Louis Cathedral chime, a jazz version of "Jingle Bells" clangs from the street, and the doorbell rings nonstop. OFFSTAGE SARA pounds the building door and screams out to DALE, who is unloading SARA'S Cadillac, then through the INTERCOM at BLAINE. BLAINE talks into the INTERCOM with one voice and to GILLIAN with another.)

BLAINE: Battered by bells.

SARA: *(OFFSTAGE. Into INTERCOM)* I'm downstairs. Loaded with boxes. Your father's things.

BLAINE: My aunt.

SARA: *(OFFSTAGE. To DALE)* Dale!

BLAINE: Ugh! We'll have to make love later.

(A crash. BLAINE jumps.)

GILLIAN: *(Breathing heavily, to BLAINE)* Don't stop. I'm on fire—

BLAINE: I don't want her to meet you like this.

GILLIAN: The only thing that's not hot is my feet.

SOUND: Banging and yelling outside.

(HE pulls on his shirt.)

SARA: *(OFFSTAGE. Into INTERCOM)* Blaine?

GILLIAN: *(To BLAINE)* Don't answer. I know it seems like an extravagance—

BLAINE : Is the door locked?

GILLIAN: You're prioritizing romance—

SARA: *(OFFSTAGE. Into INTERCOM)* Help me bring this junk up.

BLAINE: *(Into INTERCOM)* Merry Christmas, Aunt Sara.

GILLIAN: *(Erotically to BLAINE)* Say you're busy.

BLAINE: *(Relenting. Into INTERCOM)* You're two hours early.

SARA: *(OFFSTAGE)* The Christmas party is always at six o'clock.

BLAINE: *(Into INTERCOM)* Could you please get some ice?

SARA: *(OFFSTAGE. Into INTERCOM)* I've got your father's suits.

GILLIAN: I've something to show you.

BLAINE: Stop!

SARA: *(OFFSTAGE)* I donated them to the Junior League—After his funeral. But your sister bought them back.

BLAINE: *(Into INTERCOM)* I'm buzzing you in; don't leave those clothes.

GILLIAN: It's not my fault you're so damn gorgeous—and I can't take my hands off you.

BLAINE: *(Breathing heavily)* Button up your blouse!

GILLIAN: Do I need to start—the good old Southern tradition… of begging for it—

BLAINE: The third button.

GILLIAN: Begin our own Gothic history.

BLAINE: If you're going to punish me, I'm going downstairs.
(OFFSTAGE. Feet pounding upstairs. To GILLIAN) Aunt Sara's arrival is one of a series of catastrophes. I talked to her four hours yesterday. I set myself up to be tortured. Used to be there wasn't much to do but listen. I've per-

fected two phrases with her: "Em," and "There you have it."

SARA: *(OFFSTAGE)* How many flights are in this rat trap? Two?

BLAINE: There you have it. *(To GILLIAN)* Help me clean up.

GILLIAN: *(Flops back on chaise)* I'm too excited.

BLAINE: My aunt's a relic from another stratosphere. She's like… black ice. You can't see it, but it's treacherous. *(Looks around)* Where are my shoes?

SARA: *(OFFSTAGE)* I've made it to the first floor.

BLAINE: *(To GILLIAN)* She's coming in. End of sentence.

GILLIAN: You didn't tell her we're getting married.

BLAINE: I didn't want to… expose you to my family. Until I was sure… Sweetness and elegance in a relationship are such beautiful things.

GILLIAN: If she's not nice, is the marriage off?

BLAINE: No. The marriage is on with alien relatives. I know this sounds neurotic. *(He swallows dryly.)* But could you…go out into the court-yard…and come back in…*(Swallows again)* so I can present you.

GILLIAN: I don't believe this—

BLAINE: *(To GILLIAN. Clearing his throat excessively)* You have to under-stand that if you're family connected, there's a certain liability.

GILLIAN: Where in the hell's my purse?

BLAINE: Watch the expletives.

GILLIAN: Where's my fucking purse? *(Breathing quickly)* By thirty, I feel, it's time for me.

SARA: *(OFFSTAGE. Using a key)* Open up!

BLAINE: (Whispers to GILLIAN) God, she's got a key.

GILLIAN: You gave her a—

BLAINE: No…Quick, into the bedroom.

(GILLIAN ducks into the bedroom. SARA staggers into the room, out of breath and feigning chest pains. SHE is wearing a long glamorous velvet gown, a hat, and a fur and is dragging a bag of suits.)

BLAINE: Merry Christmas. You're sure enough early.

SARA: (Gasping) I'm going to have my lawyers…contact your land-lord…because I didn't have a heart condition…till I climbed those stairs.

BLAINE: (Steering her) How did you get the key?

SARA: Don't fuss at me.

BLAINE: Aunt Sara, you can't just barge in here.

SARA: (Collapses in a chair, panting) If I see one more tee-shirt with a Cajun Christmas tree, I'll vomit. (Looks about) Shall I set these suits in your bed-room?

BLAINE: I'll take them.

(DALE enters in a long velvet coat. SHE lugs ornaments, a huge nativity set, and a man's Xmas sweater. SHE gasps for breath.)

DALE: Oh, Blaine, let me hug you. I saved you Dad's sweater.

BLAINE: Wait. I don't want this stuff—

SARA: You haven't taken the time to lie and say I look pretty. My husband, God rest his soul, lied to me for three years, and I was in bliss.

BLAINE: You look beautiful. There you have it.

SARA: Dale, go put my hat and coat on the bed.

BLAINE: I'll take it.

(*Grabs the coat and hat and hurries them to the bedroom.*)

SARA: Let me look at you, Blaine.

DALE: He's not finished dressing?

SARA: I've the one good eye. I see well, but I don't see details. You don't look like yourself.

BLAINE: I haven't combed my hair.

SARA: Your buttons are mismatched. There is a great difference between being casual and being sloppy. Your character is in your shirt. You've lost weight. Why won't you come to dinner?

DALE: (*Touching him*) You used to come every Friday and Sunday. Aunt Sara would have such spreads, crabmeat au gratin, baby asparagus, and crawfish bisque. Let me fix your hair.

SARA: If you're sick of seafood, Bertha could make grilled quail or lac-quered duck.

DALE: Why not come once a week?

BLAINE: I plan to. I phone y'all—

DALE: Tell us what you want and when you're coming now, and we'll start planning ahead—

BLAINE: I can't, sugar. I'm sorry. It's hard when people move away. I know. You feel like it's part of yourself you're losing. But I'll be back. Soon as I graduate, I'll visit a lot.

DALE: Let me sit by you. Now you tell me your schedule, and I'll help you find a time—

BLAINE: (*Clenches his teeth*) Not now!

DALE: Give me your hand.

BLAINE: God, I'm loaded with my studies. I don't get off class till four—I've no time.

DALE: I don't want you to stay away.

BLAINE: Things are better now. I still miss y'all, but I'm living a saner life. I no longer drink a bottle of Maalox a day.

SARA: You're not studying too hard? Knowledge counts, but it doesn't count that much in building a practice. Medicine's still a social art. Whenever I call my plastic surgeon, which I do regularly, he's off skiing in Lake Tahoe. *(Points to a paper wallet)* Your tuition, rent, and lagniappe.

BLAINE: Thanks.

SARA: Course I've no idea how long I'll be able to help you. I've never balanced a checkbook. I shrivel at the thought. Shrivel!

BLAINE: After med school, I'll spoil you…

DALE: I kept Dad's medical kit for you. With the initials outside. Mm. The leather's still fresh. Won't you wear Dad's Christmas sweater?

SARA: Stop emoting, Dale.

DALE: A pine needle's still in the sleeve. Here, I'll help you.

BLAINE: No. *(His voice breaks)* I don't want to be like Dad.

SARA: It's horrible, but I can't show any interest in death.

BLAINE: *(Rushes to the door)* All right, that's it. I don't want these suits, this case, this sweater. I don't want to head the American Medical Association, treat all the indigents in Louisiana, bury my wife at thirty-five, and die myself at fifty-three. Take this stuff back.

SOUND: The Cathedral bells toll.

(DALE rushes out, suddenly triggered, crazed.)

DALE: Oh, no. Blaine's a monster. He hates dead people. Oh no…I must get to Church.

BLAINE: *(Yells out)* Dale. Come back. Dale.

SARA: She's off to the Cathedral. *(SHE undoes her collar. Gasps)* Your sister is a mortuary fanatic. I don't know why I took her in. You ever hear of a funeral cortege on Christmas Eve? She's given me a fever.

BLAINE: You let her run around by herself in the Quarter?

SARA: Joe will follow her.

BLAINE: Who?

SARA: My new escort. He's changed his name from Joel.

BLAINE: Shouldn't you go too—

SARA: Don't punish me, Blaine, I can't go with her. I'm too embarrassed. *(Throws herself back in the chair, panting)* Dale makes us stop by each funeral service so she can pay her respects. She wants people passing by her funeral—to drop in.

BLAINE: *(Hands her some water)* Drink this. You're dehydrated. It's not easy to understand Dale because she's so much going on inside. Her hormones are raging, and her heart is bigger—

SARA: When I said I'd take her, I thought it'd be mostly weekends. There is some weirdness in her, and I can't figure it out. She got kicked out of boarding school because they thought she was a witch. They found her in City Park feeding chicken to the alligators. Grape and magnolia leaves all through her hair.

BLAINE: You never told me.

SARA: Mud all over the car upholstery and—*(Gulps. Removes a sack of items from her purse)* Yesterday I found these strange articles of personal adornment inside her clothes: animal claws, tiny carved owls. Look in the bag. It's too dreadful.

BLAINE: They called Joan of Ark a witch, and—What's this?

SARA: A bird head. Dale's possessed. She howls at night like an inhuman soul. When half of your family is gone, you're a psychological amputee. Check my heart. The girl terrifies me.

BLAINE: (*Awkwardly reaches his stethoscope down her shirt*) If you can keep Dale busy enough, she won't notice—

SARA: You're gone? I hate to be the bad fairy, but you've got to come live with us. When you pass on an errand, Dale starts watching for your MG.

BLAINE: If she's unhappy without me, she'll be unhappy with me. Med school's intense; it's bound to strain my relationships. (*Puts away stethoscope*) You're fine, Aunt Sara.

SARA: But for how long?

BLAINE: I'll get the hors d'oeuvres.

SOUND: *Knee-tapping guitarist plays "Oh Holy Night, the Stars are Brightly Shining. T'is the Night, of the Dear Savior's Birth."*

(*SARA hurries to the balcony.*)

SARA: The Quarter is swarming with junkies. Awful signs, "I'll work for food." I suppose I should throw them some quarters.

(*BLAINE sneaks GILLIAN from the bedroom out the front door.*)

SARA: Hey Joe! That adorable man. Dumb as a post. He just drives me about. Last week, Joe dropped Dale off and didn't find her till six hours later. There's not a square block in the Quarter. It's built around bayous, rivers, and coolies. (*Sniffs and picks up a long hair strand.*) Funny smell, like lavender perfume. (*Finds a purse and snoops inside*) Whose purse? Tampax. What's this? A birth control device?

BLAINE: (*Coming out to the balcony with a tray of goodies*) Don't start.

SARA: Where did "Don't Start" go? Remember, Blaine: what one needs in the dark of the night, one tosses out in the morning. I hope you're going to Mass and confession. (*Chuckles*)

BLAINE: Chocolates?

SARA: Never eat chocolate. Rots the teeth.

BLAINE: Cashews?

SARA: I'm watching my waist now that I can see it. You have any shrimp puffs or crab dip? I didn't come here to eat from plastic. *(BLAINE passes her a dish.)* Canned cheese straws? So, who is she?

BLAINE: My life has swerved in a new direction. It's the most extraordinary thing. I met this actress—

SARA: All your breeding, and you can't get a proper date and decent canapes. I hire help in threes. Three maids, three cooks, three drivers. One always shows up, and you can fire two when necessary.

BLAINE: *(Controlling his temper)* It's hard for you to understand, you've been so grief-struck about Dad.

SARA: Grief-struck? I never saw your father. Still, it is a plunge in appearances.

BLAINE: For all the woman I've dated, Gillian's the most magical with her long hair and—

SARA: Mm. Your cheese straws are limp.

BLAINE: I'm engaged.

SARA: There's no reason not to be dreaming about marriage, but to commit to it. You spend your thirties doing that. Don't spend your twenties doing it.

BLAINE: Gillian's not like other women. She's traveled to Australia, lived in Africa. She lives her life completely from her conscience.

SARA: Hmph. Is she well connected? To have an image in the medical community, you must have a wife who appears first-rate as wives go. You've a family tree going back to...to—

BLAINE: Jesus Christ.

SARA: Who are her parents?

BLAINE: Her father was a mortician.

SARA: A mortician's daughter? And an actress. You wouldn't be accepted in any social home in the South. I can hear your table conversation. "What's the latest in shrouds?"

BLAINE: Are you relaxed?

SARA: No.

BLAINE: I'm getting married on January sixth.

SARA: In a year.

BLAINE: In two weeks. On the Epiphany. The day the angels changed the wise men's lives. I was pretty much hopeless, you see. If it wasn't for prayer, I'd have been suicidal. I met Gillian…she's so balanced. She's always— there. Even when she's away, she's always there. The problem with many marriages is there's no magic. Good woman, nice family, very competent. Those women cannot help you move out of your deficits.

SARA: That's ridiculous.

BLAINE: I'm looking for a new form, breaking the envelope.

SARA: If I'd known you had to settle down, I would have fixed you up with the LaBorde girl.

BLAINE: (Giggles) We've no chemistry.

SARA: How about English? Physics? At least you know you don't like each other. What's so funny?

BLAINE: The reason I've this giddy feeling is I keep thinking I'm not qualified for a wife like Gillian, and someday, somebody is going to call me on this. I'm waiting any minute for some shoe to drop or midnight to arrive.

SARA: You're afraid she'll be exposed as a fraud.

BLAINE: Oh, Aunt Sara. There's nothing more wonderful than to marry the woman you care about the most. Having a sweetheart, something inside of you lightens and you're not out there by yourself anymore. I thought I'd take a leave from school, bask in the happiness, but Gillian wants to get married over the break, and there's an opening at the Cathedral.

SARA: Why don't you just kill me? Hang my clothes next to your father's. Lay me out at the mortuary.

BLAINE: Please. I'm not an eel. I don't have tough skin.

SARA: How's Dale going to take this wedding? A girl who isn't even smart enough to hang around with the outcasts? Oh, some days she's normal, but I never know when those days are.

BLAINE: The family is important to me so we'll get together. Gillian's helped me thread my life together. She has more energy than other people. The energy of a singular person.

SARA: All of her family are dead?

BLAINE: Yes.

SARA: She has no relatives? No contacts? The system for success is con- tacts. *(A Cadillac horn screeches. SARA waves and yells.)* Hey, Dale. Dale. She wears James' gold cross as if she's taken on your father as a cult.

BLAINE: No one accepts death at once. We get eased into it. Dale was okay before. She'll revert back. Remember when I took her to London. We went walking on the heath, and she started to accept Dad's illness—

SARA: Dale gets depressed. Six hours a day I can't find her. I thought minding her would get easier. It didn't. The episodes got greater. But you're distracted, and my chest pains mean nothing.

BLAINE: You have nervous indigestion from getting too excited, worked up all the time. The meat. The booze. If you'd start an exercise program—

SARA: I'm turning into an old woman fast, teeth falling out, wrinkles crawling over the skin.

BLAINE: *(Giggles)* I want you to help me organize the wedding.

SARA: You don't have a knife or a gun?

BLAINE: I'm getting married!

SARA: You're gaga.

BLAINE: I'm going to have a wife!

SARA: Nuts.

BLAINE: I didn't want to get married now. But being with Gillian is like walking on the moon. Once you've done that the world has a different perspective.

SARA: The most awful thing that's happened in marriage is aunts having abdicated their traditional function as marriage-makers.

(DALE enters, breathing heavily. SHE catches her breath in the doorway.)

DALE: Who's getting…married, Blaine?

SARA: Your brother's discussing a couple he used to know.

DALE: In the…French Quarter?

SARA: No. Most households in the Quarter are selfish people, living alone.

BLAINE: Bing.

SARA: *(Shouts to DALE)* Come in. Entrance ways are for people who don't know one another.

(DALE removes her coat. SHE is wearing a nun's habit and is short of breath.)

DALE: Oh, Blaine. You missed the best funeral. Five Cardinals in the same church. Of course, one was dead. Lucky me, I arrived in time for them to make their exit. One came from Africa. One was on crutches. One was being helped by two people—

BLAINE: What's that get-up? *(Takes her coat to the bedroom)*

ROSARY HARTEL O'NEILL

DALE: It's a ceremonial habit. I've joined a religious order—the Lazarians.

BLAINE: The what?

SARA: Some lay cult obsessed with the dead. Thank God she goes out at dawn and dusk, the antisocial hours.

DALE: Let's set out the Christmas ornaments. *(Walks to the side)* I'll put up the manger. Dad used to read Saint Luke: *(Gasps)* "Mary gave birth to her first-born son and wrapped him in swaddling clothes and…laid him in a manger, because—"

SARA: "There was no room for them in the inn."

BLAINE: *(To SARA)* Her shortness of breath seems worse. I'm looking at my sister a moment ago. I've no idea what's going on in her life. A lay cult?

SARA: It's a catastrophe. I told her. If you enter the cloister, you'll have killed your aunt. I won't visit you. Stick my face behind an iron grill. *(To BLAINE)* I demand you come live with us.

DALE: Can I sit on your lap? *(Sits on his lap, unwraps statues)* Here's Balthasar, your favorite wise man. And his camel.

BLAINE: The ox, with a crack down his back.

DALE: And the donkey with one ear—

SARA: We can put baby Jesus in the cradle before his time has come. *(To BLAINE)* Tell Dale about your plans.

BLAINE: *(To DALE)* I've met a wonderful woman. She's kind and gentle—

DALE: Don't talk about her. Talk about me. Look, I've got the star from our old manger set. *(Hugs him)*

SARA: Your brother's going…to ruin his life with a certain—

(GILLIAN enters, lingering in the doorway in a superb evening dress.)

GILLIAN: Gillian Pederson-Krag. Merry Christmas.

SARA: *(To GILLIAN)* Stand up, Dale.

BLAINE: Honey, this is my aunt, Sara Birdsong. The pretty girl's my sister, Dale. This is Gillian, my fiancée.

SARA: Peculiar name—Pederson-Krag. Is that one or two words?

GILLIAN: I was married before.

SARA: What did "our" husband do?

GILLIAN: Not enough.

BLAINE: You don't have to apologize for having been married.

GILLIAN: I'm not. *(To SARA)* What a lovely pin.

SARA: I don't like snakes, but they're the symbol of medicine, and my family is in that business.

DALE: *(To GILLIAN)* They're also the symbol of fertility. Did you know that?

GILLIAN: I'm not pregnant.

BLAINE: *(Breaking free of DALE)* Dale. Finish fixing the stable.

SARA: The Dominican nuns gave your father that manger set. James treated the entire order and never charged a cent.

DALE: *(To GILLIAN)* There's my father's picture.

GILLIAN: Nice.

DALE: Look if you move back and forth, his eyes follow you around. Wonderful eyes.

SARA: With those tarantula lashes.

DALE: Just like Blaine's. Come sit by me, Blaine.

BLAINE: Not now, honey.

DALE: Oh, Blaine's so cold.

SARA: In my day, women were supposed to entertain. You talked about dogs or the weather.

(The following lines overlap as DALE interrupts to get attention.)

BLAINE: *(To GILLIAN)* Tell my family about your acting career.

GILLIAN: I got cast on this medical show—

DALE: My father was a grand loving doctor.

GILLIAN: I see. It's a hospital series for—

DALE: One call, one chat, one round of visits.

GILLIAN: Actually, I play this head nurse—

DALE: My father liked tradition. He guarded his patients.

SARA: Gillian doesn't want to talk about your father. The middle classes don't have an obsession with parenting.

BLAINE: What was that crack for?

SARA: It was a joke.

BLAINE: Don't joke about Gillian. Joke about—*(Searches for a name)* Joe.

SARA: My niece and nephew are the image of their father. Altruistic and obsessive—Of course I like being single. Most women do. Women have got to marry men older or uglier or poorer 'cause the world prefers men. And women have got to be smarter because men say they'll take care of us, but they don't. And now when you look around—there's a crop failure in men. So I suppose I'll never have another. Still, I was married happily for three years, three years out of ten, that's pretty good. *(Smiles)* Hand me the chocolates, Dale.

GILLIAN: We'd like to have the reception in your home.

SARA: Who's organizing this?

BLAINE: Of course we could elope, but in a way it leaves us bereft. We're nostalgic for the rituals that make life important.

DALE: I got something caught in my throat.

SARA: She eats too fast.

BLAINE: Swallow, sugar.

DALE: I can't breathe.

SARA: And then her windpipe is too small.

GILLIAN: Hurry.

DALE: Something is stuck.

BLAINE: I'll get it. The Heimlich.

DALE: (Coughs up the chocolate) There it is. Oh no. I'm so embarrassed.

BLAINE: Ssh. Go rest…Lie down here. Relax.

GILLIAN: Dale, I brought you a gift. A friendship ring. See, the tiny bands come entwined like wreaths.

BLAINE: Say, "thank you," sugar.

DALE: I hate jewelry.

BLAINE: That's not nice. Symmetry Jewelers even engraved it.

DALE: My father died, and left me a sapphire with forty diamonds. I would rather have had him alive. I never wear it.

GILLIAN: Not this ring?

DALE: Blaine gave you my sapphire. It belonged to my grandmother.

SARA: That ring's been around.

DALE: She stole my ring. Daddy gave it to me. No. No. No—
(*She covers her ears and runs to the balcony.*)

BLAINE: It was in Dad's bank box in a blue velvet bag with my initials on it.

GILLIAN: I didn't take your ring. Excuse me, I feel...nauseous.
(*Exits away from DALE to the bedroom.*)

BLAINE: Dad told me to use it, if I ever needed an engagement ring before—

SARA: How old is that woman?

BLAINE: Gillian—you okay?

GILLIAN: (*Calling back*) I'm a young twenty-nine...

BLAINE: You've gotten Gillian upset.

SARA: Oh, she came in upset. Live in the real world.

BLAINE: What is the real world? It's got something to do with feelings. I'm telling you, this is the most thrilling time of my life...And you're not listening. I can't be near you because of the— I want you to like Gillian.

SARA: And what about my hurt? Usually I repress my feelings, but tonight I can't.

BLAINE: Em.

SARA: My first Christmas with Dale, and you pay no attention to me.

BLAINE: You don't get a lot of attention because people are anxious around you. It's like people recognize it when they see it, but they don't know what it is—rudeness.

SARA: How dare you?

SOUND: *The Cathedral bells toll.*

DALE: *(Rushes in from the balcony)* My father was a grand loving doctor. One call, one chat, one round of visits. *(Stomps feet and removes a stuffed duck from her purse)* One call, one chat, one round of visits.

SARA: Some days Dale'll be nice, and others she throws this at you. She's doing this more this week than ever before. You have to get used to it. *(Pulls the duck out of DALE'S hand)* She sleeps with that little beat-up terrycloth duck you gave her when she was five. Carries it everywhere. *(Whispers)* Have you forgotten the boarding school? She was crying so much, she stopped eating. And all those tiresome stories about Dale trying to wound herself. The last time it was at breakfast with a grapefruit knife. *(Shaking her head)* Roll up your sleeves, Dale.

DALE: No.

SARA: *(Tears back her sleeves)* There.

BLAINE: You cut your wrists.

DALE: No. I was goofing off. The knife slipped.

BLAINE: Don't lie.

DALE: Stop screaming. They're just scratches.

SARA: She does it to torment me! This morning I was so upset, I cut my lip, and it swelled up so bad, I couldn't wear lipstick. I've got to use the little girls' room. *(SARA exits to the bathroom.)*

DALE: Come live with us.

BLAINE: I can't. Saturday, I'll visit, and we'll talk.

DALE: No, you won't.

BLAINE: Going to med school is really hard.

ROSARY HARTEL O'NEILL

DALE: I wouldn't bother you.

BLAINE: All that reading makes your brain tight. I've this pretty nice arrangement where I can go to class from eight to four, rest for an hour or so, then study all night.

DALE: You could have the whole attic.

BLAINE: What makes it possible to face up to so much work is the relaxation I get from coming home alone. That soothing interlude before study. The calm before the letting go of the day. I love it when television's off, and the phone doesn't ring. You have to be fairly independent to be a good medical student.

DALE: Then why are you getting married?

BLAINE: When you're in love, you don't have this gnawing feeling in your gut. You're fed by this wonderful ambiance. You study harder, longer. *(Looks up and sees GILLIAN)* Gillian.

GILLIAN: *(Returning from the bedroom)* I freshened up, and I feel better. *(To DALE)* I'm sorry I took your ring. Here.

DALE: I don't want it.

GILLIAN: Won't you forgive me...be in our wedding? I ordered you a beautiful dress.

BLAINE: And a rose bouquet. You can have all the Shirley Temples and petit fours you want.

DALE: *(Backs onto the balcony with BLAINE and GILLIAN following)* I don't want things! They're carrying that dead Cardinal to the hearse now. See the stream of cars. The headlights. The trumpets at the door.

BLAINE: My loving Gillian has nothing to do with my love for you. I love her in a different way, but I've loved you longer. You can spend every Saturday night with us, and after med school, we'll see about a room for you.

DALE: No, you won't. You'll forget.

GILLIAN: Soon, you'll go off to college.

(SARA crosses into the bedroom for her hat and coat.)

DALE: Not for two years. Living with Aunt Sara is horrible. The woman should collapse under the weight of her own awfulness. When she comes to my room, it's like the arrival of Valkyries.

BLAINE: I know she can be a pain, sugar, but—

SARA: *(Crossing to the balcony with her hat and the two coats)* Oh, do be nice to Dale after she's been so ugly. This has been the most dreadful Christmas. Blaine screaming at me and making me depressed. It's awful to have ugly things said about you. It's even worse to have them said in front of strangers unexpectedly.

DALE: I wanted to explain to Blaine—

SARA: *(Hands DALE her coat)* Put on your coat. I took you in so Blaine could triumph in med school, not so he could marry an overaged woman. You and Gillian are colluding against me.

GILLIAN: That's not true.

SARA: It's something when wives turn out to be nobodies. Mediocrity and availability will beat out background and intelligence any day. *(To BLAINE)* If you insist on marrying that woman, I'll keep Dale for one week after the honeymoon, then she can move in with you.

BLAINE: Dale can't live here.

SARA: It's emotionally debilitating. You're a thief. You've stolen my youth.

DALE: I'm moving in with Gillian and Blaine. Wow!

SARA: *(Waves)* Joe, we're coming!

DALE: Gee! I can't wait to live here! This is the most exciting news—

SARA: Stop raving! The French Quarter is so ugly. It's Gentilly times fifty.

(SARA leaves with DALE.)

END OF SCENE 1
ACT ONE

SCENE 2

(Continuous)

GILLIAN: *(Searches for a Kleenex in her purse)* Where's my purse?

BLAINE: *(Points)* I'm sorry. I should have warned you—

GILLIAN: I'm dumbfounded.

BLAINE: In this family, you need two personalities. The private one and the one that gets beaten on. If only I wasn't in touch with the one that's beaten on. *(Chuckles)*

GILLIAN: *(Sniffs)* Stop.

BLAINE: I'll get us some coffee. After Dad's death, I vowed I'd live in the real world, try to be generous and caring, but I tell you it's frightening. To some extent, I can comfort myself with the thought we've been down difficult paths before.

GILLIAN: Don't say anything.

BLAINE: I want to help…make the hurt go away.

GILLIAN: Leave me be.

BLAINE: *(Romantically)* My perspective is very multifaceted as a result of this lifetime in medicine. I started when I was sixteen years old by lying about my age and getting a job at Touro Hospital—

GILLIAN: Stop.

BLAINE: Because I was passionate about healing and wanted to be near doctors and at that point thought they were just a step below the gods. Of course you learn otherwise when you move around with them in the world.

GILLIAN: Don't touch me.

BLAINE: Right. Coffee? Cream? Sugar?

GILLIAN: Bourbon, if available.

BLAINE: Whoa!

GILLIAN: Take Dale this ring. How could you give it to me when—

BLAINE: She said she hated jewelry.

GILLIAN: I can't live with you and your sister. I'm not the same as the girls you've dated. Something's missing on my face. I look up and I can't find it. I think it's youth.

BLAINE: You're young.

GILLIAN: I'm thirty-four. I lied to your aunt. (Nervously) All of my problems are related to my body. I've a seriously screwed-up body. And then, there's the whole question of kids.

BLAINE: You don't want children, fine.

GILLIAN: Something you can't have is rather difficult to want. Children aren't yours, they're on loan anyway. Three years ago I was in an accident. I probably can't have kids. No portraits to ornament the parlor. No sons to champion your name.

BLAINE: (Swallows hard) Children count in marriage, but they don't count that much.

GILLIAN: I'm thirty-five.

BLAINE: You want to stop with that number now? Or shall we go on?

GILLIAN: I'm thirty-six. When you said Dale was sixteen, I envisioned this child. She's complicated and so is my career. How can an actress's life be compatible with a strong man's?

BLAINE: No point in being afraid of a strong man, you should be afraid of a crazy man. I can't live with romantic ambivalence.

GILLIAN: I am not nineteen and naive anymore. There aren't many auditions in New Orleans, and when my agent calls, I have to be ready to travel. I can't tell you when I'm coming home, if I'm on tour— What if I get a Broadway play that's held over?

BLAINE: I'll grab my suitcases, borrow money from the bank, and take a plane to New York.

GILLIAN: It's not a relationship when you're living with someone who's not there. My work is my obsession. When you're an actress, you help create soul in the universe. The theater calls for energy, a mythic closeness. You are stripping yourself, exposing your life, in all your failings, so you can provide insight to others. Acting is religious. It 's my mission. What an actress passes on is finally her soul.

BLAINE: That's wonderful. I'll save the bodies and you save the souls...Most of my friends think I'm nuts going to med school when I've got to follow him. *(Points to his father's portrait)* My dad gave his life to surgery. And he was incredible. He could tell what was wrong with a person by the way he walked. And sometimes he actually cured people by laying on his hands and saying you'll be okay. People lined up in front of his clinic for blocks...just to see him. Maybe it was because he didn't charge them. Something that made my mother slam doors and scream at him in their bedroom. If people couldn't pay their bill, he would rip it up. And at Christmas time deliveries of food, flowers, and plants would begin: overwhelming the house with the aroma of joy and gratitude. When he died, Dad had two thousand dollars in his account. He said, "Well, that's two thousand dollars more than I had when I came in." Aunt Sara bailed us out. Unless I get through med school, there won't be much future for me or Dale.

GILLIAN: Oh, Blaine.

BLAINE: What I miss most about him is his idealism, this sense of mission, which you have. Tell me we're better than any other couple.

GILLIAN: Yes. We're both so...damn needy.

BLAINE: You are beautiful. *(BLAINE whistles)*

GILLIAN: Don't whistle.

BLAINE: You used to like it.

GILLIAN: I like everything about you. That's the problem.

BLAINE: Marry me. *(Hugging her)* It never feels like you're strong, when you're doing something important, it feels like you're on the abyss. *(THEY kiss.)*

END OF SCENE 2

ACT ONE
SCENE 3

(Ten a.m., twelve days later, January 6th. Sun blasts through the windows, giving the apartment a stark reality. SARA enters in a long black dress, a veil over her face. SHE is crying. SHE sits in a corner sniveling into her champagne. DALE, who looks much paler, wears an airy pink bridesmaid's dress. SHE puts out some strawberries. OFFSTAGE, GILLIAN is in the kitchen in her wedding dress, and BLAINE, in his morning suit, is downstairs in front of the apartment.)

DALE: Pink is for dancing. *(Spins about, eating)* The Cathedral was lovely. Incense and organ music. The private wedding—

BLAINE: *(OFFSTAGE)* All the bags packed?

GILLIAN: *(OFFSTAGE)* Not yet.

DALE: I can't wait for the reception.

SARA: *(Sobbing)* Now Blaine's married. I feel so old—You'll be moving.

BLAINE: *(OFFSTAGE)* You got the Euros?

GILLIAN: Yep.

SARA: *(Sobs to DALE)* What shall I do? Take a correspondence course in antiques? Volunteer at the hospital? Have a face lift? When you're young, you're too hot to handle, and when you're ready, no one wants to handle you.

GILLIAN: *(Peeks in)* Check the passports on the mantle.

DALE: *(Checks the mantle)* They're okay!

SARA: Have you seen my neighbor? Angelina looks like a younger version of herself, like she's left town and her cousin's arrived. Angelina says to me, "How old are you? Fifty?" Let's get to the point. She was on the operating table twelve hours, with three plastic surgeons.

DALE: When Daddy was a boy, at Jesuit High School, the priests made them say "Congratulations" at weddings. *(Picking at the strawberries)* When Daddy was alive we ate lots of strawberries. I thought the stork dropped me from a planet where they made them. Daddy fed me—

SARA: If you say Daddy once more—I'll scream.

BLAINE: *(Entering)* Where are the plane tickets?

SARA: You want them now?

BLAINE: I'm going to stick them in my carry-on.

(SHE hands them to BLAINE, who starts reading them over. GILLIAN enters.)

SARA: Open them later. It's a midnight flight. And the hotel accommodations are paid for. We should be going.

GILLIAN: Thanks again, Aunt Sara.

SARA: Sara.

GILLIAN: I've always wanted to go to Paris. Then to stay in the wedding suite at the George V near the Champs Elysees with a grand piano and a balcony view of the Eiffel Tower.

SOUND: Car toots.

SARA: We've got to get to the Country Club.

GILLIAN: I dread facing your relatives again. Tough crowd. If they only pretended to care about me, I could take it. You know I once had a nosebleed during an audition, but I wanted the part so bad I stuffed a Kleenex in my nose and continued acting. The director kept yelling. Finally, I screamed, "I'm bleeding. What do you want?" "Another actress," he said.

BLAINE: You look gorgeous…You have this emotional translucence. Everyone loved your hair with the pearl insets.

GILLIAN: Why did your cousins stare at me?

SARA: Let's go down…

GILLIAN: Is it because of my age? One woman said I looked like your mother.

BLAINE: I'm sure it was meant as a compliment. My mother was beautiful, and died young.

SARA: (Checks her watch) Get my fur, Dale. My eyes are all puffy. My face looks like a tomato. My hat's on the bed.

DALE: We're not going down before Gillian. (Pushes her down) I'll sit in your lap if I have to.

SARA: (Forces her off) Get off. You monster. Let me go.

BLAINE: These tickets say January first. There must be some mistake.

SARA: It must be a seven.

BLAINE: And our hotel reservations are for last week.

GILLIAN: What's going on?

BLAINE: I don't know. Aunt Sara?

SARA: I feel so wretched.…It was the maid's fault. She was supposed to check them. But she's—illiterate. A liar. The new maid, Luella, Suella, I can't pronounce it. Why is everyone glaring at me? You don't suspect I did this? (Gasps) Joe picked up the tickets.

DALE: If you hadn't been juiced up sobbing all week—Oh…You're so mean.

SARA: Who do you think paid the caterer—

GILLIAN: Oh...no.

SARA: Ordered the roses—

BLAINE: Don't cry. Please. We'll call. We'll fix this after the reception.

SARA: Made a donation to the Cathedral. Glamour doesn't come cheap.

DALE: You ruined their trip.

SARA: Then to be attacked by a brooding sixteen-year-old...and a woman I never liked in the first place.

DALE: You're a cruel, lousy witch! *(Starts to exit)*

SARA: Fine, Dale. You go to the reception alone. Spend the night with Blaine. I was going to keep you till after the honeymoon, but you've been so vicious, you can stay with them. My niece is a heart thief on a monumental scale. She's chewed up my feelings and spit them out.

(SARA exits. DALE calls after her.)

DALE: What a thrill to move in early. Have Joe bring my stuff.

BLAINE: *(Calls after her)* Aunt Sara.

DALE: My terrycloth duck? My pictures?

(Cadillac roars off)

GILLIAN: She's left. This morning, I got dressed, put on this veil, your aunt says to me, "I suspect Dale will move in sooner than you think."

BLAINE: Let me hold you.

DALE: Where are we going tonight?

BLAINE: We could check in a hotel.

GILLIAN: With her?

DALE: I'll keep quiet and hidden like a good little mouse.

GILLIAN: *(Whispers)* You can't have sex when you don't have hope.

BLAINE: Shh. We've got to get to the reception.

GILLIAN: *(Yells)* You go. I agreed to take Dale in temporarily. Not give up my life.

(DALE circles about them, flitting about them, like a butterfly, placing objects here and there as the light fades.)

END OF SCENE 3

ACT ONE
SCENE 4

(Two months later. Early March, Mardi Gras time. The living room is strewn with DALE'S objects and Mardi Gras decorations and costumes. SARA in a long coat is talking into a cell phone. SHE walks before the set as if down a street.)

SARA: Blaine. Are you there? Pick up…No, I don't want to leave a message so you can wave my laundry over the Quarter. I'll call back. *(Hangs up and dials again)* This is your aunt. Remember? The one who is financing your education. I don't like the role, but I've got to play it. Pick up. *(Slams the phone and dials again)* Blaine, I know you're there. Medical school's over, and it's five-thirty. I got your exam grades. Need I say, I'm horrified. I don't want to be hectored by F reports showing up in my mailbox. When I said medicine was a social art, I didn't mean it was a party. You have my brother's reputation to consider. *(Coughs)* I know the roots of stupidity are complex, but I want you to get your brain out of hock. Learning is a slow system of osmosis. Eavesdrop on the smart fellows. Write a longer paper. And please do brown-nose your teachers after class. *(Coughs)* Remember the golden rule. She who has the gold rules. I'm not financing a failure.

(Blackout. Toward the end of SARA'S speech, DALE enters in a sorcerer's costume with her astrology chart. GILLIAN follows, retreating to a corner to rehearse her nurse's role in the television series. BLAINE crosses to another part of the room,

studying. Throughout the scene, street revelers scream out, "Throw me some beads," or play music, "All because it's carnival time, it's carnival ti-me, it's carnival ti-me, everybody's drinking wine," as they await the approach of a parade.)

DALE: Blaine has the most wonderful astrology chart. There's so much creative giftedness around him, I've been inhaling.

GILLIAN: Shh. I'm working on my lines.

DALE: Still?

GILLIAN: You have to make art as if you had eternity. *(Studies her script)* "The doctor will be making rounds in a half an hour if you'd like to freshen up."

BLAINE: *(Puts headsets to his ears and opens a book)* I'm going under. Do you know the Australian box jellyfish is the most poisonous one alive? Toxins, that's the theme of the night.

DALE: *(To BLAINE)* Look. I did a watercolor of your sun sign, maybe finished, maybe not. Blaine's an old soul. He's had twenty-five hundred lives.

GILLIAN: Get that out of his face.

DALE: I just goof off…nearly every day. Mama studied at the School des Beaux Arts, and lived on Beethoven Street—in Paris.

GILLIAN: "What are these pills doing here? You were supposed to take them—"

DALE: Across from the Eiffel Tower. Her apartment once belonged to a Cavalier poet from the seventeenth century. "Gather rosebuds while you may and while you're young go marry, for having once lost your prime, you may forever tarry."

GILLIAN: *(Reciting her lines)* Where was I? Oh yes. "You were supposed to take them with your milk—"

DALE: *(To GILLIAN)* Do you want me to do your chart?

GILLIAN: No! I need to concentrate. *(Grabs stomach)* Ugh. I've got these awful cramps.

DALE: You want a heating pad? Something to drink? A Coke?

GILLIAN: Get away.

DALE: I want to help—

BLAINE: *(Removes headsets. Shows her some pictures in his textbook)* Here, sugar. Did you know the cure for a jellyfish is to pour vinegar on the tentacles? Don't pull them off because they release the poison. If a brown recluse spider bites you, it can kill you. See the fiddle on its back? A black widow, you spot that, you better squash it.

DALE: Oh. No. Stop. *(Crying)* I'm an Aquarius. We're the sign of the most emotion. I feel for others you see. I believe in non-injury to living things so they can roam free.

GILLIAN: *(Puts in some ear plugs)* Time for ear plugs. Where was I ? "Supposed to take them with your milk after breakfast—"

SOUND: *Police whistles scream, announcing a parade.*

DALE: *(To BLAINE)* Parade's coming! Let's take a break.

BLAINE: I've got exams the Monday after Mardi Gras—

DALE: I could give you a quiz on the way to the parade. Make you recite all the ways to die from poison.

BLAINE: I've got those big tests coming up. Remember?

DALE: At least look at your chart? Astrology shows you how to realize the potential genius of yourself. I'm Aquarius with a moon in Virgo, and you're Virgo with a moon in Pisces.

GILLIAN: Quiet—

DALE: I've studied your horoscope and it's what one would call a "fortunate" chart.

GILLIAN: *(Memorizing)* "After your breakfast." No. After your lunch. "After your lunch."

DALE: *(To BLAINE)* You'll always be able to get whatever money you need, and you'll be protected from the worst life can throw at you. For you have the sun in Virgo and the moon in Pisces. Johann Wolfgang von Goethe, born in 1749, had the sun in Virgo and Count Tolstoy, born in 1828, had the moon in Pisces. Moon in Pisces means the aim of your life is to be in tune with the infinite.

GILLIAN: She puts me in a state—

DALE: Something of the magician hovers about you.

GILLIAN: With all the unnecessary useless banter.

DALE: For you've a guardian angel, at your side. And she will give you the power over the world that the magic lamp gave to Aladdin.

SOUND: *Sirens blare outside as a parade approaches.*

GILLIAN: Shut up!

DALE: You ruined my reading. I don't like living with you.

GILLIAN: Blaine, do something.

BLAINE: It's so exhausting—

DALE: *(To GILLIAN)* Stay in your room.

BLAINE: To have to be an evangelist.

DALE: Witch.

GILLIAN: She's off on a rage again.

DALE: Gillian's so mean.

GILLIAN: You hear her, Blaine?

BLAINE: *(Packing his books)* I'm looking for quiet.

GILLIAN: When I've suffered the—

BLAINE: The quiet I can't get.

GILLIAN: The degradation of a sister-in-law who's a loose cannon. Oh, my stomach hurts. Your sister's constantly misbehaving. She's a worthless—restless anxious—being—Oh, my stomach hurts so bad. Ah. Oh.

DALE: She's showing off.

GILLIAN: My period's so screwed up.

BLAINE: Lie down.

DALE: She wants attention.

GILLIAN: Oh. These cramps.

DALE: Last chance for an Oscar.

BLAINE: Is that blood?

GILLIAN: God. Help me.

BLAINE: Get a towel.

DALE: Where?

BLAINE: There. Call an ambulance.

GILLIAN: I can't stop the bleeding.

BLAINE: A damn ambulance.

SOUND: *A band blares as a parade marches down the street.*

DALE: The streets are roped off. A parade's coming.

END OF SCENE 4

END OF ACT ONE

ACT TWO
SCENE 1

(Two months later. A rainy Saturday in May. The living room and bedroom of the apartment. Antique timepieces, stopped at the hour of James Ashton's death, lend the rooms a sweet poignancy. The living room has been made into a sickroom for DALE. White sheets cover the chaise and furniture and her astrology and drawing supplies are everywhere. The bedroom is GILLIAN'S retreat, where, threatened with miscarriage, SHE spends most of her time in bed. DALE, in a long lace nightgown, is bedded in the living room. SHE acts slow and nervous, as if drugged. GILLIAN, glamorously disheveled, in a long satin gown, balances a looseleaf check-book on her bed. SHE is surrounded by ice cream, Cokes, and champagne. Both women look as if they could be in the medieval gowns of maidens in a golden castle. BLAINE has just finished replacing his father's portrait over the mantle with one of GILLIAN on her wedding day. HE picks up a cake and crosses to DALE.)

BLAINE: Come wish Gillian "Happy Birthday."

DALE: I'm too depressed! I'm sixteen, and I've never seriously accomplished anything.

BLAINE: The Mozart Complex. I've chocolate chip mint ice cream. You ever notice how ice cream shrinks from being a mountain to being a puddle? You get it, and it's gone.

DALE: You don't care how I feel.

BLAINE: You need to get up, move around some.

DALE: I'm too weak.

BLAINE: Learn to trust yourself. It's like someone with an injured leg. If you remain bedridden, your muscles will atrophy. Instead, you must learn to limp by building strength gradually.

DALE: I feel bad about feeling bad but—I can't help it.

BLAINE: Let's wish Gillian happy birthday together.

DALE: You do it.

(BLAINE exits to the bedroom and DALE picks up the phone. The following scenes overlap with DALE talking on the phone and BLAINE tending to GILLIAN.)

BLAINE: Happy birthday to you. Happy birthday to you. Happy birthday, dear Gillian.

GILLIAN: *(Smiles)* I celebrate birthdays, but I don't count them.

BLAINE: You get prettier every day.

GILLIAN: Men say that, but they use age as a standard of decline. *(Her hands run restlessly over her drink.)* No one says I want you to meet my pretty, old wife.

(DALE picks up her cordless phone, dials, and speaks into the phone.)

DALE: Aunt Sara. It's me. I feel sick.

BLAINE: *(Putting a hand on GILLIAN'S shoulder)* Make a wish and blow.

DALE: *(Into the phone)* Blaine and Gillian won't come out of their room. And I'm so hot.

BLAINE: What did you wish for?

GILLIAN: A boy.

DALE: *(Into the phone)* I think I've a fever.

BLAINE: I can't manage a baby.

GILLIAN: I know, but if there's any chance for me to carry a baby—that specialist says it's now.

DALE: *(Into the phone)* Blaine and Gillian are doing things.

BLAINE: And what about your career?

DALE: I can hear them panting.

GILLIAN: I didn't think I could get pregnant. The doctors said it was

ROSARY HARTEL O'NEILL

impossible, but I've almost made it to the three-month mark.

DALE: *(Into the phone)* My head hurts.

GILLIAN: I'm so thrilled. Maybe there's a chance for me to be a mom. To make us a family. To grow us closer together.

BLAINE: The doctor says there's a strong possibility you'll still miscarry.

GILLIAN: Don't talk that way about Boo.

BLAINE: What?

GILLIAN: I've named the baby, and I talk to it.

DALE: *(Into the phone)* I'll try, but I don't think I can sleep. Bye. *(Hangs up and starts falling asleep)*

GILLIAN: The doctor said getting pregnant's the hardest thing.

BLAINE: He also said there was an eighty percent chance you'd still lose the baby.

GILLIAN: Well, I've given you permission to be the glum one in this relationship, so we're moving along quite rapidly. You mustn't watch me all the time. It makes me nervous.

BLAINE: How are you feeling?

GILLIAN: You mean how's the spotting? *(Harshly)* Why do you ask that? Less, I think. I mean, who ever says more? I present myself as an example— If you have any serious aspirations about the value of rest. The blood's dark red. So, I guess it's old blood, not...I'm not up to talking about it. I'm full of nervousness.

BLAINE: Let me do the worrying. I've the number for the ambulance right here in case the bleeding gets worse while I'm away. And you have my cell phone number.

GILLIAN: Are you leaving?

BLAINE: Thought I'd catch a couple of hours at the library while you try to nap. You need to rest.

GILLIAN: *(SHE gets up uneasily, pours more champagne)* I didn't sleep with that downpour last night. No, I didn't. I'm scared to close my eyes. Sometimes I lie here, throat tight, heart pounding, waiting. Then, the room lightens, the air feels thinner, and I know it's morning. These bad nights have made me anxious.

BLAINE: With that new hormone treatment, the spotting could stop completely. If you remain calm.

GILLIAN: But what are those pills doing to me? My hair's falling out. What's wrong? Why are you looking at me?

BLAINE: *(Wipes her brow)* If I look at you, it's to admire how pretty you look.

GILLIAN: My hair was thicker once. Don't you remember? Now when I comb it, I lose a clump.

BLAINE: Your agent called. When you're feeling better, she wants you to try doing voice-overs.

GILLIAN: I've lost the desire to act now that they've fired me from the series. Only one percent of the roles are for women over thirty-five. And if you become pregnant, they send your character to Australia. I don't think anyone gets used to rejection. An actor has to obey all these klutzes. The last two plays I've seen, actors have been completely nude. It's so degrading. I ask myself, "Do I want a part that bad?" Once you start telling a director what you will or won't do, you become a "diva" whom nobody wants. You can't audition with a lousy attitude. You've got to be up, positive. Besides, all the major roles are cast out of New York. My agent thinks I should move.

(Next door, DALE dials them on her portable phone. The phone rings by the bed. BLAINE waits uneasily for GILLIAN to get it.)

BLAINE: Let me fluff your pillow.

GILLIAN: Don't fuss about me.

BLAINE: *(With nervous exasperation)* Tell me what you need to feel good, and I'll do it.

GILLIAN: Help me balance the checkbook. We're spending more than we're depositing.

BLAINE: I can't face it. I was in pharmacology class, and I'd stopped taking notes—worrying about you and our finances till I heard the class laughing. The professor had called on me three times. Like the way I felt in Gross Anatomy, when I looked around the room and saw the other kids working on their cadavers—knowing exactly what to do, while I experienced a queasy sensation of total ignorance.

GILLIAN: I don't see how we can afford these doctor bills.

(The phone stops ringing. BLAINE sits to eat cake when DALE again phones them from next door. After 8 rings, BLAINE grabs the phone, and GILLIAN retreats into her champagne.)

BLAINE: *(Into the phone upstage)* Hello.

GILLIAN: If that's Dale, tell her the Waterman pen she gave me leaks.

DALE: *(Into the phone)* You promised to read to me.

GILLIAN: From now on let me sign checks with a cheap pen.

BLAINE: *(Into the phone)* I've got to study.

GILLIAN: *(Watching him jealously)* Who's on the phone?

BLAINE: Wrong number.

GILLIAN: Why does wrong number call so much?

BLAINE: It's Dale. I was joking.

DALE: *(Into the phone)* You can work in my room.

BLAINE: Not today. *(HE hangs up. DALE hangs up.)*

GILLIAN: (Throws the checkbook aside) Must she keep phoning you?

BLAINE: She's sick, and I'm her brother.

GILLIAN: Why don't you go away with Dale?

BLAINE: (Clears throat) Getting mad at Dale won't make you feel better. (Swallows) She knows you come first. Look, I'm going to the library.

GILLIAN: Already? It's no fun being married to a dictionary.

BLAINE: (Checks his watch) It's getting late.

GILLIAN: At least when Dale was well, there was someone to scream at.

BLAINE: What time is it?

GILLIAN: Who knows? Dale's set your dad's clocks to the hour of his death.

BLAINE: (Grabs one) You don't want 'em. I'll throw them out! You think I like to sit up all night memorizing names of bacteria and diseases? I'd rather be dead. But I do it. I buoy myself with caffeine and I do it. It's a lot easier to slug about. (Tosses the clock)

GILLIAN: Don't…

BLAINE: You smile, maybe for a sentence, or in bed and poof like a match, you're out. It's not a relationship when you're living with Mrs. Gloom. It's not just the speaking; I need a happy face. And then when I hear you whine, "I'm so depressed," I think how lucky the garbage men are. They drive by, unload the dumpster, and drive on. The trick is to keep you from dumping. If throwing out the clocks will do it, let's kill the clocks. (Dumps another clock) Christ. What's gotten into me. (With a nervous panic) God, I'm sorry. I—

GILLIAN: (Her eyes meet his.) You do pretty well—being married to a phantom.

BLAINE: I'm sorry. It's just that…I'm so wound up, I forgot your surprise—(Scoops her up and carries her to the doorway) I always wanted a portrait of you over the mantle, so—Happy Birthday. It's a good likeness, don't you think? The day you look your prettiest, your wedding.

GILLIAN: And your funeral. This must have cost a fortune.

BLAINE: You're worth it.

GILLIAN: Look, one eye's lit up, one's dark.

BLAINE: You look like this nineteenth-century princess.

GILLIAN: The color of my hair is all wrong.

BLAINE: *(Carrying her back to the bed)* You've the hands of royalty—long and narrow. God, you're beautiful. Expressive eyes, that ethereal smile.

GILLIAN: *(Unzips her gown)* Are you lusting after me?

(DALE begins rocking back and forth.)

BLAINE: It's the gown. The way you unzip it. It was like John Singer Sargent. It had a nice rustle to it. *(THEY kiss.)* Kissing you reminds me of what a miracle the human body is.

GILLIAN: Lock the door. Didn't your daddy tell you about bad girls?

BLAINE: I'm a dead man's son. I make up the rules. I'm going to dance around you. Like a moth round a fire. Give myself over to chaos.

LIGHTS: *Lights fade as BLAINE crawls into bed with GILLIAN.*

END OF SCENE 1

ACT TWO
SCENE 2

(Later that evening. GILLIAN stands on a chair, adjusting her portrait. DALE watches, staring.)

DALE: Is Blaine never coming home?

GILLIAN: He'll be back when he's done studying. *(Beat)* Papa's been deposed.

DALE: *(To GILLIAN)* You don't have to feel bad about not wanting me here. I know I'm moody. My moon is in Virgo, so it's no wonder I'm Byronic.

GILLIAN: It's so difficult right now.

DALE: If you let me, I could help…

GILLIAN: I've the number of the doctor right here. *(Leans back slowly)* God, I've a headache. You can't know what it's like for us to keep going.

DALE: 'Course I do. I'm trying to live my life completely from love—

GILLIAN: Well, back off a bit.

DALE: I got your birthday gift at a little shop in the shadow of the Cathedral.

GILLIAN: *(Lifts up a crystal ball)* My, it's heavy.

DALE: It's a gazing ball. It reflects the moon and the planets. If you touch it, and meditate, the quality of your prayer will shoot up to a new level.

GILLIAN: It's chilly.

DALE: The ball can't feel weather. It's always cold.

GILLIAN: Too bad.

DALE: Lift it. The gazing ball is pink now, but it'll turn blue, lilac, and gold. In the daylight, one half of the ball is dark. Light has the same energy as love. It's true. Southerners are a people of the sun. We used to be a people of the moon, we let the stars rule us, and we watched the moonlight. Then people lived in small places between the earth and sky. God was in the sky, man was on earth, and love was the link between the two. Make a wish. Close your eyes and bare your soul.

GILLIAN: I feel quietly exalted.

DALE: I'd love to do your chart. I believe the spirit's older than the body, and if you tap the soul of another person, the body will revive. I'm resuscitating various parts of myself, opening up drawers, seeing what's there. I want you to know how much being here means to me.

GILLIAN: I do, but—your living here complicates things.

DALE: I would live with y'all anywhere...I've been reading the mystic Schaeffer, who accepts people as they are.

GILLIAN: It's too crowded. Charts and markers all about.

DALE: I could move by the washroom. I'm like jello. You can put me anywhere. I guess Blaine told you...I've this hole in my heart. I'll probably never get married. I've already lived more than they said I would and— *(Breathes heavily)* All I need is my little duck and these snapshots. You can throw the rest of my stuff out.

GILLIAN: Blaine needs quiet.

DALE: Don't lie. You don't like me living here. Sometimes, I put photos around the room, and pretend that I'm back home.

GILLIAN: I don't want to be a deliberate loser, but you're going to have to move.

DALE: *(Pulling out a knife)* Other times, I run this knife over my wrists— telling myself to simply end life.

GILLIAN: Give me the knife.

DALE: You think I don't exist as a feeling person.

GILLIAN: Hand it over.

DALE: I'm terrified I'm going to say something wrong, and that I should cut my tongue out.

GILLIAN: What are you doing?

DALE: I'd like to...rip your picture. Let you see what pain looks like. I know I can't please you. I'm stupid. Oh my! *(Runs wailing to the bathroom)*

GILLIAN: *(Running after her, banging on bathroom door)* Dale! Dale! Dale! . .

END OF SCENE 2

ACT TWO
SCENE 3

(DALE is in her daybed, GILLIAN is resting in her room, and BLAINE is in the kitchen. SARA arrives, bedecked in Oscar de la Renta and carrying champagne, chocolates, and ladyfingers. A thunderstorm rages outside. SARA opens the door with a key.)

SARA: Yoo hoo. Anybody home? I've got champagne and chocolates. It's fine to have an apartment over Jackson Square, but at least install an elevator. There's nothing but ignorance in the Quarter. What a dramatic sky. Rain everywhere, and no one's using umbrellas. The sky is like sharks' teeth. There's a woman out front with a broom. She sits under the gallery but does nothing. I said to her, "Why don't you at least sweep?" *(Removes and shakes out her raincoat)* You're all alone?

DALE: They're around. I was dreaming that y'all were burying me—

SARA: How can you ever improve if—

DALE: Under the James Ashton tree.

SARA: You don't stop the morbidity.

DALE: There's so much shade there...'cause that tree's really two trunks...that grew together. I flew to the treetop.

SARA: They should let some light in here.

DALE: *(Breathing heavily)* From there, the graveyard looked so sweet. The graves were white-washed and numbered. Some names plates had faded—

SARA: Don't talk.

DALE: I spotted some Agapanthus, Dad's favorite flower. The more they're crushed together, the happier they are...And pyracanthus. They're supposed to do well in northern climates, but for some reason they thrive here.

SARA: *(Touches DALE's forehead)* You're in a cold sweat.

DALE: I met Uncle Otto with his dog, Rip. And picked some oleanders—

SARA: *(Throws her hat off)* That's enough! Quiet!

DALE: What's wrong with your face?

SARA: Worry. Grief. What else? *(Rises abruptly, marches to the bedroom, and raps on the door)* Yoo-hoo. *(Hurts her knuckles, examines them)*

BLAINE: *(The next three lines—BLAINE'S, SARA'S, and GILLIAN'S—are said simultaneously.)* One minute.

SARA: I'm in a yucky mood.

GILLIAN: This is a bad time…

SARA: I could gobble everyone up.

(BLAINE enters. While HE, SARA, and DALE talk, GILLIAN fixes up and changes into a long crimson at-home gown.)

BLAINE: Keep your voice down. Ssh. Let's go onto the balcony—

SARA: How about a kiss? My nephew doesn't even know who I am. I have to introduce myself on the way in.

BLAINE: You should call before you barge over.

SARA: I don't think nephews ever pay you back for what you did right.

BLAINE: Over here.

SARA: You can't plan a life and say if I only do things that are high-minded, my family will admire me. They hate you anyway if you keep traveling to Paris.

BLAINE: I've not much to say to you after you—

SARA: Don't punish me for your bad marks.

BLAINE: You ruined my honeymoon!

SARA: I was operating in the best interests of the—

BLAINE: Spare me.

SARA: (Sniffs back a tear) Life has got to mean more than a honeymoon, a degree, or even your nephew insulting you.

BLAINE: You'd better go. (Looking out) Where's Joe?

SARA: Who? Gone for a ham sandwich and won't be back.

BLAINE: You drove?

SARA: You can't get killed in my Cadillac. Trains get out of the way.

BLAINE: (Getting her coat) Let me get your wrap.

SARA: (Skirting him) Blaine's such a gentleman. He'll be fighting with you, but he'll help you with your coat. It's that woman who's turned you against me.

BLAINE: Gillian has influenced me, yes. It's because of her, I'm letting you—

SARA: (Pouting) Aren't you going to ask me, "How was Paris?"

BLAINE: How was Paris?

SARA: Brilliant one minute. Boring the next—

DALE: (Rising slowly) Let me take your hat. Is that lipstick on your cheek?

SARA: It comes and goes. My nephew says it's my meanness popping out. (Gestures to DALE) Put on your robe and slippers.

DALE: Which ones? I don't know what season it is. I sort of drift through the universe.

SARA: The child suffers from neglect. She's stopped eating and batters me with phone calls. (To BLAINE) Are you making your classes?

BLAINE: I go to class. Any class after eleven, I'm there.

SARA: You're failing. Your body can't keep up with your mind. You look awful. Bags under the eyes. Your skin's sallow—How many articles have you published? None? Blaine had fourteen articles published by twenty-one, Dale. He was our shooting star. In February, he barely passed his combined tests.

(HE stares at SARA contemptuously, then turns his eyes toward the door as if HE fears GILLIAN is coming.)

BLAINE: I wanted to take a leave, but Gillian wouldn't have it. I've been studying a lot…over the past few days.

SARA: Do you have a nervous condition? Speaking in bursts.

BLAINE: I'd like to hear you out, but—

SARA: Boys raised in an elegant household can be highly vulnerable. How's Gillian?

BLAINE: I'm sure Dale told you.

SARA: She lies on the couch eating chocolates and turning into the great white blimp. I'd take any spouse, even a blimp, but there aren't too many tall, good-looking men left. There're not too many short ugly ones either.

BLAINE: She's pregnant.

SARA: I know.

BLAINE: And the baby's in trouble.

SARA: She's too old.

BLAINE: Doc Ryan says Gillian needs absolute calm.

(BLAINE forces his face into a kindly expression. SARA examines a plate of ladyfinger cakes.)

(GILLIAN enters, tipsy, in a red dress. SHE holds a glass of champagne which she

has been guzzling. She gives BLAINE a nervous look, her manner self-conscious. BLAINE grows increasingly agitated with GILLIAN's drinking.)

GILLIAN: What about Doc Ryan?

BLAINE: You should be resting.

GILLIAN: *(Gestures to the portrait)* I wanted to see y'all's reaction to my birthday gift. Well, what do you think?

DALE: That picture's so…peculiar.

SARA: It does capture a certain *"Je ne sais quoi."* Perfect for over a casket in a funeral parlor.

GILLIAN: Or over a mantle in the Baroness de Pontalba's apartment.

SARA: You've gotten so pale. And puffy.

GILLIAN: Arthritis—

SARA: I never knew what arthritis was till I was forty. Men do need a fecund woman coming from good stock.

GILLIAN: *(To SARA)* What a fancy outfit.

SARA: I worked with my designer to "do" this dress. Oscar won't design for anyone who won't wear him exclusively, so I had to throw out all my clothes—you want his number?

GILLIAN: *(Starts to pass her and stumbles, a bit tipsy)* I didn't say I liked it. I said it was fancy— *(Dryly)* Actually I do…like it. Let's open the champagne.

BLAINE: *(To GILLIAN, regarding the champagne)* Careful. I love your dress.

GILLIAN: I got tired of all that black. With Blaine gone all the time, the neighbors thought I was a widow. So I went and bought a scarlet dress in a miracle fabric.

SARA: Let's prudently change the subject.

GILLIAN: I've been putting up with you damned people…trying to create a personal life. But you're like bats; as soon as I get rid of one of you, another one flies in through the belfry.

DALE: I'm praying for you. That you'll find the courage to risk letting God in your life.

GILLIAN: I know about your spirituality. Fanaticism sometimes used to counteract a charmlessness in a person. Some people make themselves more intrusive than anyone thought they'd be.

DALE: (Sobbing) Oh my…Oh my.

SARA: The girl is grieving.

GILLIAN: I'm trying to dislocate the sensor that makes me resent the hell out of you.

BLAINE: (To GILLIAN) Honey, you've got to rest.

GILLIAN: Later.

SARA: Since Dale's moved here, her new doctor says she sleepwalks at night. I talked to Dr. Ryan on the phone. The man's more radical, but somehow sincere.

DALE: All of a sudden I feel this presence. Like someone is in the room. (SHE races to the bathroom.)

SARA: Midnight ravings, and the doctor's prescribing more antidepressants for her mood swings. He can't figure out why Dale's running a low-grade fever. It's more than the shock of her father's death; they know that much now. He feels Dale isn't being appropriately monitored, and that Gillian isn't sensitive to her condition. I'll stay with you for a few days. Access the situa—

GILLIAN: Ah-ha! There's the hitch. I don't want family snoops. (Waves of anxiety rush through her. SHE grasps her stomach.)

BLAINE: Will you get in bed?

GILLIAN: (To SARA) You invade my house. Come barging in and think you can do that.

BLAINE: Aunt Sara was leaving.

GILLIAN: *(To Sara)* You're a neurotic criminal. A swindler with no sense of consequence. Casting a spell by disapproving of me. I've a right to my own body, my own privacy. *(SHE clutches her stomach.)* Ah. Ooh!

SARA: Tut. Tut. Sick people, they use up the living.

BLAINE: *(To GILLIAN)* Why must you punish me? Let's go to the bedroom.

GILLIAN: No.

SARA: No. I must talk to you. I bought y'all a house. It's one of those marvelous Gothic Revival houses. Delicate in appearance in this soft, rose shade. The style takes its inspiration from twelfth-century cathedrals. With pointed arches, and diamond-shaped lights. And it's on St. Charles Avenue.

GILLIAN: *(To SARA)* Near your house?

SARA: Down the block. Blaine used to make his nurse pass it. So I said to myself, why not buy the boy something?

GILLIAN: But I like this apartment!

SARA: Surely you want what's best for Blaine—The boy's exhausted. I can't in good conscience watch you both flounder.

BLAINE: It's stupid to imagine awful things, but I worry when I leave—

SARA: If you were nearby, the servants could help out.

GILLIAN: I'm not moving.

SARA: *(Takes a sandwich)* Since y'all married, I've been poised for catastrophe.

BLAINE: We don't have to make a decision right away.

SARA: *(Screams OFFSTAGE)* Dale.

GILLIAN: She's in the bathroom.

BLAINE: *(To SARA)* Get her. I need to talk to Gillian alone.

SARA: I'm starving. Where's your kitchen? *(Exits)*

BLAINE: *(To GILLIAN)* You should eat. I don't get it. What's so horrible about her buying us a house?

GILLIAN: I want to live uptown, I do, but when I think of them next door, I hyperventilate.

BLAINE: *(Passes her the contract)* The contract's already been signed.

GILLIAN: Interesting. Ha, ha! The house was bought for you and your sister. See your names and Social Security numbers here.

BLAINE: A formality. Aunt Sara has seen so many marriages fail, she doesn't count on—

GILLIAN: Ours to last.

BLAINE: I'm sorry my family's so screwy. I was born into an insane asylum; I got out.

GILLIAN: *(GILLIAN clasps her stomach and moans.)* Ooh.

BLAINE: God, no—

GILLIAN: I've known women like your aunt.

BLAINE: Sit. Oh, please—

GILLIAN: Egomaniacs living for themselves—

BLAINE: Gillian, please—

GILLIAN: They destroy their in-laws' lives…because nobody stops them. *(Grabs her stomach)* Ooh. Ah.

BLAINE: It's going to be all right. I'm here.

GILLIAN: The new wife hopes she can make it because the sex is good, and the sister's spells of brooding are short. I want to destroy this paper.

BLAINE: Yes. Yes. What is it? Are you bleeding badly?

GILLIAN: I lived with bullies like your aunt. Wouldn't buy you a house—but where they wanted it. They need a man to control because they're out of control themselves.

BLAINE: Look, I just talked to her. Rest for a while, eat something.

GILLIAN: Talking to your aunt doesn't work because the woman lies. And you? You believe her excuses.

BLAINE: Close your eyes for a second. It'll do you a world of good. When Dad died, I was practically crazy with loneliness. He died three times—wiped out totally—but the doctors kept bringing him back. But then he was gone, see. Really dead. I was shaking in my shoes for weeks, shaking like a little hard stone. I put myself in a situation in my classes where I had to work at a speed that allowed no time for sadness. I had my family and my studies, but was constantly lonely. And then I met you. And I had this awakening experience. Just being near you I feel this burst of energy around my heart like it's all white, exploding full of love. Unconditional love. That's why I can love you as I do and Dale at the same time.

GILLIAN: Do you think we could live far away, after med school?

BLAINE: Trouble is, you grow up in New Orleans and you like to have it around. I could compromise. (BLAINE looks grimly away and walks to the window. GILLIAN runs her fingers nervously over her stomach.) I know I shouldn't trust Aunt Sara, but the situation here isn't working. I'd like to hire a companion for Dale. Pay for her to see the best specialists and for you to—But what will I use for money? Move to that house for a year. For the love of Jesus, let's do this.

GILLIAN: I was so fit before this—You remember. Making love with you night after night. When the doctor told me I couldn't have kids, I handled it. But when I found out I was pregnant, I felt young again. Like a teenager. I want Boo to live, Blaine. I want to be a family. I can't live by your relatives. I feel myself disintegrating when they're around.

BLAINE: Listen, Gillian. I want a family more than anything. But why can't you accept that Dale is part of our family? *(Clears throat. Pulls out a report)* Dale is just having problems creating a new structure for herself. Her medication works, but only for a period of time.

GILLIAN: Oh Lord, don't—

BLAINE: Dale's got to continue living with us—here or in that house.

GILLIAN: Won't your aunt take care of Dale?

BLAINE: She's not going to care for my sister alone. She's never had to do anything alone, and she's not going to start now. If Dale is near us, I can keep an eye on her. Why are you against living uptown? We'll have our own house. You don't have to go to their—

GILLIAN: I've sympathy for your sister, but you made a promise to me. I see myself getting sicker every day. And if I lose the baby, it'll be your fault.

BLAINE: Don't say that. Can't you see? I'm desperate, exhausted. Dale's in a very heightened state. It's a restorative measure the body is taking on for—

GILLIAN: I'm not moving.

BLAINE: That's it? You're going to leave me...hanging? You go do any nasty thing you like. It's pretty horrible to...Dale's young.

GILLIAN: And I'm not.

BLAINE: She has feelings, for God's sake.

GILLIAN: And I don't.

BLAINE: You want me to pretend she hasn't suffered shock.

GILLIAN: My first husband was a stuntman. Caught on fire, jumped off cliffs. He was a man who punished you when you said "No." Once my husband got so mad, he cracked an egg on my head. Another time, he busted my lip. See, here's the scar. The day I left him, he held a gun to my head and screamed, "I'm going to kill you." *(GILLIAN'S speech accelerates. Thunder crashes.)* See where he put out a cigarette in my scalp? Do you know what it's like not to be able to sleep because your heart is racing so fast? To have this permanent shakiness in your fingers? *(SHE grasps her stomach as if SHE'S just had a cramp.)* I spent my marriage forgetting details of events that took place hours before. Wore turtlenecks to cover the bruises. After I found the guts to leave him, I never let fear stop me like it did before. And now my body's alive again, and I'll do anything to keep our baby.

BLAINE: I'm sure Dale's condition will improve…if we move her. God, I'm betting it will.

GILLIAN: Do as you like. Send her to your aunt's, to boarding school, to the hospital. Feel free to live with Dale if you want. But I will not. I've got to rest.

(GILLIAN starts to exit.)

BLAINE: I taught her how to walk, how to tie her shoe. How to flatten a penny on the tracks.

(GILLIAN exits. BLAINE picks up a medical book, skims it, hurls it down. Stuffs the contract in his pocket. Blues music drifts up from the street. HE walks out onto the balcony as SARA enters looking for BLAINE with chocolates and some liqueur glasses.)

SARA: Cabernet Sauvignon?

BLAINE: Here. On the balcony. Gillian's gone to bed. She's very edgy. She needs rest, but she can't rest.

SARA: It's difficult to control someone you care about.

BLAINE: Will you stop?

SARA: She's an actress! The stage is her God.

BLAINE: She's quit acting.

SARA: Chocolate?

BLAINE: Thanks.

SARA: Chocolate should be enjoyed with a dessert wine. Look outside at the light and the land. Dale says light defines experience but I think it's the land. Jackson Square. Your sister's in the bathroom sobbing.

BLAINE: There's no heros in the real world, just in bad fiction. You're going to have to hire someone to live with her in that house.

SARA: A stranger. When she has a brother?

BLAINE: Then you'll have to take her back in. *(Calls)* Dale, come here.

DALE: *(OFFSTAGE)* Coming.

SARA: *(Reaches for a drink)* I can't handle it. Her willful attempts to get attention, the suicide threats. The trigger can be almost anything—ice, an unexpected rainstorm. Look, I've chewed my lips so bad, they're bleeding. Thank God for Drambuie.

BLAINE: Are you going to numb yourself to sleep?

SARA: They say if there's no support structure at home, she'll have to learn limits inside a clinic. Of course, they do have that adolescent program at De Paul, but it's all so humiliating.

BLAINE: I can't toss her in a bin with the freaks. I've worried about Dale so much longer than you. Since she was born.

SARA: At seventeen, she'll need to go to the adult ward. Then Dr. Ryan talks about some experimental studies with needle electrodes…that have a higher response rate than drug therapy.

DALE: Y'all, it's so exciting. *(Runs in)* A bat's on the ledge by the window.

BLAINE: Calm down.

DALE: I cracked the door, and when I went to open it, that bat's pointed face looked up at me with its wings fanned out.

SARA: Don't buzz about me.

DALE: I once had two bats in my room. I woke up one night to this whirl flying about. When I saw it was a bat, I scrunched under the covers.

SARA: Stop emoting.

DALE: The next day, Daddy died. Are bats a sign of death?

BLAINE: I don't know. Dale, listen. Gillian and I may not be moving to that…house on Saint Charles.

DALE: But Aunt Sara's already bought it.

BLAINE: Gillian likes it here.

DALE: If only you'd show it to her, she'd be mad for that big house. It has a side entrance—under a *porte cochere*. There's a room with a view of a garden with a kind of early evening dark. She'll have such energy in that house.

BLAINE: I'm upset about it—

SARA: *(To BLAINE)* Blaine's upset, but not so upset it galvanizes him to compassion. Gillian will change her mind. Take your time and seize the right opportunity to show her the house. To catch prey, leopards lie in wait in tree branches. When the animal passes below, the cat pounces on it.

BLAINE: *(To DALE)* You think you'd like us all in that house, but you wouldn't if—Have you never felt bad about hanging around married people so much?

GILLIAN: *(OFFSTAGE)* Blaine!

(BLAINE exits)

DALE: It's Gillian who's poisoned…him…against me.

SARA: I've got to go to *les toilettes*.

(SARA exits. DALE gasps and wails after them.)

DALE: Gillian lies because she wants…Blaine for herself— I've tried to reach her. But I can't. She's so cold, vultures get out of her way.

(A tropical storm descends. Thunder, lightning and darkness. DALE gets a suitcase out of the hall closet and begins collecting pictures, paperweights. Her nervous state is extremely apparent. SHE is a young girl who has cracked up before and is going to crack again—perhaps repeatedly. DALE's eyes dart away, picking objects out of the gloom. The scene is bathed in a deep silver, almost bluish light; the heavy furniture gleams with dampness from the rain outside.)

GILLIAN: Lightning hit the balcony.

DALE: *(Tossing objects in the suitcase)* Blaine's losing it. Screaming because I want to…live near…you. I can't stand y'all…I'm taking my basket. My picture. My tray.

GILLIAN: You feel helpless?

DALE: I'm going away. Where's that locket of my baby hair and my picture—Blaine kept on the mantle?

(GILLIAN clutches the back of a chair and draws a few deep breaths as if SHE had sudden cramps. DALE gasps for breath.)

DALE: If I thought Blaine would never see me again, I'd set my body on fire, burn myself up. Might as well talk about the clinic…People telling me not to do what I want to do, not to feel what I can't help feeling. Worry eating me alive.

GILLIAN: Love Blaine, but let him have his own life.

DALE: I'm not taking it from him!

GILLIAN: What am I supposed to do—Forget that I'm married?

DALE: I want my gazing ball back.

GILLIAN: Never lead an adult life—

(DALE grabs a suitcase and tosses the ball in, yanks down some clocks.)

DALE: And Daddy's clocks. On any one night he'd have forty clocks ticking in the house. This picture of Blaine belongs to me.

GILLIAN: I know it's difficult for you…

DALE: Half of that big house was mine. You wouldn't have had to see me.

GILLIAN: You've got to accept certain unpleasant things about Blaine and me, that we're married and want to be alone. I failed so miserably before—

DALE: I'm taking my baby cup Blaine was keeping. These bronzed baby shoes. And this locket of hair. (DALE runs to the door, but GILLIAN seizes her by the wrist.) Oh, I can't breathe.

GILLIAN: Blaine's the first decent thing in my life—

DALE: I knew what you were from the first. Taking everything for yourself and…I'm running away—

GILLIAN: It's not normal how you cling to Blaine.

DALE: I'm never coming back.

GILLIAN: Whenever you're in the room, I look up and I see you either glaring or gazing at him. You don't want him to be happy because you want him scared, hopeless, shaken to the bone. It's a lifestyle I won't move into. I won't let you jump, hop, and scurry your way into my life.

(GILLIAN forces DALE to her knees, crying hysterically.)

DALE: I've a right to my own brother. Get away. Back off. You witch! I'll hurt you if you don't let me live here. You want to get rid of me? Why don't you kill me? (Takes a knife and pushes it in GILLIAN's hand) Hurry up and get it over with. Kill me!

(Entering, his face haggard, BLAINE pulls them apart. The storm builds outside. The wind over the Mississippi rises, sweeping over Jackson Square. Lightning streaks the sky.)

BLAINE: Gillian!

DALE: She's making up lies about me.

GILLIAN: I'm not!

DALE: *(Her breath quickens.)* It's like this fist's...closing...over my...My heart's pounding, hammering, beating flip-flops.

BLAINE: What have you done to her? She's burning up.

GILLIAN: She's crazy.

DALE: My heart.

BLAINE: Get her pills.

GILLIAN: Dale, you mustn't pretend.

DALE: This roaring's in my ears.

BLAINE: Put a pillow under her.

DALE: *(Gulps air furiously. Her body stiffens in apprehension.)* Don't leave me, Blaine.

BLAINE: I won't.

DALE: *(To GILLIAN)* Blaine wouldn't have said "no" to that house...if you didn't...hate me.

BLAINE: I didn't say no.

GILLIAN: What did you say?

SOUND: Thunder crashes.

DALE: How would you like it if someone threw you away?

GILLIAN: *(Clutches her stomach)* No. Ugh.

BLAINE: You're cramping.

DALE: Faker. I hate your apartment.

BLAINE: *(Leads Gillian to the chaise lounge)* Rest.

DALE: I hope it burns. I hope you burn in hell.

BLAINE: *(The lights flicker and go out.)* Dale. Quiet.

DALE : I hope you lose…everything you love. I hope God kills your baby.

(BLAINE slaps DALE in the face. HE walks slowly and sits by GILLIAN. Rain pours. Lightning flashes. The lights go out. DALE crosses with a candle as if seeking a ghost. Thunder claps and the sound of rain closes in. DALE drifts to the balcony as a diamond-like sheet of rain descends, catching the light and quietly gleaming. DALE extends her hands under the rainfall, turning them as if to cleanse them. Then she scoops up water and cools her forehead. The rainfall increases. DALE takes her hands from her burning forehead and stretches them through the rain as if reaching for someone beyond the moon.)

DALE: *(To DADDY, laughs)* Daddy. How'd you find me?

BLAINE: Who are you talking to?

DALE: *(To DADDY)* Magic. I'm the empress of Louisiana, remember? *(To BLAINE)* Blaine, that's disgusting. I think most men who desire virgins are insecure about sex. They feel since the girl's never had any, she'll think they're good. My, you're a hustler. Button your shirt up. *(To DADDY)* Go kill me. Get it over with. *(Searches about. DALE grabs SARA'S purse. BLAINE starts toward DALE.)*

BLAINE: I don't know how to help you.

DALE: Say your rosary, get in bed. Daddy's come. He's alive. He can come out the grave. Let's take a joyride. *(Exits)*

BLAINE: We've got to catch her.

GILLIAN: *(Blocks the door)* Just trample me down. Hurry up and get it over with.

SOUND: *An alarm blares. Sound of cars braking over a sodden road.*

BLAINE: Move.

GILLIAN: No. If she can't have you, she's going to— put herself in the emergency room. One pays for relatives, if relatives don't learn.

SOUND: *An alarm blares. An engine rushes OFFSTAGE.*

SARA: *(Running in from the bathroom)* She's gunning my Cadillac like a missile. I saw her from the bathroom window. We'd better go down.

(SARA exits. BLAINE peers about, wild-eyed. GILLIAN'S facial muscles twitch and she draws in her breath with a sharp sound. Picks up the phone. The alarm cuts off.)

BLAINE: I can't watch her kill herself. Go and identify the body.

GILLIAN: Call the police and her doctor. *(Dials the phone)*

BLAINE: What are you doing?

GILLIAN: Stopping this. *(Into the phone.)* Hello. This is Mrs. Ashton. Could you send...a patrol car over? The Pontalba apartments. Saint Peter. My sister, Dale Ashton is...heading down Chartres Street in a stolen vehicle.

(GILLIAN drops the receiver and grabs her stomach. HER lips form a mute O. SHE cannot talk. SHE stands motionless, breathing heavily. HE watches her. Rain pours outside. Lightning flashes.)

BLAINE: God! Get off your feet. I'll be right back.

GILLIAN: *(SHE lies down.)* We've got to finish this. I know you've been excessively close to Dale.

BLAINE: Go lie in our room—

GILLIAN: Your long walks. And all those nights you tucked her in bed when your dad was ill.

BLAINE: You think our relationship was as rotten-minded as—All of Dale's problems are related to my father. He worshiped her. It wasn't anything crude and incestuous. Just an aging father loving a pretty daughter who reminded him of his young wife. She reflected his youth back to him like a twisted mirror. And when Dad died, Dale became a sort...of widow.

GILLIAN: Oh, it's so attractive to be a helpless waif buffeted by the seas of an unfair world. Well, the wild ride is finally ended. You have a choice. I know this is painful, but are you going to let her destroy both of you?

(*Sounds of someone running up the stairs. SARA rushes back in.*)

SARA: Dale's started up my Cadillac. If you care about Dale, don't let her die.

GILLIAN: I wish one of these times she would die. She's inflicted so much pain on Blaine.

SARA: And what have you given Blaine, a barren future.

(*DALE charges in, disheveled and muddy, with a gun.*)

DALE: That's it. Hands up. Faces to the wall. All of you.

SARA: My gun.

DALE: Going to see if this works.

SARA: Put that down, it's loaded.

BLAINE: Give me the gun.

DALE: Faces to the wall, I said.

(*SARA and GILLIAN turn.*)

BLAINE: Wait!

DALE: Turn around.

BLAINE: Look—Dale. Hold on a minute.

DALE: I'm racing the engine and I realize it's not me I want to kill. It's her. Her, Aunt Sara, and that baby. Everybody, lie on the floor now.

BLAINE: Don't move, y'all.

DALE: Put your faces on the ground, or I'll shoot. (*Waves the gun around*)

BLAINE: Why are you doing this?

DALE: Drop, I said. *(Shoots the ceiling)* Think you can ignore how I feel? That I'm that dumb? Lie down, bitch.

SARA: Oh.

GILLIAN: Ah.

DALE: Listen or I'll blow your heads off.

BLAINE: *(Steps forward)* Hand me the gun. I'm walking to you now. If you shoot someone, it'll be me.

DALE: Stay back.

BLAINE: No.

DALE: I'm warning you.

BLAINE: The gun—

DALE: Back or I'll shoot.

BLAINE: Hand it—*(DALE shoots the gun.)*

BLAINE: Awl.

SARA: You almost hurt Blaine.

GILLIAN: You nearly killed him.

DALE: It's Gillian's fault. She made me do it.

(SHE ducks from him, runs into the bedroom, locks the door.)

BLAINE: Dale, open up.

DALE: I'll kill myself. Cause she made me do it.

GILLIAN: Oh, God.

BLAINE: Open the door.

SARA: Oh, please, Dale, please.

(*BLAINE breaks down the door as police sirens resound from a distance. DALE is stretched out in a pool of blood. They cross to her moaning, "Oh no. Please. Lord. What did she do?" when DALE jumps up.*)

DALE: Surprise! I think I should go on stage with Gillian. You like my death scene? (*Police sirens grow louder out front.*) Fake blood from the magic store. Great joke, ha-ha. I really scared you. Ha.

BLAINE: (*Crosses to the phone and picks up the receiver*) Hello? 911? My sister Dale Ashton has attempted suicide. Could you send someone up? Please contact her doctor. Dr. Howard Ryan at Touro, and have him meet her at the hospital. Then deliver my sister there. (*Gets out suitcase*)

SARA: What are you doing?

BLAINE: Packing. I'm going away. (*To GILLIAN*) You coming?

GILLIAN: With wings. (*Begins to pack*)

SARA: Are you crazy?

BLAINE: Maybe. Buddhists believe great fortune belongs to those who release living things. I release you, Dale. I release you, Sara.

SARA: Don't you care about your sister? She needs—

BLAINE: This time, the authorities will handle the situation.

SARA: The authorities!

BLAINE: Aunt Sara, I'm putting Dale in your capable hands. I know it's going to be a rough time for her, but you can get through it together. You've lived a fearful life, Aunt Sara, now you can come into your own. A wife has to come before a sister. A baby before anyone. I'm leaving for a much needed rest. My wife never had a honeymoon. New Orleans is the city Rhett Butler took Scarlet O'Hara to after their wedding. Bye, Dale.

(*THEY exit*)

SARA: *(Screams)* What hotel are you going to? Blaine! Answer me! Tell me!

BLAINE and GILLIAN: *(Their voices overlap OFFSTAGE)* We'll call you.

END OF SCENE 3

ACT TWO
SCENE 4

(A rainy Christmas Eve, seven months later. 6:00 p. m. At rise of curtain, a street version of Jingle Bells resounds, a clock chimes, and Cathedral bells ring out. A bassinet with blue bows dresses one corner. BLAINE hurries in, wearing a raincoat. HE unloads snacks: cheese straws, caviar, egg nog, a metallic tree dressed with tinsel and gold babies. HE pours himself some egg nog in a mint julep cup and reads a card.)

BLAINE: *(Drops card and talks to his son)* "Merry Christmas to my Louisiana Gentleman." I am not a Louisiana gentleman. I'm not sure what that is. But if any of the predictions of the doom of my family are true, I want to be there with my own life when my family dies....Last year, when they put your Aunt Dale in the hospital, I lay on the railroad tracks and prayed that a train would hit me. It was pouring outside, just like tonight. I resigned myself to death, and it was easy. I woke up with the sound of fire scorching metal, and walked off the tracks. Most times, fire puts you to sleep....Your Aunt Dale is coming home from DePaul Clinic tonight. That's a place where they fix people who are broken in the head. She's better. Aunt Sara visited her once. She'd go more often, but she remarried and travels a lot. I go twice a week with Dale's dog, Voyager. Woof. Woof. Now and then, Dale looks to see if he's standing up or lying on the ground. Robins have adopted her. She fed them some crumbs and now they peck away. Scratch. Scratch. She says they got those red breasts from picking the nails out of Christ's hands. *(Places some sketches about the room)* Most times I visit, Dale draws and I sit there and listen to the wind chimes ringing out. You can do too much for fear of the need to do something. Drawing's become an obsession. She's done a series of spring dresses. You know the story of Persephone, the goddess of spring? Persephone was condemned to Hades, but Zeus said she could return to earth six months a year, if she could row down the River Styx past her relatives who screamed out for help and not stop. Dale says becoming an adult feels like that.

SOUND: *A pounding on the door.*

BLAINE: Who is it?

SARA: *(OFFSTAGE into the INTERCOM)* Mrs. Claus.

BLAINE: You're early, Aunt Sara.

(BLAINE flattens his hair and opens the door. SARA enters in a long Christmas gown with an extravagant coat and hat.)

SARA: Titanic weather. Some woman's walking a duck down the street. There's a drunk by the doorway. A man shooting some film let me in.

BLAINE: Merry Christmas.

SARA: *(Sticking her cheek out for a kiss)* Thank you, darling.

BLAINE: *(Takes her coat and shakes out droplets of water)* Mm. Fabulous coat.

SARA: I dress like I want. I don't owe anybody anything.

(HE exits to the kitchen.)

SARA: Where's beauty boy?

BLAINE: *(OFFSTAGE)* Asleep.

SARA: Ooh. What an adorable snore. *(Talks to the baby)* For my baby, Saks is delivering three flying monkeys, a teddy bear, and something with tiny feet, a head, and a big spindly back. It looks like a roller toy, but it's an African porcupine. *(Crosses to the door)* Weather's ghastly, somewhere between a mist and a drizzle. You can almost taste that old Creole dust. Driving down here, the traffic was barely creeping, and the wreck was on the other side of the road. *(Waves at the car)* Francois, I'm over here. My husband forgets where you live from trip to trip. We'd come more often but—*(Looking out, screams)* Francois, come inside. The man knows no strangers, because he talks to everyone. Artists. *(Sniffs, calls out to BLAINE)* The Quarter is a place I'll never get used to. Rancid odor? I could go all year without smelling that River. You got canapés?

BLAINE: *(OFFSTAGE)* On the table.

SARA: *(Examines the tree)* Your tree's too small. And dried out.

BLAINE: *(OFFSTAGE)* Gillian fixed it for Boo.

SARA: That explains the color clashes and that avalanche of tinsel. Is everything in metallic this year?

BLAINE: *(OFFSTAGE)* The better for Boo to see it.

SARA: Cute. I suppose a little frivolity is good for the soul.

BLAINE: *(Pokes his head in)* The ornaments are gold babies. Hang one.

SARA: You do it. I hate fun. We have three parties tonight. You? Medicine's still a social art. Now they don't allow smoking at Touro, so half of the hospital is chatting on the roof. Glad to see your grades are improving.

BLAINE: *(OFFSTAGE)* Solid honors.

SARA: Your father was first of his class.

BLAINE: *(Pokes his head out the door)* I gave up trying to be first. Too much stress on my family.

SARA: Francois runs around catering to everybody. *(Calls out)* Your house is a perpetual mess. Dust can't be good for the baby. How often does your wife clean? Hmph. The word maintenance isn't in Gillian's vocabulary....I have a man general clean our house. It's easier for me to ask a man to do something. For some reason it's always appealed to me. You want his name? *(When BLAINE doesn't respond SHE screams)* Caviar's soggy. *(Calls out to the street)* Francois. *(To BLAINE)* Thinks you are on Saint Anne. He's none of the bad qualities usually associated with social climbers.

(BLAINE enters dressed in a red sweater, fresh shirt, and slacks. HE carries a silver pitcher of egg nog and cups.)

BLAINE: I'm glad y'all are happy. Egg nog's nice and hot.

SARA: Good, because your cheese straws are limp. *(Checks her watch)*

Where is Gillian? I know this is a snobbish comment. But no woman in the Garden District would keep an in-law waiting. It would never happen. *(Waves to the street)* Francois! Will you come up here. He couldn't find a spot so he's waiting in the car. The category is gone for what Francois does. A true gentleman.

(GILLIAN and DALE enter, dressed in matching long velvet dresses. DALE acts alert, but fragile.)

GILLIAN: My dream is to belt out a slightly bawdy song in a low-cut dress.

SARA: I didn't see you.

DALE: We came through…the back.

GILLIAN: I spent hundreds on a seamstress. Matching dresses in Dale's design.

BLAINE: *(Opens his arms to DALE)* For your first visit home.

DALE: I've got to …be back…by eight o'clock. *(Points to the dresses)* They're not too expensive.

BLAINE: Have I ever denied y'all anything?

DALE: *(Glancing about)* Things look…so bright…and tin…sel…ly.

BLAINE: Sit here, girls. I don't want y'all to get a draft.

SARA: *(To GILLIAN)* What do you do to make men dote on you so?

BLAINE: She exists. *(Puts out some mistletoe and kisses GILLIAN.)* Mistletoe.

SARA: Dale, precious, come give me a hug.

BLAINE: *(To DALE)* You look splendid. You've gained weight. Your skin's shiny.

DALE: Is it? I…used that new makeup you sent…Blaine, people at the hospital…make me feel good about myself.

SARA: Don't talk about it.

DALE: I was lost somewhere inside my bad thoughts…but I'm learning how to hold my feelings in check.

GILLIAN: That's great.

BLAINE: Wonderful.

DALE: I've been doing…well in workshop. I drew…some baby clothes…for Blaine, Jr.

GILLIAN: Marvelous.

BLAINE: They're fantastic.

SARA: Yes. The sketches are quite good.

DALE: I'm so breathy…about them. I…designed…a series…for each…month.

GILLIAN: *(Lifting a design. Doorbell rings.)* How adorable.

SARA: *(Rummages in her purse)* Where did I put those clippings from *Le Monde*? Big purses. You can find everything and nothing in them at the same time. *(To BLAINE)* Look at Dale's drawing. Francois thinks one day she'll go to the School des Beaux Arts.

SOUND: *The doorbell rings.*

SARA: That's Francois. Tell him I'll be coming along.

BLAINE: You just got here.

SARA: We're on our way to the country club. That's the thing about New Orleans. There're too many parties. Other places, you eat and drink between Thanksgiving and Christmas, then you have a break. Not here, you go right into Mardi Gras, Easter, Saint Patty's day and the Fourth of July. Maybe you should wake the baby so Dale can say goodbye.

DALE: I don't want…Francois…to drive me back. I want Blaine to take me.

SARA: (Gestures to the rain) But there's no reason for Blaine to brave this…sleaze. We have to pass the clinic—

BLAINE: I want to drive her. We could look at the Christmas lights. I'll drive you later.

SARA: What a darling boy.

DALE: It's not…too…much…trouble?

BLAINE: 'Course not.

DALE: Thanks.

(Doorbell rings again. DALE exits to the front door.)

SARA: I don't know if you realize what a darling boy Blaine is. He's a regular Louisiana gentleman. If I could've had sons like Blaine, I would have peopled Louisiana. (Hands him a money envelope) Merry Christmas early. I've commissioned a painting of Boo. I detest portraits. Nevertheless we must have them. A good portrait is one of the niceties of civilization. Portraits, and lockets, and silver baby cups.

(DALE returns)

DALE: Oh, you put out…my drawings. And I…love the…tree. With gold…babies.

GILLIAN: Time to put the angel on top.

BLAINE: (Lifting DALE) You do it.

SARA: (To BLAINE) Don't drop her.

BLAINE: Geez, you're heavy.

SARA: You'll muss her dress.

DALE: The angel's…smiling…on our family.

GILLIAN: Let's turn on Christmas music and get a picture. (Puts on music)

SARA: I'll take it. I've a horror of photographs.

GILLIAN: Everybody smile and squish together.

DALE: *(To BLAINE)* Get in the middle.

SARA: A wife, a sister, and a new baby. That's rough.

BLAINE: Should be a banner year.

(The camera flashes, "Have Yourself a Very Merry Christmas" plays as the curtain falls.)

CURTAIN

Photo: Christian Raby
Pictured: Shelley Poncy,
Soline McLain

Solitaire

A PLAY IN TWO ACTS

First performed in November 1993
American Center, Paris

CAST OF CHARACTERS

IRENE DUBONNET (MIMI). 60+. Strong, stylish widow of one month. Wears a hat cocked over one eye, a neck smothered with pearls, a 5-caret solitaire. Irene dresses young—dying her hair a richer version of red to offset her violet eyes—and flashing a fan, color coordinated to each outfit, against the heat. Irene could pass for forty.

ROOSTER DUBONNET (ROO). 30. Her son, an artist and a dreamer with the boyish charm of a college freshman. Very careless. Rooster appears pale, sickly, with flushed cheeks and locks of hair tumbling in disarray over his forehead. An uncertainty is at the center of all his choices. Rooster forgets to change his clothes.

QUINT LEGERE. 45. Irene's son-in-law, a driven accountant. Very neat. No matter what Quint wears, his broad shoulders and smooth tan make him look first class. Quint changes his shirt four times a day to keep crisp in the summer. Quint feels it's important to dress your best when you feel your worst.

BUNKY. 20. The only son of Quint and ex-wife Kitten Dubonnet Legere. Nonchalant and seductive in blue jeans and boots, he refuses to relate to school. He wears a tee-shirt which reads, "Protect Wild Life. Throw a Party." Bunky is a rebel—with a wild streak of fun. He quells his passion for adventure by absorbing himself in blues music and busywork for his relatives.

JASMINE RUSH. 36. Adopted daughter of Irene Dubonnet, glamorous actress. Dresses outrageously—over the edge of Italian fashion—with heavy eye make-up and ensembles contoured to her body and legs. The most famous hand model in the world, Jasmine needs help doing ordinary things like opening bottles, zipping gowns, dialing the phone—so she won't rip a nail.

THE TIME

The not-too-distant present. July 4th weekend.

SETTING

Gallery of "Serenity," a summer mansion, Pass Christian, Mississippi.
ACT ONE: SCENE ONE. "Serenity." Sunday, July third. Late afternoon.
SCENE TWO. "Serenity." The next day. Twilight.
ACT TWO: SCENE ONE. "Serenity." Sunday afternoon, one week later.

ACT ONE
SCENE ONE

(The gallery of a Greek Revival home facing the Gulf of Mexico. Pass Christian, Mississippi. The Gulf Coast is the haunt of wealthy but weary New Orleanians: people wearing seersucker suits and white sundresses, people who might otherwise dine at Antoine's Restaurant in New Orleans. The mansion (one of the few intact after Hurricane Camille) reminds one of plantation culture, of that doomed if circumspect way of life.

The gallery overlooks a paradise of flowers and veil after veil of shrubbery, a pool, a duck pond, gardens with birds, marshes and woods. Dubbed "Serenity," the estate remains the heart of a kingdom of wildlife, their final refuge from a world grown too strange, too hard, and too disturbing.

The action passes on a gallery, with baskets of blue hydrangeas and colored garden furniture placed over soft brick. A rotating ceiling fan is spinning shadows overhead. Windows catch reflections from the trees and moss, their shutters, perfect for eavesdropping, trembling ever so slightly. The sturdy columns of plastered brick evoke nostalgia while appearing lost in space. They seem to ascend into the sky. The place has a haunted elegant quality, as if it had been constructed for a reception after a defeat. The ghost of old fears, the gallery fuses light and shadow in the unrelenting heat. Today, the gallery feels luminous, public, and safe, i.e., conducive to mindless chatter.

A lazy Sunday tableau. A tray of scotch and bourbon, a bucket of ice, and hors d'oeuvres: olives, celery, pickles, caviar, and cheese straws are set out for Sunday cocktails.)

SOUND: *Throughout the act, there is heard the soft cries of sea gulls and the lapping of waves. Jacques Brel music resounds.*

LIGHTS: *A surreal light fades up on IRENE DUBONNET playing Solitaire.*

(As IRENE speaks, silhouettes of the other characters stroll through the scene as if SHE is calling up memories.

IRENE: I belong to a part of society rarely viewed by outsiders— the Southern top drawer. We're the handful of families who live on and above the rest. East Coast boarding schools and junior year abroad. Mint juleps and Russian caviar. We slip inside a private door at Antoine's Restaurant and phone for our personal waiter to escort us to a back room. We are the people the great Louisiana hotels were built for—the lobbies showcasing the Mississippi River, the silver service steaming with jasmine tea, the harpist strumming the "Clair de Lune." Our women have been plumed and manicured, and our men steeled to position themselves for the slightest financial advantage. White suits in summer. Navy blazers for fall… a nurse to sleek down every wisp of hair, we dress exquisitely. No white shoes before May. No straw after July. Patent leather always a second choice. Taste is so inbred that we are impulsively stylish. My family is, I suspect, the most miserable one I know.

IRENE slams down the cards. Black out! All the characters exit.

SCENE ONE

(German shepherds growl outside, hurling the scene into reality. ROOSTER is in a rumpled white suit, loafers without socks. QUINT enters in smart business clothes.)

QUINT: Tie up your dog, why don't you, Roo! Good-for-nothing guard dogs… won't let you in your own house! *(Wipes off the cuffs of his slacks)* Will you look at these pants!

BUNKY: Dad! Uncle Roo pulled another all-nighter!

ROOSTER: I watched the sun rise from Hancock Hospital emergency room.

QUINT: Too much partying!

ROOSTER: An overdose of pleasure. My lady love slipped and broke her toe.

BUNKY: What's that on your leg?

ROOSTER: A spider bite.

BUNKY: A black widow?

ROOSTER: No. An ordinary brown recluse.

QUINT: That's not the cancer returning.

BUNKY: You had cancer?

ROOSTER: A little melanoma. On the side of my nose. And on my neck.

BUNKY: What does it look like? Maybe I have it.

ROOSTER: Please! *(Wafting a mushroom)* Look! A mango-colored marvel from that landfill out back!

QUINT: Don't discuss the rear property.

ROOSTER: Only thing that catches your eye.

QUINT: Why do you walk back there when you get these reactions?

ROOSTER: I'm a hedonist living for pleasure in a state of disadvantage. Polyester, soap, dust! I'm allergic to practically everything!

QUINT: I love Mississippi! If I had $50, I'd buy it!

SOUND: The phone rings. QUINT grabs it and hangs up. It rings again.

(QUINT pours a scotch and water. ROOSTER peers through some binoculars.

ROOSTER: Things on the beach aren't what they seem. A patch of sand is scurrying away. Silver mackerel are flipping on the shore. Their habitat's vanishing!

QUINT: No one gets the Sunday paper here?

ROOSTER: My life's evaporating, too. I've no cash flow, and no credibility.

QUINT: Cash flow has nothing to do with credibility! Ha! You've no financial credibility as a part-time illustrator.

ROOSTER: I'm an artist.

QUINT: *(Picks up a book from Tulane University)* A law school catalog?

ROOSTER: I thought maybe I'd study criminal law. I need to find something with meaning.

QUINT: Criminal law? Do you want to wash your hands after shaking your clients' hands?

ROOSTER: *(Pouring a drink)* I'm almost thirty, and I've never had a job that could support me. *(Gestures to a wing of the house)* I open the icebox in my quarters, and see my reflection in the rear wall... Maybe I should get a master's degree in social work.

QUINT: Your Mama's property is worth a thousand dollars a square foot!

ROOSTER: I live high on the hog at Mama's but on my own... I'm just a scavenger sniffing around for loot!

QUINT: Take the nipple out of your mouth.

SOUND: *The phone rings. QUINT answers it and changes his voice.*

QUINT: *(Cont.)* No, Quint isn't here... call back after five... No, I can't take a message. *(QUINT bangs down the phone.)*

ROOSTER: Are you upset about something, Quint? You're the closest thing to a brother I've got.

QUINT: Brother-in-law.

ROOSTER: What's the difference?

QUINT: In-laws ain't family. Rules are different for in-laws than for family members.

SOUND: *The Our Lady Star of the Sea Church bells resound.*

(BUNKY *dances in wearing a Mexican shirt. He shakes Mexican jumping beans.*)

BUNKY: *Buen-os Dios! Sino-ritas! Donde es los sombreros, pinatas!* Hey, Uncle Roo. These Mexican jumping beans are alive. Uncle Roo and I want to start our own gallery business in Tijuana.

ROOSTER: Now that the will's in probate, no one's supposed to ask Mama for money. I hope the lawyers will rush things.

QUINT: Your Mama has the lawyers paralyzed. Your old man had safe deposit boxes in every bank, up and down the Mississippi. Now she's bombarding the lawyers with conflicting information. You'll have to wait in line like the rest of us… for her to parcel out the estate.

BUNKY: Want a pickle?

(BUNKY *pops an olive and nervously wipes his hand on his t-shirt. HE exits*)

QUINT: Your mother is a power, a Cro-Magnon, Roo. You hit her with a crowbar, it don't make a dent.

ROOSTER: She bought a house for you and your wife.

QUINT: Ex-wife. Your mother has my best interest at heart except when it conflicts with her own.

ROOSTER: Bunky's still her only grandchild.

QUINT: Thank God I had a son. Look, this family's a circus! I've learned to jump through an increasingly difficult series of smaller and smaller flaming hoops. There's a world of private decisions being made around your dad's properties. Your mother and her advisors are inside the monastery, and we're out here in the bar.

ROOSTER: You're her accountant.

QUINT: She's hired a front man to frame me.

ROOSTER: Not Mama.

QUINT: A third-rate attorney, but a blood relative, her second cousin once removed.

ROOSTER: Clovis DeBango?

QUINT: He's a merger and acquisitions guy. He buys and sells people. Clovis's caught me before and he's going to get me big now.

ROOSTER: What did you do?

QUINT: I took out a note against the family insurance policy. I'm vice-president.

ROOSTER: You stole money!

QUINT: It's a paper deal. The account was flush.

ROOSTER: It wasn't your money.

QUINT: DeBango's frozen all my accounts. He's going to shut my firm down and send me to jail. DeBango's setting me up to be the fall guy for these dishonest family partnerships. The man's a gold-digger. He'd take a ring off a dead man's finger.

ROOSTER: What's DeBango's motive?

QUINT: Do I want to analyze Frankenstein?

ROOSTER: Mama never hurt you.

QUINT: One person can do tremendous violence to another within the confines of a "happy" home. I saw a tomb with a sign on it, "I told you, I had high blood pressure."... Talk to your mother?

ROOSTER: I don't know how. Our conversations start happy and become more and more tragic.

QUINT: Just like life... I gave you a job in my CPA office.

ROOSTER: So I owe you?

QUINT: I'm trying to be as decent as possible in an indecent situation. My creditors are clobbering my brains out. Your dad was giving me his rear property for a wildlife refuge. I went in hock to grab all the adjacent land, but he kicked the bucket! Your mama pulled out.

QUINT: I had hoped you'd found the steel in your back—to ramrod things and take control.

BUNKY enters and hands QUINT a Federal Express envelope.

QUINT: *(Seizes another drink)* Thanks.

BUNKY: Booze, so early!

QUINT: Just bracing myself for the lawyers. *(Perusing papers from the envelope)* I've been vaporized! That's corporate slang for terminated!

BUNKY: You're so calm about it.

QUINT: I feel a certain triumph that I won control over my emotions. That for now I can keep them at bay. *(Reviewing the envelope)* This is the real fear in life—being framed by your family, persons of integrity, with your interests at heart—not losers. The scent of money draws them out. The corpse is barely cold, but the kin approach, in packs, like mice. Each one squealing for a bite.

BUNKY: Sssh! Grandma'll be home from church soon.

QUINT: Let's not rile her up. We can upset Dad, though! Clovis DeBango hurls me this dart—this lethal document. *(Tosses an envelope at BUNKY)* Tiny print destined to destroy. We're in Louisiana, redneck country. There are more lawyers licking their chops off bankruptcies here… than rats.

(ROOSTER puts an ice pack over his eyes and stretches out on the couch.)

ROOSTER: I don't want to get in the middle of this.

QUINT: Tell your mother to call off DeBango. Lend me fifty thousand dollars. This is not some typhoon that's wiping out South America. I'm your brother-in-law.

ROOSTER: I don't feel good.

QUINT: If your mother thinks you're on my side, she'll help me out.

ROOSTER: I think I'm coming down with the flu.

QUINT: Talk to her. If not, I lose everything: the house, Bunky's education…

ROOSTER: Don't take this the wrong way, but nobody in the family trusts you. You lap up the booze. I'm sorry.

QUINT: Go on. You slit open the wound, dig your finger in it.

ROOSTER: Mama says you have a credibility gap downtown. Important people refuse to work with you.

QUINT: I'm telling y'all my neck's on the chopping block, and you're lifting the blade. They got the Mafia after me. Those guys compete in violence. Their currency is blood. They don't get their money, they'll hang my head on the gate.

ROOSTER: My advice to you, Quint, is to be a bit patient. She's an old woman… you'll outlast her.

QUINT: You're living off her and advising detachment. That's good.

ROOSTER: You asked for help.

QUINT: I asked you to do something.

ROOSTER: I'm an artist, you're the businessman.

QUINT: You're not going to weaken your position to help me. I see. You're an artist, so you can't think. You can't play politics. You can't zip your pants.

ROOSTER: I don't know how to say this, but I've been promoting DeBango. I recommended they remove your name from all family documents, and we slip you some money.

QUINT: (Shocked, gasps for wind) The… most… unsuspecting people… are turncoats.

ROOSTER: DeBango says that you keep having "credibility gaps."

QUINT: "Credibility gaps."

ROOSTER: Quint! We're saving the family land… for Bunky.

QUINT: DeBango's set up an irreversible trust to lock me out!

ROOSTER: That paper's a formality.

QUINT: You never had to hustle.

ROOSTER: Mama'll give it all back to you, Quint!

QUINT: You lie around here whining… like a weasel in heat.

(QUINT seizes an umbrella and swings at ROOSTER)

BUNKY: Dad, he's sick!

QUINT: Not too sick to think of his own interests. Decapitation is too good.

ROOSTER: Just rave away!

QUINT: This family has shut its doors on the murder of my career. They think my failure is beneath them.

BUNKY: *(Restraining QUINT)* Roo just wanted to help me.

QUINT: Y'all can't deny my pain as if you could silence it beneath a river of booze.

ROOSTER: It's Mama's money.

QUINT: We were in a partnership. But it was never enough for her because she couldn't control me. *(Swigs a drink and imitates IRENE)* "Don't worry, Quint. I'll help you if you get desperate. You can live in Clarence's room out back and repair the villa."

ROOSTER: Mama's losing her faculties one by one. Sometimes I'm the only person she confides in all week.

QUINT: Tell her to make a friend. What's missing is compassion for the individuals and issues involved and a set of standards for the restoration of

ROSARY HARTEL O'NEILL

decency. It's my fault that I trusted this family. A warning light should flash on whenever y'all approach. *(QUINT exits)*

ROOSTER: So much has changed since I was a boy. Maybe I've changed. I'm surrounded by memories that have led me astray. I don't believe life's real. It's an illusion, so it doesn't bother me. If I thought it was real, I'd kill myself.

BUNKY: You promised to buy fireworks for the Fourth of July!

ROOSTER: I've got those catfish sketches to draw.

BUNKY: For that science textbook? Forget it! Dad's mad at Grandma. No one can tell her off because they want her money. And she's old.

ROOSTER: Cruelty doesn't come with age. All old people don't act like that. They eat their young here.

SOUND: *Dogs bark offstage.*

(IRENE enters.)

IRENE: Quint! Roo! Tie up your dogs! Dogs mating on the lawn. Why can't Quint get a male dog or keep his dog in the pen?

ROOSTER: All right, Mama! *(Exits)*

BUNKY: Welcome home, Mimi!

IRENE: Bunky, get that—dog!

BUNKY: Do I have to?

IRENE: Father Fannen focused his sermon today on money. He looked at the congregation and said: "Probably none of you have ever seen real pearls." Of course, it was the one day I wore mine to Star of the Sea. Undo these pearls, Roo. Father Fannen announced my age in Daddy's obituary in the church bulletin. He wants me to bequeath these pearls to Star of the Sea.

ROOSTER: Those real pearls you were willing me.

IRENE: After Mass, I managed to keep my graciousness and my distance simultaneously. I've never worn fake jewelry a day in my life.

ROOSTER: Irish priests may force you to change your ways.

IRENE: Ruthy May! *(Yanks off her pearls and places them on the table. Calling.)* That maid is probably lying lengthwise across the bed with my portable phone.

SOUND: *The phone rings. IRENE grabs it.*

IRENE: *(Into the phone)* Hello. Who?… It's for Quint. *(To QUINT)* Aren't you going to say, "Good morning"?

QUINT: Good morning.

IRENE: I hope you didn't ruin my Cadillac hauling your speed boat. Well, aren't you going to say, "Thanks"?

QUINT: Thanks. *(Into the phone)* Unifirst Bank for Savings went belly up! *(Flattens his hair back from his forehead)* No! *(QUINT dials another number and crosses upstage)*

IRENE: Roo, I want to update y'all all on that bill to preserve Mississippi wildlife.

QUINT: One minute! *(Exits)*

IRENE: I hope you're not tying up my phone. To continue with my story, the agent for the Department of the Interior and Forest Service is *(Spells)* R-o-a-c-h. It's pronounced "Ro-ach."

ROOSTER: Roach, no way!

IRENE: *(Correcting him)* "Ro-ach" wants to buy up Daddy's marshes.

ROOSTER: Do we have to talk about money and ruin cocktails?

IRENE: Listen, you might learn something. It's hardly possible.

ROOSTER: *(Gnaws a piece of celery)* I feel like I'm swimming upstream.

IRENE: "Ro-ach" needs a thirty-year net lease on my rear property. *(Pause)* This will affect your grandchildren. My attorney has reservations. The land would be worth much more if sold commercially.

ROOSTER: We've heard all this before.

IRENE: I'm trying to get to what happened last week.

ROOSTER: By returning to the beginning? Every person has a lifelong conversation with himself. What am I but an alien point of view entering your conversation?

IRENE: Right! I do better with folks who can't talk back, babies, people in a coma. That's why I volunteer at the hospital. Once the coma victims start getting better, they're difficult to deal with. Irresponsible!

(IRENE takes a Bloody Mary. QUINT enters. HE cradles the phone and searches for the paper.)

QUINT: No, I haven't seen the business section.

IRENE: That's why I've put the whole preserve idea on hold.

QUINT: *(Shocked, to IRENE)* You said you were reconsidering.

IRENE: I don't remember anything of the sort! *(Deferentially)* Won't you join us for cocktails, Quint?

QUINT: *(Hanging up the phone)* No, thanks. I've got to see what the Times has to say about the real estate market. Doesn't anybody bring in the paper?

IRENE: They keep throwing it in the duck pond. We should cancel the subscription. *(Sipping the drink)* There is too much tabasco in this Bloody Mary, Roo. Taste it?

SOUND: *There is a moaning sound, like a baby crying, as BUNKY returns from the yard.*

BUNKY: A tomcat. He followed me from the woods. I named him Phantom.

IRENE: Ye gods! He's stuck in the walls.

BUNKY: He's been there for three days.

IRENE: Quint, you should keep Bunky out of those woods.

QUINT: Phantom. *(Exits for the paper, mumbling)* That's some name. Phantom.

SOUND: The cat groans faintly from inside the walls.

IRENE: *(Takes another Bloody Mary and draws deeply through the straw)* Bunky, there's too much hot sauce in the Bloody Marys.

BUNKY: Is there anything I can do to earn money here? Straighten the garage?

IRENE: I'll pay you to leave my house alone. Y'all put your glasses back.

BUNKY: *(Collects the glasses)* I feel like a bean bag thrown back and forth.

IRENE: *(Rises)* You're my only hope. Your father's one step ahead of the sheriff, and Rooster's totally lazy.

(IRENE and BUNKY exit for the kitchen. Quint's phone rings.)

ROOSTER: Another arrow. Being respectful doesn't mean you invite a massacre. *(ROOSTER picks up the pearls, pockets them, and retreats to the beach.)*

QUINT: *(Returning)* I'm so disgusted, Roo. I'm not reading a wet newspaper. I have certain standards of cleanliness… *(Changes his voice to answer the phone)* No, Quint is not here. You'll have to collect payment. *(Talking naturally)* Oh, Jay, it's me, Quint. They're drilling offshore? Sift through the oil companies… see who wants a track of marshland. A guy named Fatswell's been sniffing around.

SOUND: An alarm blasts.

(QUINT hangs up the phone. BUNKY rushes in.)

QUINT *(Cont.)* Boon's triggered the alarm. How do you stop the dang thing? Is there a switch! *(BUNKY laughs)* I'm not laughing! You think it's funny, but these sirens are giving me high blood pressure!

BUNKY: Push the red button, the panic button, then 34960. The code's *(Spells)* F-O-O-L.

SOUND: IRENE's phone rings. QUINT answers it.

QUINT: Fool! Not you, stupid. It's… the code word, FOOL.

BUNKY: Not fool. *(Spells as HE exits laughing)* F-O-O-L.

QUINT: *(Spells)* F-O-O-L.

SOUND: The alarm stops. We hear someone strolling up the drive, whistling through her teeth.

(QUINT leans out the gallery.)

QUINT: *(cont.)* Jasmine! Welcome to Serenity. *(Hangs up the phone)* You're a one-woman parade.

(JASMINE enters, dangling her custom-made shoes over her shoulder and dragging glamorous luggage.)

JASMINE: My driver dropped me at the gate. This house is a fortress. It looks like a fat lady who's been to the orthodontist. All that metal work!

QUINT: We're broke, but safe!

JASMINE: I want a ride in your big, bad Jaguar.

QUINT: Sold it.

JASMINE: I can't think of you without a Jaguar. It's part of who you are. *(SHE peers out)* I can't find it. It used to be I could find your car right away. *(Pointing)* It's not that old raggedly thing by the duck pond. You're driving a Japanese subcompact!

QUINT: A rental car, darling. I should have sold my interests in the company. Then I could drive a BMW instead of a Saab—which is in the repair shop.

JASMINE: *(Removing her gloves)* I'm a parts model. I might break a nail! I flew home via New York. Elizabeth Arden. They sent me through the revolving door and *voilà*!

QUINT: *Voilà!*

JASMINE: I believe one should always dress as rich as possible. I want my clothes to make a fashion statement, and these clothes definitely talk! *(SHE spins around)*

QUINT: *(Seductively, pants like a dog)* Arf! Arf!

JASMINE: They're from a shoot in Australia! I don't like to encourage foreigners, but I do like variety in my clothes.

QUINT: You remind me of my ex before therapy made her so difficult.

JASMINE: I like dressing up and dressing down. I don't like dressing in the middle.

QUINT: You don't?

JASMINE: I've joined Debtors Anonymous. This group of shopping addicts. But, I can't stop myself. When I see something I want, I buy it. I've run up an incredible bill on Pete's company Visa.

QUINT: Pete?

JASMINE: Daddy Dubonnet…

QUINT: You said "Pete."

BUNKY: *(Enters and plops down another tray of Bloody Marys)* Running back and forth between yesterday and today. Hey, Jasmine! I saw your hands on "General Hospital" and "One Life to Live." *(Reaches for JASMINE'S hands)*

JASMINE: *(Slips her hands in her pockets)* These fingers are insured against chapping. When I'm broke, they go to work.

BUNKY: I taped your "Silk n' Soft. I'm Dripping Charisma!" commercials.

JASMINE: I'm sorry I missed the funeral. We were in the middle of shooting. No one would accept my collect calls… Did Mimi like my red blanket—for the casket?

BUNKY: No! She said you charged it to her.

JASMINE: I'm paying her back. Thanks for the rose you had laminated in plastic. Smells sweet. Such a pretty purple.

BUNKY: Now, Mimi… always talks "property."

QUINT: Relatives are not like property. Property is valued in this family.

SOUND: *A squeal comes from JASMINE'S luggage.*

JASMINE: It's my Yorkshire Terrier.

QUINT: Not another pet!

JASMINE: Cornelia Bronte Shambles. The smallest dog alive. She's ninety-seven, and can't control her bladder. She just lifts her skirts and goes anywhere. *(Shaking her little bag)* See!

QUINT: Put her up, son.

BUNKY: Inside?

JASMINE: Leave her in the top drawer in my back room. She won't wet there. My underwear is more sacred to her than all your orientals.

(BUNKY exits with the dog. JASMINE meanders about.)

QUINT: Have a Bloody Mary.

JASMINE: Just water for me. Caviar on toast. Marvelous. *(Savors the caviar, then tosses it into the trash)*

IRENE: *(Entering, she stalks JASMINE)* I wondered how long it'd take you to show up.

JASMINE: Mama Dubonnet! *(JASMINE puts her hands in her pockets)* Just picking! I... I... I have "fear of fat." All my friends are fat, bald, married with kids. I don't eat; I graze. I can get as much satisfaction from looking. Really!

IRENE: You're on a diet?

JASMINE: It's not a diet. It's a way of life. When I get hungry, I eat a banana. Quint, could you peel this?

IRENE: Jasmine, you still live on the same postage stamp? You've got to drive thirty-five miles into the brushes, Quint, to get to her house.

ROOSTER: (Stumbles in, in a hiking outfit, shirt unbuttoned) Wow! What started as a walk ended up an adventure! Oh, hi, Jasmine.

(BUNKY dashes onstage with a pot of steaming fish soup.)

BUNKY: Gumbo is served! Jazz, will you recite something from a movie later?

JASMINE: No. (Twitches BUNKY'S ear and whispers) They don't pay the entertainment in this family, like they don't pay the help.

IRENE: We certainly do pay the help, even when they don't show up!

(Everyone sits. IRENE signals for BUNKY to say "Grace." HE does so, rapidly, with no emotion, then they dive into dinner.)

QUINT: My boy got 1570 on his SAT, a near-perfect score, but something's missing. Sewannee, the University of the South, said: "Nothing in his application sparked their interest."

ROOSTER: It's chronic fatigue syndrome. A yuppie disease from having too many college applications. He's allergic to the twentieth century.

BUNKY: Ha! That's good.

QUINT: I should have sent Bunky to that military school in Alabama... where the colonel comes to your house to get you!

BUNKY: I was voted the boy most likely to die from a violent death.

(Phone rings.)

IRENE: *(Pauses, taunting QUINT)* It's for you, Quint.

QUINT: *(Withdrawing with the phone)* Where? Who?... DeBango wants a Dunn and Brad report from the New York Stock Exchange on me?

ROOSTER: Have you got any Pick-a-pepper sauce?

IRENE: Roo's problem in life is he jokes too much, and of course you have to eat.

ROOSTER: Pick-a-pepper! Yum!

IRENE: He puts that sauce on everything.

ROOSTER: Some sauces have flavor, but pepper is what makes a sauce great.

IRENE: You have to hit him in the head with a two-by-four like a jackass to get him to stop. Either way he'll have to answer to God, not just to his mother.

ROOSTER: "Gran Sangre de Tore." Great blood of the bull! Yum! Conversation isn't just talk, it's blood sport if it's worth having!

IRENE: Be careful, Roo. I could cut you completely out of the will.

ROOSTER: You insult me and forbid me to react.

IRENE: I don't compete with preadolescent mouths. Bad taste doesn't condone politeness. *(Puts down her fork and wipes her eyes)* I don't know why I go to all this trouble to create Sunday dinner.

BUNKY: For me, Mimi. Excellent turkey gumbo.

ROOSTER: *(Eats and talks simultaneously)* I fill up here, so I can starve on my own money.

IRENE: Don't eat with your fingers, Roo.

ROOSTER: I've got plenty of ice in my refrigerator, but no food.

IRENE: Close your mouth, son.

ROOSTER: Whenever I rent a movie at the video store, they say, "You're late on your payments."

IRENE: You can't socialize with the manners of a pig.

ROOSTER: (Gulps his wine out of the bottle) That cheap box won't hold two bottles of wine! Ha.

IRENE: You come to the table with your gut hanging out.

ROOSTER: (Adjusting his cap) When I go out, I look presentable.

IRENE: There is a code of behavior in acceptable society. You eat with your fingers. Talk with you mouth open. Drink nonstop!

ROOSTER: I've got to fill up with booze to sit at this table. Like a blow-fish, I inflate until I burst. There are dead blowfish shattered all over the beach. Being polluted to death. They swell up because they're terrified… expand until they pop. But it's not worth it for one meal ticket! (Dumps his plate over) For one lousy meal, it's not!

IRENE: I'm so mad at Pete. He went and died on me. He used to handle this. I'm the easiest person in the world to get along with. You can ask my dead husband. (Exiting) Clean up, Bunky.

BUNKY: My night hasn't begun until I've picked up somebody's shit. Good night.

SOUND: Music. A dreary version of "Columbia, the Gem of the Ocean" drifts in from Star of the Sea.

QUINT: (Sips coffee and peers into his cup) No, it's not a good night. It's another lousy night.

(BUNKY mops up the drenched table. JASMINE flips her address book.)

JASMINE: (Seizing a phone as if it's a life preserver) Being around this family in the country… It's the saturation that gets to you.

QUINT: Coffee?

JASMINE: That stuff is toxic!

(JASMINE hands QUINT a phone, and HE punches in the numbers. JASMINE'S hand slides over QUINT'S when taking the receiver.)

JASMINE: *(Cont.)* Is this the Hilton? The Hilton that has the rain forest? Don't put me on hold! Shit!... Get me Chuck Feingold, Big Star Productions. No, I won't wait! This is long distance! *(Presses the phone against her shoulder)* This receptionist from hell!

SOUND: The phone rings, JASMINE grabs it.

JASMINE: *(Cont.)* Oh, Chuckie... What?... Who put 'Midnight Rapture' on hold? It's canceled... Oh, no. How can I advance you the money? Good night, "poochie poops." *(JASMINE slams down the phone, and forgetting her hands, rips open her purse.)*

QUINT: Try some coffee.

JASMINE: I've already drunk my allotted cup.

QUINT: Ah, ha! Middle age has you in its claw—you're counting coffee cups.

JASMINE: *(SHE massages her nails ferociously)* I need a loufa sponge and a herbal wrap to lift the dead cells! I can't believe this fat vein. Yeek, a ripped nail!

QUINT: After thirty, y'all have to hang up your spurs.

JASMINE: I've peaked. I know I'm old. My hands are old. I'm two years older than God.

QUINT: Nature discriminates!

JASMINE: Men discriminate! The biggest part of acting is attitude. And Doctor Wiseman can't find the right pills.

QUINT: There's a bankruptcy every five minutes. For sale signs like postage stamps stuck on houses along the beach. I can't relate to your cosmetic problems.

JASMINE: Those deals don't concern me.

QUINT: Well, they must pay you a lot for M.C.ing the L.A., S.P.C.A. dog walkathon?

JASMINE: It's volunteer work.

BUNKY: That's not a salaried position.

JASMINE: Mama Dubonnet told me I didn't have to trouble myself with any family meetings. It's a simple will.

QUINT: On paper, yes, but in practice… This is the last outpost where people make a will prioritizing the adults they can control. Without this agenda, everyone scatters. It's time you get your own attorney instead of relying on this family's.

JASMINE: What can I do at six on a Sunday?

BUNKY: (Swatting the air) Nasty horseflies.

(JASMINE inches over so her breasts almost touch the middle button of QUINT'S starched shirt.)

JASMINE: Can we talk tacky? Daddy Dubonnet promised me ten million dollars for this picture.

BUNKY: Mimi won't like "Midnight Rapture"!

JASMINE: When I decide to do something, I pick up and do it. You don't have to show me more than once!

BUNKY: Another horsefly.

QUINT: We must make haste—slowly for two reasons. There's no forced heirship in Louisiana, and you are an adopted child.

JASMINE: She won't cut me out!

QUINT: You're tough! Good.

(A horsefly spins overhead, but QUINT catches it in his fist and squashes it midair.)

QUINT: *(Cont.)* You'll need that resistance because here everything's changed. The only thing a bear respects is a bigger bear.

SOUND: *A phone blares. JASMINE goes to get it, but QUINT puts his hand over the receiver.*

QUINT: Keep 'em dangling. That'll keep 'em interested. *(Tracing a question mark on her hand)* Warm hands.

JASMINE: Cold heart.

BUNKY: *(Throwing napkins on to a tray)* Mimi says, "If it looks like a duck, walks like a duck, and quacks like a duck, it's probably a duck."

(QUINT marches back to the table, pulls out an alligator-skin checkbook, and scribbles a check.)

QUINT: Get yourselves some fireworks. *(Tosses him some keys)* Drive below eighty.

BUNKY: Quackidy quack! *(Skips out)*

JASMINE: Mama Dubonnet's scared of me because I've got insanity in my blood. There's nothing I'm afraid of. My real daddy was a crazy man. Pushed me in the Mississippi River when I sassed him. So I've seen the rush of death. When Pete adopted me, I weighed eighty-nine pounds. My stomach was so swollen it looked like a balloon. But Pete loved lost causes. We went walking every Sunday. Pete treated me like a treasure.

QUINT: *(Removing his jacket and tie)* You weren't one of the secretaries he slung against the couch… who made "her" walk blindfolded.

JASMINE: He preferred me to his real son and daughter.

QUINT: Relationships for him were like ducks in a shooting gallery. He knocked one down and another popped up in its place. No wonder Roo's so screwed up.

JASMINE: You're responsible for Roo. He's imitating you. Following some penchant for power, disguised by psychological bullshit!

QUINT: I don't have to take this from a hand model!

JASMINE: I'm more than a hand model. I had a T.V. series! I did commercials—temporarily. Now they've become my specialty. But for how long? Even silicone injections won't stop veins from popping up. There are no hand lifts. I want to work. To do that, I need massive plastic surgery, a liposuction, and ten million dollars. Well, just think about it. I deserve the money!

SOUND: *Low romantic music floats under the scene.*

JASMINE: *(Cont.)* I know you weren't there for… Kitten.

QUINT: My wife? She left me. Sailed to France with her new independence! Maybe husband number two will thaw her out.

JASMINE: You cheated on her.

QUINT: Once Kitten returned to college, she never came to bed. Students arrived at the house in groups like tourists.

JASMINE: You were outnumbered.

QUINT: I would sit up at night watching your movies. "Boys Night Out," "Color Me Red," "Slippery Sunday," and remembering those slow summers. I should have left my wife then, but Bunky fell ill. Wasted away to a little pile of bones on a chair. You make concessions.

JASMINE: Too many concessions.

QUINT: Sex is a tyrant. It pops up its head and demands your flesh. *(HE touches her back.)*

JASMINE: Stay away, Satan! Just because somebody liked it once doesn't mean they'll like it again.

QUINT: I'm new and improved. *(QUINT twitches her ear.)*

JASMINE: This is wrong!

ROSARY HARTEL O'NEILL

QUINT: Does it feel wrong?

JASMINE: Not now, but maybe later.

(JASMINE and QUINT kiss. IRENE observes from a side door.)

QUINT: *(Putting his arm around JASMINE)* Let's go to the beach.

JASMINE: Okay, but don't touch me. Just don't touch me. *(THEY both exit.)*

(BUNKY enters loaded with fireworks, followed by IRENE.)

BUNKY: I've got cherry bombs, snakes, hand grenades! *(Dumps them and calls)* Hey, Roo! It's going to be a battlefield! Roo! Better tie Boon up! He'll get his face blown off if he sniffs around these fireworks.

IRENE: I can't take one more forced celebration.

BUNKY: Where's Roo?

IRENE: He'll be better in the morning. I should be panicked, but it's all in a day's work.

BUNKY: Did he have another spell?

IRENE: Since Roo was born, I have ceased to be Mrs. Dubonnet. I am Rooster's mother. *(Wipes her mascara)* I live with an inner panic button stuck on alert.

(IRENE picks up the sketchbook. SHE has the urge to rip it up, but SHE rests it on the table.)

IRENE: *(Cont.)* He's becoming too… sensitive. I realize some parts of society don't consider white males useful, but this family needs one. I might as well do a fire dance. I tried to be sweet to him. I don't need him.

BUNKY: He's painting his signature work!

IRENE: Art's consuming him.

BUNKY: *(Reverently opening the sketch book)* Such talent!

IRENE: Depraved drawings. Talent is something the world decides about us later, Bunky. It's not anything we can know in our heart. Artists have lives, they don't have careers.

LIGHTS: *Bonfires blaze from the beach. BUNKY picks up the binoculars and crosses downstage.*

BUNKY: They're starting up some bonfires! Wow, will you look at that!

IRENE: Try looking for a happy artist.

BUNKY: Don't start, Mimi.

IRENE: I just try to keep on going with some quality. That's not easy. I've been a mother longer than you realize. Motherhood is a series of letdowns. The same old conversations, rushing to nowhere. When I'm really mad at my son, I ignore his drawings. He gets back at me by drawing, incessantly. Art allows him to punish me in a disguised fashion. The amount of carnage created by him is immeasurable. I don't think mothers ever truly forgive what sons do to them.

BUNKY: Don't get paranoid.

IRENE: Roo's growing suited to the life of an artist. He's developing the mettle for cruelty.

BUNKY: Sure is hot! I like the smell of summer. These scorching July nights.

IRENE: I have spent forty years of my life building my name in this community. I don't want it destroyed by this garbage.

BUNKY: I don't care how hot it gets.

IRENE: Stray artists rattling around in the French Quarter like dice in a cup. You have to breathe life in them. They're so drugged. Most decent people don't go into the Quarter anymore.

BUNKY: But sometimes with three lines he'll make me homesick for a place.

IRENE: If I want a painting, I want a real painting. I don't want an overgrown cat or some fish guts.

BUNKY: He's trying to tell a story. Try to understand. *(Exits)*

IRENE: Vile images. That's art. *(Swoops up the sketchbook)* It's the freak show characters that push this trash. Damaged personalities. Obsessed with the obscene. There's nothing lonelier than being the mother of an artist. I got a lot more by being mean than by being kind.

(IRENE begins tearing up the pages.)

SOUND: *Phantom moans in the walls.*

IRENE: *(Cont.)* Still alive, are you? *(Exits to the beach.)*

SCENE TWO

LOST SKETCHES

(The next day, July Fourth, twilight. QUINT is wearing a T-shirt, "He who has the most toys wins," and fixing a crab trap. Sporting a bird-watching outfit, JASMINE is manipulating a telescope overlooking the Gulf. BUNKY is stretched out, filling out job applications. Nearby a silver tray of scotch and bourbon, a bucket of ice, and leftover donuts, croissants, and coffee idle on a table. The sun is set-ting—red fire bleeding through the sky. The Star of the Sea Angelus resounds as ROOSTER limps into the room. HE looks half-dead.)

ROOSTER: *(Reaches for a donut and searches around the room)* A three-donut day! Got to jump-start that body. My eating habits are terrible, and I'm not going to change them...

JASMINE: That's stupid.

ROOSTER: Sometimes it's better to be stupid. Smart people realize we can't figure things out. *(Collapses—throwing his leg across the arm of a chair)* I keep forgetting where I put things!

QUINT: (*Shocked by ROO'S leg*) You've got a lump that big on your ankle!

ROOSTER: Whenever you're sick, you must face the wheel of fortune.

BUNKY: He could need a transfusion, Dad!

ROOSTER: I don't want blood.

JASMINE: Please!

QUINT: (*Noticing streaks on ROO'S ankle*) God, you're turning pink in spots. Bleeding through the skin. Hold out your foot. Oh, my God...

ROOSTER: Spider bites. We are all terminal! As soon as it's out, people start treating you differently. I have something wrong with my chart, but they can't tell what it is. I can't find my paintings!

QUINT: You should stay off that foot.

ROOSTER: Find my sketchbook, Quint. I haven't drawn anything today... I need that book to see where I left off with my life. It's got all the memories that I've been collecting, like the sensations in the leaves when the sky turns white in July.

JASMINE: Just draw them again.

ROOSTER: You think my memory can sustain these details?

QUINT: Maybe they're not so important.

ROOSTER: (*His throat is rasping*) You act like my sketchbook's a calendar or something. It's not a fucking date book, y'all! See the dentist. Repair the car. Have lunch with Mama.

(*Nudging BUNKY to patronize ROO, QUINT pretends to bidding at an auction.*)

QUINT: I'll offer a ten-dollar reward!

BUNKY: I'll add five to that!

ROOSTER: Y'all think I can start, stop like some computer. I know paint-

ROSARY HARTEL O'NEILL

ing doesn't ring up the checking account.

QUINT: Make it fifteen, fifteen, fifteen, no, twenty dollars.

ROOSTER: No one's going to furnish my office or buy me a desk.

JASMINE: Here's twenty-five.

ROOSTER: Twenty-five dollars for the entire series!

ROOSTER: It's amazing I'm still in my right mind!

SOUND: *A group of the town's boys are parading along the beach, playing "When the Saints Go Marching In."*

(QUINT *and* JASMINE *begin dancing, waving hankies, doing the cake walk. The strained sounds of their dancing shoot through ROO'S heart, calling him to task for his lost youth.)*

ROOSTER: *(Cont.)* That band again! I've got to reconstruct my life… the past week.

BUNKY: *(Steering ROO offstage)* Let's check out front.

QUINT: Poor bastard.

JASMINE: *(Dancing with QUINT)* Don't let Roo's theatrics worry you. You should feel sorry for me, stranded in the boondocks… You could sprout roots here from just lying around. If I don't keep busy, I rot like the trees. My idea of fun is lounging by a pool in the Beverly Hills Hotel. I don't ask for much: elegance, someone nice to talk to, like Julia Roberts. God, I miss Los Angeles! Let's go to the beach! Watch the birds visiting for the day. Sandpipers are going extinct! They're mating on the beach.

QUINT: In exile.

JASMINE: It's part tradition, part assumption, part desperation. Come on. Let the sunset caress our skin. The water's pearly— blues, grays, all shades of gray. See the waves… lapping everywhere… and foam!

QUINT: A done deal! Watch out for that ant hill covered with poison.

JASMINE: Look at the clover all over and honeysuckle. *(Offstage, their ripples of laughter trail off)*

ROOSTER: *(Wanders onstage with a wildflower)* I discovered this red honeysuckle. It has no scent. I'll study one fragile, delicate vine. Memories are all I have left.

SOUND: *The phone rings off the hook.*

BUNKY: We'll find those sketches. Don't worry.

IRENE: *(Shrieking offstage)* Bunky, run get the phone!

BUNKY: I've never run for anything in my life. *(Answers the phone like a calloused receptionist)* She's not here. It's for Quint. He's not here. *(Slams down the phone)* I'm right on the edge.

(IRENE hurries onstage to the howling of dogs. SHE looks unusually glamorous and uneasy with her Panama hat in one hand and a paper bag in the other.)

IRENE: This place sounds more and more like an animal shelter. *(SHE pops off her jewelry and shrieks)* Quint! Jasmine!

(ROOSTER has set himself up with a fantastic oil lamp and a fifth of Jack Daniels.)

LIGHTS: *Moonlight streams across his face. Periodically, firecrackers, Roman candles, and smoke bombs sizzle in the sky. ROOSTER rings a bell.*

IRENE: Ruthie May.

ROOSTER: The seven o'clock cry. Every twenty-four hours, she screams from the heart.

IRENE: *(Hunting around)* I've mislaid my pearls, son. Can you help me find them? I guess I'll have to crawl on my hands and knees. Well, say something!

ROOSTER: What day is it?

IRENE: Monday!

ROOSTER: All day?

ROSARY HARTEL O'NEILL

IRENE: Don't you like that?

ROOSTER: *(Swigs his drink)* I have to be loaded Monday, or I won't come home.

IRENE: You're at it again.

ROOSTER: This isn't me. I'm standing in for a friend. Do you know who I am? Well, neither do I. Do you know where my money is? Well, you don't know much.

IRENE: *(Rooting around for the pearls)* I've had experience with weepy eccentric people. Spoilt, we used to call them. Don't let the normalcy of my life interrupt your creativity.

SOUND: *There is a deadly silence.*

LIGHTS: *Moonbeams begin falling like diamonds across the gallery. Around it, Spanish daggers, palmettos, banana trees are starting to stretch their jagged limbs toward the moonlight. Roman candles explode streamers of red, lavender, and silver through the sky.*

IRENE: Actually, I came out here to accept your apology. A poor peace is better than an excellent war. Such a starry night. It's a blue moon, the second full moon in a month. They said forty percent chance of rain tonight, and it's beautiful! Remember that game we played on the pier, "Light My Candle"? One person runs from corner to corner saying, "Light my candle," and everybody switches seats behind him screaming, "Next door, neighbor!"

LIGHTS: *Roman candles shoot over the Gulf, exploding color everywhere.*

SOUND: *Fireworks crackle like pork skins frying; sizzling, hissing.*

IRENE: *(Cont.)* Come watch the Roman candles?

ROOSTER: I hear them.

IRENE: It's easy to start drinking, son, but when do you stop? The wee hours of the morning.

ROOSTER: It's better to drink with steam coming out your ears.

IRENE: I read about a commercial artist who makes three million a video. He's outlined five steps to success: be brief, be winning…

ROOSTER: If there are so few steps, why isn't everyone successful? *(Drinks violently)* Some artists are happier if they don't see their paintings hung.

IRENE: It's time to switch when you begin losing your hair! No one's ever going to hang your painting!

ROOSTER: Watercolors.

IRENE: Painting, watercolor, whatever.

(ROOSTER taps his foot, a habit that reminds her of his nervous breakdown.)

LIGHTS: Moonlight streams across his face.

ROOSTER: Never stare down a fish because they have no eyelids.

IRENE: No eyelids!

ROOSTER: You're a loudspeaker. I whisper something in your ear and it comes out your mouth.

IRENE: I dislike seeing you sick.

ROOSTER: It could be worse. I could be dead. My nervous breakdown hasn't healed.

IRENE: Shh. Depression.

ROOSTER: I need a few days off from the world to recover each week.

IRENE: You want to rent that villa in Italy? Take a Mediterranean Cruise. What do you want?

ROOSTER: When did this shrinkage of your mind occur? You started smart. Valedictorian. But you've been thinking the same thoughts for thirty years. I have no more status than a parlor entertainer.

IRENE: I'd hoped you had enough distractions with the textbook.

ROOSTER: Distractions! Is that what you call my work?

IRENE: You have to face reality, son.

ROOSTER: Do you think people walked on the moon by doing that? I'm like Cassandra, balancing the gift of prophecy with the curse of madness. Despite blistering summers, I'm drawing every species of vegetation, animal, and insect. I have penetrated the thickets on hands and knees. Slept in lagoons to make my perception of nature's paradise.

IRENE: Pipe dreams! You're living in a pipe? Who's bought one drawing but me?

ROOSTER: You have a bad mouth and you say cruel things to people.

IRENE: You've got to paint in a style closer to the center where the majority is.

ROOSTER: I'd rather go back to the hospital.

IRENE: The curator of the museum said plain as day, your style has... no appeal.

ROOSTER: He promised to hang one piece.

IRENE: If I give him five hundred thousand dollars. It's your connections he's after. You said, "Teaching interests me."

ROOSTER: (Tapping his foot) I don't want to as-ss-ociate with those people!

IRENE: Why not catalog slides at the Historic Collection?

ROOSTER: Still trying to buy me that job!

IRENE: You could work at your dad's agency.

ROOSTER: (Chugs more Jack Daniels) I've received an ancient legacy. A commission! I can't think of myself as not being an artist. Painting either brings you to the cocktail circuit or to God.

IRENE: You don't dress like a priest.

ROOSTER: I practice to get it right. One aspect of perfection.

IRENE: And what aspect is that?

ROOSTER: Dodging the predators. That isn't easy because the laws of the sea don't apply. Out there, the predators have names: the electric eel, the swordfish, the hammerhead shark. Here, humans are perverse. They poison the artist through emotional blackmail. You've got loved ones like piranha hungering to extract your talent. Going into a frenzy for a drop of genius. A piranha's teeth snap like a steel jaw. You don't stop one by patting its head, Mother. I survive by keeping a low profile like a flatfish, pressed to the sea floor. I was born like a regular human, but my eyes have rolled around to the top of my head from crawling along the bottom. It's easier for me to change me than for me to change you.

(ROOSTER stretches out on the floor with the whiskey bottle.)

LIGHTS: Automatic yard lights flash on silently as if some god has magically lit up the gallery like an exhibition hall.

SOUND: The radio inside plays Henry Purcell's "La Mort du Roi"—its haunting sounds blend with the rising wind.

IRENE: You and I were close before.

ROOSTER: Before, I was inclined to do what you wanted me to do.

IRENE: I don't see life as a series of victimizations.

(ROOSTER starts to draw—valuing the light replacing the dusk.)

IRENE: You've drawn for a while. Why not move on to something else?

ROOSTER: Did you find my sketches?

IRENE: I prayed about them at Star of the Sea. Father Fannen talked about families living in cardboard boxes. One person losing some sketches is not terminal.

ROOSTER: It's not terminal, but I can see it from here.

IRENE: You're punishing yourself over something no one appreciates... it's like wanting to play a symphony in a barroom south of Houma in a place called "Whiskey Pass." Ha! Ha!

ROOSTER: People are things, Mama. Artists! Ax murderers! You don't like my sketches because they reveal too much about the endowed violence of this family...

IRENE: I found your sketches. I didn't want to give them to you until I had them fixed.

(ROOSTER *peers in the bag as if it contains a rotting corpse. HE extracts bits of wet paper—wiping his hands on his pants and shaking his head. ROOSTER limps around the table looking at this piece and at that in an attempt to salvage something.*)

ROOSTER : Oh God no! They're torn to pieces. Drenched! Where did you find them?

IRENE: On the beach.

ROOSTER: When?

IRENE: A few hours ago.

ROOSTER: I can't repair these sketches. I never realized there was a time clock for artists. In the wee morning eye of night, I feel like I'm in this river of fire. Millions of artists are screaming, "Help!"

IRENE: Please! I'm not a vicious person.

SOUND: *We hear the lapping of the waves in the distance and the buzzing of locusts circling the house.*

(ROOSTER *watches her, sensing her uneasiness like a dog spotting a cat.*)

ROOSTER: You tore them up, didn't you? You think what's yours is yours, and what's mine is yours. You were afraid my artwork might bring me glory. Independence that would distance me from you.

IRENE: (*Flattening the wrinkles in her designer skirt*) You want to blame someone.... all right, blame me.

ROOSTER: Cut my heart out! It's all right, Ma.

IRENE: Son, I'm trying to protect you. Do you want to go back to the hospital?

ROOSTER: *(The pain in his leg firing him to attack her)* Vulture! You go through the motions of motherhood, the meals, the stories, the meetings. You never missed one. But underneath the fuss, you're a buzzard, mangling the weak without a pause of remorse. You feed on the dying. Suck up feelings. Hook yourself into another's flesh and rip. We are responsible for each other's soul. You have annihilated my self-esteem.

(IRENE crosses, weak-kneed, and with all the power in her manicured hand slaps him.)

IRENE: I'm your mother.

(ROOSTER grabs his face and sinks back, catching himself on the table and crashing over the scotch and bourbon, donuts, and bucket of ice. ROOSTER sinks down into a chair, depression weighing like a coat of steel over him. Seizes sketches from under the alcohol and olives. Dumps the scraps back in the soiled bag.)

ROOSTER: I wish you'd never given me life! I don't believe life is real. It's a big movie written, produced, and directed by God. If I thought my life was real, I'd blow my brains out! *(Shoves the bag at his mother)* Put it out back with the plastic bags and the bottle tops. Pollution!

IRENE: Get drunk, indulge yourself. Life is a big soap opera and you're the star!

ROOSTER: *(Removes the pearls from his pocket)* Here, strangle your neck like you strangle everybody else's!

IRENE: You're drunk!

ROOSTER: I'm drunk, and you're a bitch, but I'll be sober in the morning.

LIGHTS: Sparkles flash in the sky.

(ROOSTER begins ripping her pearls and spraying them across the gallery.

CURTAIN

ACT TWO
SCENE ONE
THE WOULD-BE INVALID

(Four o'clock on a Sunday afternoon, a week later. The furniture is draped in white duck cloth, and the chandelier wrapped in netting. A day-bed canopied with gauze protects the patient, ROOSTER, from mosquitoes. Near it is a mammoth bowl of goldfish that BUNKY feeds periodically. Dead leaves from a recent squall are scattered around some plants. The stereo resounds Henry Purcell's "La Mort du Roi." Its lament blends with the rising wind and waves. Moments later, BUNKY bounds down the stairs, acting out a blues song to amuse ROOSTER.)

IRENE: Bunky, turn off that music!

SOUND: Bunky flicks off the blues and hides. Seeing the gaunt expression on ROO'S face, IRENE cringes.

IRENE: *(Cont.)* Roo. I've never understood motherhood. Bruised camellias are all I've successfully nursed. We found someone to repair your paint-ings—a disaster specialist from Orlando, Florida.

(IRENE folds back some cheesecloth. ROO coughs again, responding to an eerie sound, like trembling shutters.)

IRENE: *(Cont.)* Who's there? *(Spots BUNKY)* Bunky, stop eavesdropping.

BUNKY: *(Staring over at ROO)* I can't rest. I closed my eyes and I felt vio-lated. Uncle Roo looks so… weak. *(Pause.)* Every time he veges out, I'm afraid he'll never come back…

IRENE: Most patients improve at home where they recognize their sur-roundings… These Mississippi doctors have just learned that. They're from nothing. Climbing with both hands. My great-great-grandfather was a surgeon in the Civil War, and he knew that.

(IRENE ensconces herself at a tiny table. She begins shuffling cards.)

IRENE: *(Cont.)* Don't you want to play cards?

BUNKY: Card games are boring.

IRENE: Their predictability is comforting. Solitaire's a game one person can play. Thank God, since that's the direction the world's going in.

BUNKY: Did Doctor Boudreau call?

IRENE: No. Solitaire's the American name; the English term is Patience.

BUNKY: Face up, Mimi. With his allergies, it could be the beginning of the end.

IRENE: A King of Spades—the black suit again. There are so many medical decisions to make in a lifetime. You can afford to get a few wrong; you still come out ahead.

BUNKY: Father Fannen wants to give him Extreme Unction, Mimi!

IRENE: The Sacrament of the Sick, not the dead! All sickness does not go on to death, son.

(ROOSTER moans. BUNKY runs his fingers through his hair.)

BUNKY: Listen!… Is he having trouble breathing? He's so swollen.

IRENE: The doctors are taking him to Oschner Clinic tomorrow for more tests.

BUNKY: You never told me! That clinic is terrible. Needles and tubes everywhere!

IRENE: *(Aligning a sequence of spade cards)* Your sophomoric ideas on medicine don't interest me.

BUNKY: Shit. He'll just get worse there. No one empties the garbage, they yell in the hallways, and patients keep buzzing for nurses. It's like being in a cage at a zoo. People pass you with curiosity. But when you need someone, you can't get help.

IRENE: (*Mechanically plays a new hand of Solitaire*) That's not true.

BUNKY: Not when you're there, of course. You barely touch the buzzer and they fly in like hawks. It's your money they're after. Unfortunately, the sick are less attractive. They moan from meal to meal like broken screws in some machine. And their food is like crap. I used all my allowance sneaking Grandpa fast food—in case you'd care to know. Fine, Mimi. You want to make a pincushion out of Roo, then don't come bawling to me. I won't start dialing specialists from New York and L.A. like we did for Grandpa… after it's too late. I'm not going to get hysterical or anything. I'm just moving out.

IRENE: I'm the responsible party. Not you.

BUNKY: I'm the only member of this family willing to face reality. Uncle Roo's a hypochondriac. I heard one doctor say it. Roo gets sick to get attention, because when he's healthy, people won't let up on him.

IRENE: Grandpa was right—he was always warning me about letting you get too bossy.

BUNKY: Rooster wants to stay home on the couch. Jasmine and I can rotate taking care of him.

IRENE: Jasmine! Ha! She spends her time mixing her mud mask and dousing her fingers in oil.

BUNKY: (*Paces nervously about*) When I nurse him, he gets better. Today he asked me if I fed Boon.

JASMINE: (*Rushing in*) Damn! Greta almost bit me.

IRENE: Even well-fed pets will hunt for the fun of it.

JASMINE: (*Screams, bending over and shaking her hair like a mop*) Something's loose, an extension.

IRENE: Jasmine, stop emoting. Read something to Roo from <u>Remembrance of Things Past</u>.

JASMINE: Not now! My hair's falling out! Does it have to break off?

IRENE: You lack stamina! You haven't faced the vilest quarters of life. *(Jangles a bell vigorously)* Ruthy Mae!

BUNKY: She hates that bell.

JASMINE: Oh God, another extension's slipping!

IRENE: *(Violently)* Ruthy Mae!

BUNKY: She's left for choir practice.

IRENE: I have no use for Ruthy Mae. She has a nursing degree, but it's such a waste. She just sings spirituals and wears that bandanna.

BUNKY: *(Exiting for the soup)* Why force-feed him?

IRENE: Sick people never want to eat. I was a volunteer—a candy striper at Mercy Hospital. *(Demandingly)* Jasmine!

JASMINE: *(Storms out, shrieking)* I can't feed him, when my hair's falling out.

IRENE: He'll eat, if he knows y'all want him to. *(Raises his pillow)* Well, Roo, your temperature's down.

BUNKY: I thought you said he looked bad…

IRENE: *(To ROOSTER)* Ruthy Mae made you some bouillon. It's made from the blood of baby cows. *(ROOSTER moans)* You boil the meat in water, then extract it to make this liquid with chunks of the richest beef. Rooster… Now take a few sips.

(ROOSTER coughs and flails.)

IRENE: Remember the airplane game you made Bunky play?

BUNKY: *(Making landing gestures with his hand)* The airplane is flying around—ready to land—one for Mimi, two for—Bunky.

ROOSTER: *(Flails his head away and coughs)* No. Not now!

BUNKY: Oh gosh, he's choking.

(For the first time, IRENE knows in her marrow that ROO wants to die. SHE glares out at the estate, looming before her like a ghastly cemetery.)

IRENE: *(Cont.)* Roo. I know I was against the preserve idea for Quint, but an artists' retreat for you might work. You could paint in the main house. And build cabins under those oak trees for your friends. I'll move back to town.

(IRENE hovers over ROO, searching for the slightest twinkle in his eyes. IRENE lifts up his limp hand.)

IRENE: *(Cont.)* Just squeeze my hand if you like the idea.

(ROOSTER'S fingers fold down over IRENE's jeweled hand.)

IRENE: *(Cont.)* Fine, son. I had Clovis draw up this document, to transfer the rear property. *(Slips out a paper and a pen)* It's been witnessed, notarized, and now I'm signing it. Your only obligation is to be candid with me about what you do and for whom. *(Draws the net curtains about ROO'S bed)*

BUNKY: I wonder how Dad will take this.

IRENE: Shh! You're not going to tell him.

BUNKY: *(Exits inside, shaking his head)* He's a sophisticated investigator.

LIGHTS: As the sun sets, shadows stretch across the walls. Stripped of light, the gallery resembles a mausoleum.

IRENE: *(Calls sternly)* Jasmine! I plan to face many issues… that Quint's been knowing about. Jasmine, let's sit in the shadows. You used to be so good-looking. Now, whenever I come near you, there's only this scent.

JASMINE : It's Opium.

IRENE: *(Pulls out a box)* What would you call your hair color?

JASMINE: Ice brown.

IRENE: And your eyes?

JASMINE: China blue.

IRENE: My husband's Mississippi office just sent this to me. Pandora's fantasies.

(IRENE casually opens a metal box and places a pistol on the table. She removes pictures.)

IRENE: *(Cont.)* Photos of you and Pete… He had them all over his corporate apartment.

JASMINE: Our relationship was of no importance.

IRENE: *(Whisking up a gold-framed photo)* What's this of you two in bathrobes?

JASMINE: Old press shots.

IRENE: And these? *(Slips out videos and reads a box)* "Psycho sexual films with a spin."

JASMINE: You shouldn't concern yourself with that.

IRENE: *(Removes a paper)* And the insurance policy—leaving you ten million dollars?

JASMINE: I am legally his daughter.

IRENE: We're in redneck country. You can't go much further South.

JASMINE: I have my rights.

IRENE: There's no judge in this county going to give you a nickel.

JASMINE: I'm not like your limp-wristed children. I know where I'm going, so you can't cut my hands off.

IRENE: You think your little arrangement shocks me! Ha. I was married to Pete for forty years, and him to me for four, but not consecutively.

JASMINE: *(Her eyes drawn like a magnet to the silver pistol)* We never did it.

IRENE: *(SHE puts the gun away)* How much will it take for me never to see you again?

JASMINE: The insurance policy.

IRENE: Well… you'll have to subtract that from the money you owe me. *(Gestures casually to the stack of canceled checks)* DeBango's listed these checks drawn to you and the charges on our accounts, some ten point five million. He'll deduct that amount, with a fifteen percent interest over a ten-year period from any money willed you.

JASMINE: Oh, my God. Another clump of hair's falling out.

IRENE: Or shall we just call it even.

(IRENE rips the insurance policy in half.)

JASMINE: Oh my God! All these years, I thought of you as my mother.

IRENE: You should have put some savings aside.

JASMINE: I hoped one day you would love me, too.

IRENE: I've got to provide for my retirement.

JASMINE: Like when you built me that doll house. It blew down in that hurricane. But it was there. A miniature of yours with columns, a gallery, blue shutters. Inside I had your china dolls. No one else wanted them. The play furniture. I would rock for hours there, a princess in her castle, pretending she was you.

IRENE: Where was that house again?

JASMINE: On that slab. Near the grape arbor, yes. *(Shakes her head)* It's in my memory now, only in my memory.

(JASMINE rushes to the beach, and IRENE disappears inside. ROOSTER has overheard all. HE pushes out of the mosquito netting, stares after IRENE and JASMINE. HE picks up the deed, studies it. QUINT leaps on to the gallery. HE has a bottle of champagne in one hand and crystal glasses in the other hand.)

QUINT: Rooster! Rooster! You feeling better? Champagne for the hospital report.

ROOSTER: *(Waves the deed)* Well, it worked! Grief made Mama generous.

QUINT: You're kidding. *(HE fills the glasses)*

ROOSTER: This acting is a gas!

QUINT: Relax. You're still weak!

ROOSTER: Mama didn't allow for one character development—that you could rush me to town, and my shrink could glue me back together.

(ROOSTER presents the paper to QUINT magisterially. QUINT skims the paper.)

QUINT: All the rear property?

ROOSTER: Just a dot on the map of Mississippi. Now you can travel by yacht from here to New Orleans.

QUINT: Miles and miles of swamp land. You don't mean it?

ROOSTER: I'm trying to be as inextravagant with extravagances as possible. It's a process that involves vigilance and finesse.

QUINT: Roo, you shouldn't do this.

ROOSTER: I enjoyed being a boy here… fishing at dawn, hiking with a stick, launching paper boats. But some gifts have translucent strings.

QUINT: You're signing it over to me? Even the mineral rights?

(QUINT interrupts the euphoria of champagne and tobacco, and starts to dial the phone. HE balances it with one ear, and refills his glass. HE imitates the vocal quality of the Texan on the line.)

ROSARY HARTEL O'NEILL

QUINT: *(Cont.)* It's Quint speaking! Roy? Roy Rogers? The Lone Ranger. Well, are you still mounting Dale? I got the papers in my hand. Bring Silver on over. Let's get hitched. *(Hangs up)* Roy Fatswell. He never talks. You never know if he's a genius or a complete idiot.

IRENE: *(Enters)* Roo.

QUINT: *(Lifting the glass)* We got a good report at the hospital.

IRENE: You're not drinking my good champagne. I was saving that.

QUINT: Doctor Boudreau says Roo's been playing possum. Ha!

IRENE: Don't act foolish, Quint. Rooster Dubonnet, you get back to bed! I'm calling your doctor.

(IRENE dials the phone as QUINT and ROOSTER giggle over champagne. BUNKY rushes into the room. BUNKY glances around for ROOSTER and seeing him, cries out.)

BUNKY: God! Is Roo over-medicated? For God's sake, sit down.

IRENE: *(Idles the phone on her shoulder)* I'm a hostage of Gulf Coast Bell. Get my toddy, Bunky!

QUINT: How many times did you flunk out of school, son?

BUNKY: Four, Dad.

QUINT: This is loser's paradise. Jasmine's a "hand model"! Roo's a hypochondriac! And I'm a hack! Last week, I overdosed on Quaaludes, but Rooster kept me walking, walking, and talking!

ROOSTER: *(Waving his champagne)* We boys concocted this plan!

IRENE: *(Shouts into the phone)* I want Doctor Boudreau? Women doctors are harder than men, and she's the hardest woman doctor I know. What do you mean, she doesn't know what's going on? Rooster Dubonnet has gout! Ha! Gout!

QUINT: The disease of kings!

IRENE: Gout!

BUNKY: How could that doctor get the facts right and be so wrong!

IRENE: Let me speak to Dr. Boudreau. You sent her away! To silence her! *(The phone clicks off)*

SOUND: *The phone rings. BUNKY picks it up.*

BUNKY: *(Into the phone)* Hello? Who? Dad... It's a Mr. Fatswell. The one Mimi says sounds like a snake oil salesman.

QUINT: *(Bellows into the phone)* Roy! Hi-yo Silver! You want it? Well, you've got plenty of money. You've just got to turn it loose.

IRENE: Don't come to me when y'all overextend yourselves.

QUINT: No... Irene's thrilled with the refinery idea.

IRENE: *(Polishes her diamond against her skirt)* I don't have one note on any of my property.

QUINT: That tract in back, it's worth much more commercially.

IRENE: You're drunk with debt.

QUINT: *(Hangs up the phone)* No, drunk with life. I'm officially cutting the cord. Snip. I'm going to buy confidence with cash. Build dreams.

IRENE: *(Baiting him)* The bank must have approved another loan!

QUINT: Set the boys up in Tijuana. They won't have to pawn their youth for a little "blood money." *(Lifts his arms as if launching a ball)* I want y'all to live!

BUNKY: I've already lived! Now what do I do, Dad?

QUINT: Sunbathe on the Riviera. Scuba dive in Hawaii. Cruise to Greece! Life is for the beautiful and the young!

ROOSTER: *(Cheers as he heads offstage)* The signs of success! Yahoo! I'd better change. Yahoo!

QUINT: Well, let's get packed!

IRENE: You're one step ahead of the sheriff!

QUINT: Yep, you can't make a living in oil, but you can occasionally make a killing. Imagine yourself walking inside a portrait... this house and that Gulf. Underneath is a money machine spewing oil.

IRENE: Preposterous. Any oil would have gushed into the lines of our well.

QUINT: That's not what Roy Fatswell thinks. Yep! He wants to construct an oil complex. Storage tanks for holding. Housing for the workers.

IRENE: He's not going to ruin my land.

QUINT: Well, these acres and acres of currency don't really concern you!

(QUINT slips ROO'S deed out of his pocket—unfolding it like a king unrolling a decree.)

QUINT: (Cont.) You were Roo's chief beneficiary... Now I'm the one with deep pockets.

IRENE: You want to play hardball? I'm on the board of every bank in Mississippi.

QUINT: I know, Mrs. Dubonnet. But Roo's given the rear land to me. And I've sold it to the snake oil salesman.

IRENE: Oil field trash! It's greed like yours that's polluting the South. Nature's screaming and you're going to pay.

QUINT: This oil company's donating fifty million dollars to preserve sea life—going extinct.

IRENE: You can't turn the sacred into the profane that easy. There is that bill.

QUINT: Which will be reversed. Go get packed, son.

IRENE: Claw your way to the top, and you'll get nowhere. My family owns this town.

QUINT: No one cares about your ancestry. It's whether or not this deal's lucrative. The bad boys are in politics. It's a gangster's business, not a gentleman's profession. The South is driven by greed, by little bitty politicians with little bitty men's hang-ups. They'll take my money.

IRENE: Bribery!

QUINT: Ignorance! Without politics for a living, most of them would raise dogs!

(A fog horn booms. QUINT rushes down the stairs— revitalized by the sounds coming from the yacht. HE squints out over the lawn, flicks the gallery lights, and bellows, "Ship Ahoy!" BUNKY peers through JASMINE'S telescope as IRENE walks to the edge of the gallery. JASMINE, at an upstage window, her eyes swollen with tears, observes the events.)

BUNKY: There's a tremendous ship gleaming under the moon. Looks like a space ship!

QUINT: That yacht's my ticket out of this hell hole. Bunky, start packing for Florida.

IRENE: Florida isn't even the South. It's lower Manhattan. We'll discuss this in the morning, Quint.

QUINT: At dawn, I'll be off on that yacht. Fatswell's taking the President of Hancock Bank in Gulfport and the Whitney in New Orleans to a… very rich lunch… you get my picture. He's going to be handing out a lot more than food.

IRENE: That's illegal.

QUINT: That's Louisiana! Are you ready, son?

IRENE: *(Presses her hand over her chest)* Bunky, my heart pills are in my tan purse.

BUNKY: *(Running for the pills)* She's been pacing up and down all day, Dad!

LIGHTS: *The gallery glows with the warmth of the gold moon.*

ROSARY HARTEL O'NEILL

(JASMINE enters.)

QUINT: Did you get your insurance pledge?

JASMINE: I let her burn it up. You're dallying with danger, Quint. I overheard.

QUINT: So? Just put on my tombstone, "He was fearless."

JASMINE: Irene Dubonnet's all the family I've known.

QUINT: Family!

JASMINE: I told you. I didn't do it…

QUINT: Just above the waist. I've reserved the use of the entire grounds twice a year for entertaining.

JASMINE: Who wants to party around an oil rig?

QUINT: Me.

JASMINE: You have this callousness that's quite seductive.

(JASMINE strolls down front to hear the crickets and the rush of the Gulf water. JASMINE breathes in the salty air. For the first time, SHE realizes she won't see Pete Dubonnet again. Modern technology—mud, wires, and metal braces—will replace her memories. QUINT'S hand touches JASMINE'S shoulder.)

QUINT: It's not yours, sugar. No one gave the land to you.

JASMINE: God, you're uncouth!

QUINT: This place was meant for the family sons. It dropped into my lap like a dead leaf, because the last uptown prince didn't care.

JASMINE: Irene Dubonnet's greedy but she's… refined.

QUINT: The plantation mentality. "*Debutante-ti-tis.*" No one schooled your people to put back. They were raised to think that they were owed service by birthright. Fool notion's been bulldozed into their heads.

SOUND: Horn.

JASMINE: I'm not ready to gloss this over with a deluxe cruise, with yet another hustle to erase the past. Screwing your family has repercussions.

QUINT: Life has repercussions. It's the start of the new South, of a more democratic way of doing business. Once the news of oil hits the street, these mansions will be nothing but shells. That's reality, honey.

SOUND: Once again there is a signal from the yacht.

QUINT: *(Wrapping his arm around her shoulder)* Let's go.

JASMINE: I've no clothes packed.

QUINT: For the daytime, I'll buy you a trousseau from Paris.

JASMINE: And for the nighttime?

QUINT: *(Pressing her hair back behind her ear)* Nothing. I want to marry you, Jazz.

JASMINE: Me too. My enemies are going to drool. They drooled over your Jaguar and now they'll drool over our yacht.

QUINT: God, I love to make you happy!

JASMINE: Buy me a big diamond, will you, Quint? A solitaire. What's the largest they make? Twenty carats?

QUINT: Yeah. You'll sail past forty with more diamonds than Elizabeth Taylor.

(QUINT puts his arm around her, and THEY saunter out the front gallery. QUINT yells back.)

QUINT: *(Cont.)* Rooster, boy. We're sending someone back for you.

JASMINE: So much of everything, so little of nothing!

QUINT: Don't look back!

(IRENE and BUNKY enter and hear tires crushing the oyster shells.)

IRENE: There they go—running on quicksand. I haven't a single trump card except privilege. They're spoilt, so they'll be back.

BUNKY: A temporary star. Temporary stars destroy themselves in one explosion…

ROOSTER: *(Enters humming, sporting a cane with a silver pelican head)* Kierkegaard said, "Don't finish with life, until life is finished with you."

IRENE: You're such a ham actor. You should join the St. Louis Cathedral Drama Society.

ROOSTER: I'd rather recuperate with a nurse on that yacht. It'll be hectic but fun… like sipping water from a fire hydrant! Water my plants! Chase the ducks! And feed Boon. Can't forget him! You ready, Bunky?

BUNKY: No.

SOUND: *The walls rattle as Phantom runs off.*

BUNKY: *(Cont.)* Phantom's run off. He was playing possum, too!

ROOSTER: Bye, Irene! *(Goes to kiss her but she raises her hand to stop him)*

IRENE: All animals can think. What sets humans apart is our ability to deceive ourselves.

ROOSTER: *(Blows her a kiss)* I'll send you a sketch.

(BUNKY crosses and feeds the goldfish.)

BUNKY: Goldfish will eat until they burst.

IRENE: *(Opens some shutters to reveal a splendid cake.)* It was supposed to be a surprise birthday but everyone's left. When home life is bad, people take it out on the person in charge.

BUNKY: I can't eat.

IRENE: Go on!

BUNKY: Remember when I went away to St. Paul's Boarding School. You wrote me twice a day… with a program for my career.

IRENE: You returned the letters—stamped "addressee unknown." I knew you were alive because you kept cashing checks. It's not me you love, it's my function!

BUNKY: After Mama left, I wrote.

IRENE: *(Glancing in a mirror, touches her cheekbones)* Men of the South, if they have white hair, people say they're so distinguished. A woman with the same hair, they say she should color it.

BUNKY: Will you listen to me! *(Rocking back and forth on a chair)* I might as well dive into a tank of sharks.

IRENE: Don't do that! You're going to fall on your face.

BUNKY: Like Houdini, just tie me inside a box and toss me in the Gulf. I'll get out. I'm living in the gray zone… I have to hurt myself to get attention.

(BUNKY raises his arms theatrically, acting out various circus acts.)

BUNKY: *(Cont.)* Blindfold myself for the high wires! Race a cycle down a silver cord! Flip from one trapeze to the next with a sword in my teeth!

IRENE: I ordered you an Arabian stallion. It's all white.

BUNKY: Give him to Clarence. *(HE pulls out a silver gun)*

IRENE: Where did you get that?

BUNKY: In the box—next to the photos. Everyone has one!

IRENE: Put it back.

(BUNKY stretches his arm in the air like a trained marksman and points at three spots over the Gulf.)

ROSARY HARTEL O'NEILL

BUNKY: Here's to Dad, to Jasmine, and to Roo.

IRENE: Give it here!

BUNKY: Our home life is a nightmare. There's this machine—*(Gestures with the gun)*—that needs feeding, and a staff that's overworked! People are so trapped in their own panic that no one notices anyone else.

IRENE: Hand me the gun.

BUNKY: Don't tell me how to act! *(Squeezing his hand over the gun)*

IRENE: What's wrong, son?

BUNKY: I have this anguish inside me. I don't know where it's coming from.

IRENE: Life!

BUNKY: *(Stroking the barrel with his finger)* I've been dreaming about Mama. It's funny, but I can never recall Mama holding me as a child.

IRENE: That's Southerners! We miss the people we hate.

BUNKY: And now it's August.

(BUNKY takes the gun and strolls to the edge of the gallery.)

BUNKY: *(Cont.)* At midnight, I'll be twenty-one!

IRENE: *(Never taking her eyes off the gun)* You don't want the horse, we'll return it. This is the most important birthday of your life.

BUNKY: *(Stares at the water, the salt air bites his cheeks)* No one's here.

IRENE: We'll celebrate again next week. Make a list of your friends.

BUNKY: Sure. I feel like a jellyfish on the beach. I'm flopping around with no direction. There's this Cajun restaurant near Mama that needs waiters. I could work there and sleep at a youth hostel.

IRENE: You don't know anything about… "hostels"! You're not going to go out hawking yourself.

BUNKY: Thought I'd hitchhike across the U.S. and then go overseas.

IRENE: What will you do?

BUNKY: Experiment. Living to a formula prevents chances that might happen along the way. Maybe I'll join the Marines. I've got so much despair inside, it'll take boot camp to get it out. I'm spending the night at the Gulf Shores Hotel.

IRENE: People go there to live out their fantasies... from the ridiculous to the sublime.

BUNKY: I want to go to dangerous places, where I have to defend ideas that feel right... even if I can't express them. You'll never be far from me.

IRENE: I'm sixty-plus, son. I'm old South. We come on this earth for a short time when you consider all the centuries. We make a little tour and we're gone.

BUNKY: I won't drop out of sight.

IRENE: Stay the night!

BUNKY: I can't. There's this old rage creeping inside me... I can't shake it because I trusted the wrong people. My family! People who raised me, who I thought were right... Y'all told me stories about life that aren't true. Misrepresentations! Nothing matters here unless it can be measured in money.

(BUNKY begins checking the barrel of the gun. It shines like a diamond in the moonlight.)

IRENE: For God's sake, will you put that up? You expect too much. You're just a student. The only duty of a student is to...

BUNKY: Learn well... I don't know how to gauge myself... Everyone's gone and left me with these lies.

(BUNKY rushes off stage.)

ROSARY HARTEL O'NEILL

LIGHTS: *The moonlight streams in, glistening like glass across the cold floor.*

(IRENE dashes for the phone.)

IRENE: *(Screaming offstage)* I'm still here.

(BUNKY reenters, putting on his backpack. HE slams down her phone.)

BUNKY: There's too much of you inside and not enough of me. It's emotional plagiarism!

IRENE: It's not a question of plagiarism. We're all appropriating each other.

BUNKY: Since Grandpa's death, I've been copying your rules, and they're shackling. I figure I'd better develop my own smoke alarm. I'm not stable inside. If I don't leave, Mimi, I'll be headed for trouble.

IRENE: I've been counting on you to lead this family. You're our bright star! *(Removes a money clip)* Throw away money. Buy whatever you want! Talent doesn't pass from father to son, but money does.

BUNKY: No, thanks.

IRENE: The rewards here are fiduciary, not emotional. Grandpa's left you and Rooster everything… if you finish your studies.

BUNKY: If? What about Jasmine and Mama?

IRENE: Girls don't count. Same thing happened to me! *(Pressing the money at him)* Take this.

BUNKY: No! *(Puts the gun in his pocket)* Nothing! My favorite stimulus is panic. *(HE laughs)* Da! Da!

IRENE: It'd make me happier if you'd leave the gun.

BUNKY: I'm not going to stop loving you because I'm away.

IRENE: Switch on the lights before you go. Flick the air conditioner on "super cool."

BUNKY: I thought you were saving money.

IRENE: For what?

LIGHTS: *The lights flick on behind IRENE, illuminating the mansion like a giant mausoleum. The air conditioner bumps on, and the door slams. The yard lights flash on. IRENE flips cards—occasionally she blots her eyes with a lace handkerchief, sniffs and runs her tongue over her teeth. A calliope from the church fair plays in the distance.*

(IRENE addresses the audience.)

IRENE: I belong to a breed of Southern women—now going extinct—who dedicate their lives to finding rich husbands and having sons. Harmony that's all I'm after... peace in the family. Dissension jeopardizes the simplest things: a lovely dinner, a quiet afternoon, an evening stroll. What is life but a chain of little pleasures? Breakfast in bed, fresh cut flowers, a steam and a Swiss massage...

SOUND: *Jacques Brel music plays.*

IRENE *(Cont.)* French cabaret music, your grandson's smile, fireworks on the Fourth of July... We have anything you'd want on the Gulf Coast. Passion for us is having an affair with your eyes. Where else can you grow such glorious hydrangeas and hear a calliope from the church fair? My house only looks good when there are a hundred people inside. I wouldn't live any place you couldn't hear the waves lapping the beach, see the shadows from the oak trees, where it's never too early or too late to have mint juleps on the veranda. *(Flips a card)* The red suit looks good. *(Turns a queen card)* The Queen of Diamonds! Sometimes the queen must go into her tower and cry. All great queens do. And sometimes she must say, "Off with their heads."

LIGHTS: *Blackout.*

SOUND: *Blues music comes up for the*

CURTAIN

217

Black Jack
A Thief of Possession
A PLAY IN TWO ACTS
First Performed in June, 1995
Alice's Fourth Floor, New York City

CAST OF CHARACTERS

IRENE SONIAT DUBONNET: (Nicknamed MIMI), sixty+. A ravishing matriarch. Her family has roots in the nineteenth century, and she still presides over a vast Garden District house in New Orleans. Irene is artful in her choice of clothing, with baroque blouses, adding glamour to any occasion and Gucci accessories. Her conversation is studied light and overlaid with a contrived naiveté which is often cruel, a distemper agitated by failing health. She can only leave her wheelchair for brief periods. Smart, Irene manages to fasten onto something peripheral about a subject if it concerns her and make it central to the conversation.

LUISA GARCIA: Early twenties. An Hispanic medical student, too pretty for her office as Irene's companion. Sleek and firm, she is poured into a shirt, jeans, and a nurse's jacket. She has vitality, a wondrous optimism, and thick hair resembling the mane of a stallion. An essential sturdiness of character and largeness of spirit flow into her work. Luisa has an instinct for pleasing people, for finding out what they like to do, and for somehow arranging for them to do it.

BUNKY DUBONNET LEGERE: Mid-twenties. A rock star and Irene's grandson. He has mood eyes that change colors and wild hair. Alternately deceitful boy and outraged actor, Bunky dresses in a rhinestone cowboy outfit and suede boots. His reactionary clothing defies his background from a formidable if oppressive family. Talking rapidly and cleverly, he is a magnet for attention, rendering familiar words exotic through emphasis. There is something pernicious about him—a haunted awareness behind the wry smile. He has considerable talent but is somewhat volatile and insecure, picking up on people's moods quickly.

JAMES BEAUREGARD ELLIS: (Nicknamed BEAU), fortyish. Bunky's stepfather. Athletic and tanned, he dresses in Ivy League, navy and black blazers with shirts and sweaters of gray, blue, and wine. The streaks of gray in his hair give it a transparency like gilding from the sun. Beau learned the art of Southern story telling as simply as he breathed, his family having been landed gentry in Saint Martinville for generations. He went to Harvard at age 16, wrote his first novel when he was 18, and was a professor at Tulane

University by 25. While heir to the revenues from an oil and gas plantation, Beau with the help of his third wife Kaitlin has exiled himself in Paris and created a brilliant career as a novelist and lecturer on romantic poetry.

KAITLIN ELLIS: Bunky's mother, fortyish, a delicate beauty with the clearest eyes and a porcelain complexion just beginning to crack from the strain of illness. Kaitlin moves with nonchalance, an elegance acquired from living languidly in rooms festooned with ancestral portraits and lush furnishings. Even when unkempt, Kaitlin dresses with breathless wonder. She has a reputation for vagueness which she finds useful not to discourage. From her earliest days, it was obvious Kaitlin had a destiny and was different from everyone else. She may seem self-absorbed but is in fact very observant, very shrewd about people.

RORY DEBANGO: Mid-forties to fifties. Single. There is something striking about her, an exotic strain of wild, unpredictable whimsy. Rory is precocious and charismatic with absolutely wonderful eyes and a devious smile. Socially ambitious, Rory is a dizzy, desperate woman with a zigzag character. Rory is flirtation, fey with the determination of a deliciously coquettish tart. Teenagers follow her around like puppies, infatuated with the flashy clothes, the too-high heels, the outrageous earrings. Most men are utterly charmed by the way Rory talks and moves, and they fall one by one.

SETTING

The deck and lounge of the Dixie Queen paddleboat, departing from New Orleans, Louisiana, up the Mississippi River to Natchez, Mississippi.

TIME

ACT ONE: The present. New Year's Eve. Four o'clock.
ACT TWO: Later that night.

ROSARY HARTEL O'NEILL

ACT 1

(The lounge and deck of the Dixie Queen. The abstract set seems timeless as the characters relate to the expansive horizon: the brown Mississippi River and transparent skies. Luxury is felt through detail: crystal glasses, a vintage brass lamp, blush carpeting. The set evokes grandeur and isolation, elegance on the verge of collapse.)

SOUND: *The paddle wheel churns.*

LIGHTS: *It is the coldest New Year's Eve in New Orleans in thirty years.*

(KAITLIN ELLIS waits, sipping a second glass of sherry and reading a program.)

KAITLIN: When I was a girl, I wouldn't pray for power, for the end of the world, but for a perfect marriage. Perhaps in the South, I thought marriage would be great because I was bored so beautifully as a girl. All those long, lonely Julys on the Mississippi Gulf Coast. Swinging in the hammock, staring through the oak trees at the endless sky. My cat, Visalia, lying by me, her green eyes shining, licking her paws. *(Combs the dock, her eyes welling with tears)* My husband is a writer with a certain reputation. Beau Ellis, that's right. We live in Paris. After eight years, my hormones are finally cooling down. They like to drove me stark raving nuts in the beginning, whenever Beau brushed my hair, rubbed saffron on my skin, or kissed me with the fullness of pleasure. In Beau's study when it rains, I can still smell his cologne. *(Checks a diamond watch on a chain round her neck)* Lord, where's Beau? I can't face my mother without him. Same faces at the same cruise table for one long week. *(Smiles)*

SOUND: *Throughout the play, we hear canned programming through the speakers.*

RADIO: WELCOME ABOARD THE DIXIE QUEEN'S NEW YEAR'S CRUISE, A WEEK OF PLEASURE FROM NEW ORLEANS TO NATCHEZ ON THE ONLY PADDLEWHEEL STILL IN EXISTENCE.

(LUISA GARCIA pushes IRENE DUBONNET in a wheelchair. IRENE is crouching under a wide-brimmed hat, sunglasses, and a lap blanket. ATTENDANTS follow, dragging IRENE'S luggage. IRENE barrels over LUISA, who is shouting in Spanish.)

IRENE: What awful decorations. Glamorous but not daunting. It's not the beauty that stuns you, it's the gaudiness. These shocks of temperature do violence to the skin. Stop that Spanish.

LUISA: *(In Spanish.)* How splendid everything is. Glamorous like Beau Ellis, your son-in-law. The Dixie Queen, the only paddlewheel boat still in existence.

LUISA: *(In English)* Miss Irene. It's your daughter.

IRENE: Nice of you to identify her. Every time I see her, she gets messier and messier.

RADIO: THERE WAS A TIME WHEN THE CRY "STEAMBOAT DEPARTIN' WOULD STIR THE SOUL AND FAMILY MEMBERS WOULD JOIN TOGETHER WITH LOVE AND AFFECTION.

(KAITLIN is shocked by the wheelchair)

KAITLIN: Mama. You always look lovely. I'm glad you sent the annual cruise invitation.

IRENE: Did you have to drag along your husband? I suppose Beau's here to see how soon you'll be inheriting my money. Kitten…

KAITLIN: Kaitlin, I changed my name. Remember?

IRENE: How annoying.

KAITLIN: I didn't know you'd trouble walking, Mama.

IRENE: I'm tired at the beginning of a trip. It's called age.

(IRENE glares over her sunglasses, then, satisfied that SHE has upset KAITLIN, SHE tosses off her hat and lap blanket, and rises.)

KAITLIN: Oh, Mama!

IRENE: There's a lot you don't know, Kitten.

LUISA: *(In Spanish)* It's Kaitlin.

KAITLIN: Who is the pretty girl?

IRENE: *(Ironic)* A student caring for me since my daughter won't. It's extortion at forty-nine bucks an hour.

LUISA: I'm Luisa Garcia. A trained nurse.

IRENE: Sit over there. No one asked you to talk.

LUISA: *(In English)* Aaaah. Whatever, Miss. Irene.

IRENE: Stop calling me that. I don't want to be your friend.

IRENE: The sitters are taking my pills. Aspirin. My heart patches. Agnes finally quit on us. I hid them in my safe. Agnes found the combination. Stop the Spanish.

LUISA: *(In Spanish)* For what do I want to hear this? Neurotic bullshit!

KAITLIN: *(Laughs)* Why keep obsessing about pills?

IRENE: I started hiding my pills in the lining of my luggage. But I'm already thinking of a new place for when she finds them. *(Brooding)* I don't have any real children or help. These maids come and go. They call them sitters. Aptly.

LUISA: You're married to Beau Ellis?

KAITLIN: Yes.

LUISA: Beau's a … a giant of the page. And you've got that famous son. Bunky Legere. What do you do?

KAITLIN: *(Laughs)* Fortunately I don't have to feel guilty about not making any money…

IRENE: Everyone should see Beau, but everyone shouldn't have to see him over and over.

KAITLIN: I went to my twenty-fifth high school reunion, Mama. Black tee shirts, extra-large, with Bugs Bunny slogans, "That's forty-three, folks."

Silver balloons. And Sazerac drinks.

IRENE: There were thirty-one girls in your class.

KAITLIN: Nineteen showed up. Six are on unemployment. Eight are childless. Five have serious health problems. Most are single, remarried, or divorced. The unfocused ones, they're the happiest.

(BEAU enters, noting something in his writer's journal)

RADIO: THE WORLD HAS CHANGED SINCE STEAMBOATS RULED THE RIVERS. BUT THERE IS NO MORE THRILLING SIGHT THAN ONE OF THESE SOUTHERN LEGENDS. QUEENS…

LUISA: *(In Spanish)* The king of romance. That's him. So gorgeous, and he writes like a god. All those readers…

BEAU: *(Crosses and kisses KAITLIN)* Darling. Have you been waiting long? All those women wanted signatures— Hello, Mrs. Dubonnet.

IRENE: Hello. Who can stop the "inheritor of the mantle of Thomas Wolfe"?

BEAU: *(Smiling, he puts his arm around KAITLIN)* We're sailing into the sunset.

LUISA: *(In awe, aside)* Ageless body.

IRENE: *(To LUISA)* Back.

BEAU: *(Nuzzles her hair)* In life, there're moments of grace. Life's on hold, like in a parenthesis.

LUISA: Pardon me, Mr. Beau, could you sign this cocktail napkin?

IRENE: Have you resolved to move home, Kitten?

KAITLIN: Kaitlin. My goal is to get you to Paris.

IRENE: So you can spend my money? Yes, daughters should be a comfort.

ROSARY HARTEL O'NEILL

But now I'm able to do less, 'course I don't see Kitten.

KAITLIN: Kaitlin.

BEAU: Mrs. Dubonnet, my wife is here because she wants to renew her relationship with you.

IRENE: Well, so do I. But in France they believe that husbands are harmless, which is something I've never adhered to.

BEAU: What exactly are you after, Mrs. Dubonnet?

IRENE: Never ruin a conversation for the sake of honesty.

(BUNKY enters)

BUNKY: Hi, Grandma.

IRENE: Don't call me Grandma.

BUNKY: Mimi. Everybody. I'm on Hollywood time, ten minutes behind.

BEAU: He's up, but he ain't running.

BUNKY: My chauffeur looked for a parking space while my bodyguard walked me in.

IRENE: Terminally disorganized.

BUNKY: I always arrive with what I need. I don't want to be too late for the things I'm late for already.

KAITLIN: You're so tall, muscular. I can't get over it... grown up.

BUNKY: The worst thing I have to do, Ma, is walk center stage and sing a famous line.

IRENE: After awhile even traveling around the world becomes ordinary.

KAITLIN: I'd nothing to do with your success.

IRENE: I raised Bunky. Someone had to cover the guitar lessons and the bounced checks.

BUNKY: A broken family. Who doesn't have one?

KAITLIN: I didn't know when I left you with Mama at sixteen that she'd steal you.

BUNKY: Aw, look at men in history, Ma. Their mothers were the brains behind them.

KAITLIN: You've forgiven me? Why didn't you return my calls? Or come visit.

BUNKY: I thought about it. Lots. But I never got 'round to it.

IRENE: Better buy yourself a "round to it," you want to see this son.

(KAITLIN removes a crystal pendulum from her pocket and squeezes it in her fist)

KAITLIN: Bunky has meaningful eyes, like Baudelaire.

BEAU: Don't start.

KAITLIN: Born April ninth, the same day as Bunky. But reborn every day. Reading Baudelaire is my secret passion. Baudelaire was searching for God. The last year of his life was spent in complete silence.

BUNKY: A voiceless poet?

(BEAU pulls KAITLIN to the side)

BEAU: You want them to find out about the hospital?

KAITLIN: No.

BEAU: Then, keep quiet.

RADIO: LADIES AND GENTLEMEN, WE'VE REACHED THE OPEN ZONE. THE CASINO IS OPEN FOR BLACK JACK. TAKE THE MONEY AND RUN.

(The conversation of LUISA and BUNKY on one side of the stage overlaps that of KAITLIN and BEAU on the other)

LUISA: *(Coyly to BUNKY)* Your boots are held together by a pin.

BUNKY: They were my father's riding boots. He's dead.

BEAU: Smell the air, darling. It smells different.

KAITLIN: Lighter.

LUISA: Your father.

BUNKY: Whenever I wear these boots I feel, "I'm ready."

LUISA: Ready for what?

BEAU: My skin comes alive by the water.

KAITLIN: Good to get away.

(BEAU hands KAITLIN a white Christmas rose; KAITLIN strips the petals)

KAITLIN: Mmmm. He loves me. He loves me not.

BEAU: In Paris, they say, "He loves me. He loves me a lot. He loves me passionately. He is crazy in love with me. He doesn't love me at all."

KAITLIN: He loves me passionately.

BEAU: How're you feeling, Kaitlin?

KAITLIN: You're always so concerned.

BEAU: Seriously?

KAITLIN: Seriously.

RADIO: YES, WE'RE STEAMBOATIN' INTO OUR SECOND CENTURY. PURSUING A LEGEND AND EXPECTING THE UNEXPECTED.

(*RORY DEBANGO enters flustered, reattaching a giant earring*)

RORY: I thought that rain was gone. But it's raining on one side of the ship. In New Orleans, you need pockets. You can't carry purses.

IRENE: The older the woman, the bigger the earring.

RORY: I only wear jewelry when I take a taxi, but I couldn't find one.

IRENE: The cab business in the daytime is gone.

RORY: At night, taxis are great because people are afraid to die. Last time I went out to dinner I almost got mugged. I felt so bad I forgot my Mace.

(*RORY shows the group the Mace SHE carries*)

RORY: I travel alone throughout Louisiana without being harassed, molested, raped, and beaten. I'll kill any bastard who bothers me.

BUNKY: There's a dark quality about that lady.

BEAU: I can't get a handle on it. It's like grabbing smoke.

RORY: I read you boys were here in the Social Column. So I said, now's the time to take a vacation from power. Deliver that tax folder in person and enjoy stars up close.

IRENE: You shouldn't be in taxes. You should be selling hats on a beach.

RORY: (*Hands IRENE a folder while watching BEAU*) Rory DeBango.

IRENE: Rory's a boy's name.

RORY: They use it at the firm to pass me off as a man. I'm from the black sheep side of the family, the cousin who committed suicide. Daddy called me Crummy at birth, and it stuck.

BUNKY: I remember Crummy. You have a short brother.

RORY: With an equally short wife.

BEAU: But you've gotten so—

RORY: Old. When you're old you've more estrogen, less wrinkles. You know the saying, "Off the hips, onto the face." And "Practice makes perfect."

KAITLIN: Who's practicing?

RORY: Are you anybody? The little wife? You look fresh as a daisy. Or should I say, "As a magnolia"? I'm single by choice. Married women are more nervous than single women. They're more tired. And less competent at every task, including childcare.

BUNKY: I can't get enough of Rory.

BEAU: Because she's so toxic.

RORY: I don't want to be married. I don't want to be bound. I walk by myself and feel great. *(Passing BEAU her autograph book)* Indulge me. I've the signatures of three hundred celebrities. A harmless obsession.

BEAU: What shall I write?

RORY: *(Whispers)* I'd like to take a long nap with you in the rain.

IRENE: Miss DeBango has her B.A., her M.A.

BUNKY: Her B.S.

IRENE: Everything but her M.R.S.

SOUND: Lifeboat drill, a whistle sounds.

RADIO: LADIES AND GENTLEMEN, FOR SAFETY REASONS A MANDATORY LIFEBOAT DRILL WILL NOW BEGIN. LIFE PRE-SERVERS ARE LOCATED UNDER ALL SEATS AND BEDS. SELECT THE PROPER LIFE PRESERVER FOR YOUR BODY SIZE. YOU CAN INFLATE THE JACKET BY BLOWING INTO THE MOUTHPIECE.

(BUNKY hands out life preservers)

BUNKY: Get your bulletproof vests.

RORY: Somebody help.

LUISA: *(In Spanish, assisting IRENE)* Come here, Miss Irene.

RORY: I'm going to drown. Yeeeeek.

(BEAU crosses to RORY)

BEAU: You can scream all night long. The jacket's not going to hook any better. Lift your arms, Rory.

RORY: I didn't learn to swim until I was thirty years old.

BEAU: This strap goes through here.

RORY: I'm still petrified of water. *(Sighs as BEAU pinches her)* Ooh. You got me. That felt good.

BEAU: *(Embarrassed)* There's no way to gracefully get these things on, and look like—

RORY: James Beauregard Ellis? An unusual name separates you… gives you something to fulfill.

BEAU: You're all zipped up.

RORY: I've been in love with your name since I first heard it.

RADIO: LADIES AND GENTS. THE DRILL HAS ENDED. RESUME YOUR NEW YEAR'S ACTIVITIES.

(The characters retreat to various activities. BUNKY exits, returning the vests. KAITLIN watches BEAU and RORY.)

KAITLIN: *(To herself)* This is not happening. I don't exist. I'm screaming to the marrow of my bones. You've got to see that woman there. And ignore her. You didn't marry a hometown boy who wanted a small-time life.

RORY:*(To BEAU)* Don't assume anything unless you've tried it. *(Exits)*

KAITLIN: *(Paces downstage talking to herself)* Women like her are parasites. Remnants from the ice age. You can't annihilate them. They survive because they'll do the ultimate. They've no guilt.

LIGHT: *Twilight sheds its fragile mauve over the pale wood.*

(KAITLIN removes the crystal from her pocket. SHE shivers in the harsh breeze, buttons up the sweater, and talks to the audience.)

KAITLIN: I love cashmere at night. It's extravagant. When my soul hurts, I put on cashmere. This sweater is twenty years old. It's the most famous sweater worn in my high school class. At least thirty girls looked good in this thing.*(Lifts her arm, exposing a rip)* There's a rip up the seam, but this sweater won't unravel. Cashmere is immortal. Just like crystal. *(Shrieks out suddenly.)* I've got to visit the little girl's room.

IRENE: Go smooch on some lipstick—

LUISA: Your daughter moves like she had surgery.

IRENE: *(To LUISA)* I had a hysterectomy at forty. What a relief it was, too. I never go to gynecologists who fuss with me. My brother-in-law took care of me. After he died, I never go. *(Smiles)* Kaitlin's forgotten that slogan, "Don't Work for the Next Wife." The first wife, she lets herself go. Roams around disheveled as a mad fairy. Only to have the next wife loaded with minks and jewels travel around the world.

BEAU: I'm pretending I didn't hear that.

IRENE: Why bother? For God's sake, Kaitlin, run a comb through that hair and change that awful sweater. *(Exiting with LUISA)*

BEAU: *(Crossing to KAITLIN)* Are you all right?

KAITLIN: *(Takes a pill)* If I were you, I'd eat that question.

BEAU: You can't take those pills all the time. They'll make you dizzy.

KAITLIN: *(Laughs, squeezing the crystal)* It's the crystal. Makes me feel jittery. Don't you just love it? Rory's striking?

BEAU: She's okay.

KAITLIN: Do you think I'm that striking?

BEAU: You're great.

KAITLIN: Should I fix my hair like that?

BEAU: I like you the way you are.

KAITLIN: You think I'm pretty as Rory?

BEAU: I met her by chance—

KAITLIN: The only way to keep you is to never let you out of my sight.

BEAU: Look, we're in the middle of the river. Weather's so variable. Mauve skies and thin slips of cloud.

KAITLIN: Are you taking notes?

BEAU: When I write, I'm trying to explain our life to myself.

KAITLIN: Or your relationship— *(Exiting with BEAU)*

RADIO: THEY'RE LIGHTING TORCHES IN THE PLANTATION FOR A WEDDING CELEBRATION. ROMANCE IS IN THE AIR.

(BUNKY and LUISA enter, inhaling the salty air. BUNKY walks to the railing and LUISA follows)

BUNKY: The Dixie Queen. Can you feel the energy in the wood? Nothing's been changed since the nineteenth century. It's a big dream for you to ride the Dixie Queen?

LUISA: Yes.

BUNKY: The older I get, the more I realize I'm addicted to travel. Yeah. Keep me infected.

LUISA: You live in Hollywood?

BUNKY: The entrails of civilization. They kill people with real bullets there. Hollywood has always attracted the mentally unstable. But now they carry guns. Ribs of buildings with no cement. An earthquake a night. It's the most depraved place I've ever been… Actually I kind of like it.

LUISA: Being surrounded by killers!

BUNKY: My limo has dark windows, so I'll be okay…

LUISA: I thought people went into singing for the glamour?

BUNKY: It's hand to mouth. Only it's a bigger hand and a bigger mouth. *(Resignedly)* The music industry is in deep shit. Yeah. Every new star is ten or twelve years old, and one person a week kills himself. My agent would voluntarily steal from me. The man wears a coat and tie to the beach.

SOUND: We hear a blues song—sung by BUNKY—blaring over the radio.

(LUISA rushes over and turns it up.)

BUNKY: My last hit.

LUISA: You are…*(Searches for the right word)*… in a dry period?

BUNKY: A desert, yeah.

LUISA: What's the trend?

BUNKY: The trend is sometimes I work. And sometimes I don't. All I've got is a bag full of jewels.*(BUNKY removes a pouch from his pocket, leans over the railing)* I traveled from Los Angeles to the Fiji Islands with a sack of stones at my side. Diamonds, sapphires, pearls. I'd pull one out when I needed a connection. Have one.

LUISA: I couldn't.

BUNKY: I worked my whole life for a fistful of stones.

LUISA: *(Enthralled)* How's your career?

BUNKY: I just made a jingle for a Brer Rabbit cartoon. If you're in it for the art, now's the time to get out. I'm still a major—"to do" in California? But I'm blocked. I've to drag myself kicking and screaming to the guitar. If I don't do anything, next year, I'll be just important. If you have a hit, they'll talk to you for a while.

LIGHTS: *Lights flash on upstage. The lounge door swings open and IRENE enters, followed by BEAU. HE seats IRENE, then walks vaguely to a newspaper rack, slips out a New York Times.*

IRENE: *(Calls out indignantly)* Bunky, leave my sitter alone.

RADIO: NOT TO WORRY. SEEMS THE MISSISSIPPI TAKES A STRANGE LOOP HERE THAT SENDS US IN THE WRONG DIRECTION FOR ABOUT A MILE.

(The boat dips, and LUISA falls into BUNKY's arms, her lips turned toward his mouth)

RADIO: *(Cont.)* BUT SOON THE RIVER STRAIGHTENS OUT TO A SENSIBLE DIRECTION.

(BUNKY and LUISA drift upstage)

IRENE: *(Hollers)* Luisa. I'll have to run her down because she sneaks off. On a scale of one to ten, this is the dumbest sitter in the world. She gets a one. Beau. I want to applaud you for this rudimentary form of conscience in returning South. With your…ailing wife. How many miscarriages have you put her through?

BEAU: I had hoped maybe we'd start out polite.

IRENE: You don't plan to inherit my money? Oh, I know you have means, Beau, but not big money.

BEAU: What are you after, Mrs. Dubonnet?

IRENE: I'm considering setting up a trust for you and your novels. Then you can focus on creating, not hawking yourself.

BEAU: What's the hitch?

IRENE: I want Kaitlin to spend some time with me.

BEAU: *(Adjusting the paper in the twilight)* You're so unpleasant.

IRENE: Don't play the troubled husband.

BEAU: *(Talks into his paper)* Anybody is obliging until you ask him to do something. I'm asking you not to pry into my marriage.

IRENE: Kitten's had two miscarriages, I bet.

BEAU: *(Rustling through the papers)* I don't want to be an in-law in this family.

IRENE: My daughter won't talk to me, because you've brainwashed her against me. Fine. Egocentric couples.

BEAU: She's here now.

IRENE: Hardly… You wouldn't notice because you're so absorbed—

BEAU: My wife has to put an ocean between you and her. Kaitlin wakes up to your voice like some broken tape. She even loves that specter-like picture of you at the Rex ball. Her body's frail.

IRENE: Why not let her spend some time with me? —Wouldn't you like some writing time?

BEAU: No, I'm independent. I work like I want.

IRENE: You're sufficiently shallow to write anywhere and please the public?

BEAU: Excuse me, Mrs. Dubonnet. I don't know how your daughter can stomach you.

SOUND: *The cruise ship orchestra practices faintly at a distances.*

(KAITLIN enters, pale with an obsessed look to her eyes. She slips a pill between her lips.)

BEAU: Come inside, honey. Remember how we used to dance? *(Motioning toward the music.)*

KAITLIN: *(Smiles and rambles on to herself)* I dread the holidays because I recall less—

IRENE: I hope you're not hitting up the pain pills again. Ruining my holiday with total self-absorption. With that prescription, Kaitlin can sleep standing up. They're a dead man's pill.

KAITLIN: *(Her fingers twitch as SHE crosses her arms)* A critique is fine, but a capsule would be better. Can't wait until it kicks in. *(Laughs shrewishly)* Maybe I'm not a wife today or a daughter. I've multiple personalities. Put me in a room, you get a group.

IRENE: A river cruise is a good place to glamorize ailments. There're so many people to make over you. It's like the maternity ward, where Luisa used to work.

KAITLIN: I didn't have a baby.

IRENE: Well, that should make you happy.

KAITLIN: I've had one child and everyone else's. Beau's here tonight; maybe we'll have one by tomorrow.

IRENE: You've no time for children, Kaitlin. You're the wrong type.

KAITLIN: What do you mean, Mama?

IRENE: At the zoo, there's a glass room where students dressed like monkeys care for the chimps whose mothers have left them. Some females reject their offspring.

(KAITLIN clutches the crystal)

KAITLIN: I can't understand whether Mama is alien to me because she's sick or whether she's sick because she's so alien.

IRENE: Tell me about your miscarriages, Kaitlin?

BEAU: Darling, let's go—

IRENE: With the last miscarriage—

KAITLIN: What are you talking about? Beau!

IRENE: How bad was the surgery?

BEAU: I didn't go into things. I simply said—

KAITLIN: It's amazing. To find myself living inside and outside my life. In a way I never expected to.

BEAU: I'm trying to love you—

KAITLIN: Now the men in my dreams are beginning to look good.

BEAU: My job's… taking care of you—

KAITLIN: You told Mama! What should I do in the good Southern tradition? Take an overdose? Seek revenge? *(KAITLIN runs downstage, grabs the crystal, spins it)* Do you know how to use a crystal? It's got a soul different from the person holding it. Ask it a question. It'll swing one way for yes, another for no. I'm going to tell you this. Because I can see you'll understand. I use the crystal to contact Baudelaire. Watch. Baudelaire, should I punish my husband? Now don't trick me. Sometimes he fools me. *(The crystal swings for no)* No! Ha. Marriage is a complex activity. It both connects you and underscores your solitude.

SOUND: *A band plays* La Vie en Rose.

(RORY charges in, flaunting a vulture headdress and a robe of Cleopatra.)

RADIO: YOUR STEAMBOATIN' VACATION BEGINS WITH THE MISS FLOOZY COSTUME CONTEST. LET THE GOOD TIMES ROLL, LADIES. *LAISSEZ LES BON TEMPS ROULER.*

RORY: I gave my asp to the captain and my bangle to the bartender. That just goes to show that men are interested in mature love affairs. *(Parading around in her costume)* I'm Cleopatra. The Egyptian queen. At mating time, vultures perform exciting displays. They will shoot upward, and join claws in midair.

IRENE: There's one in every group that's the strangest.

RORY: I was born on Saint John's Eve, June 23. It's a mystic day from

Celtic times when women went mad in the heat of the night. I'm not a nice girl. The first thing I read is the obituaries. That's where the money is. And you've got no client to negotiate with.

(BUNKY *enters costumed as Hamlet, followed by* LUISA, *dressed as Ophelia.* BUNKY *waves a bottle of champagne*)

BUNKY: A round of bubbles for anyone? For any two? I'm Hamlet and she's sad Ophelia.

IRENE: (*Assessing* BUNKY) For any beverage, use real crystal, darling, never plastic. You can't buy class, but you can be very visible with your money.

RORY: (*Glancing around*) Beau's lost his wife. Good. (*Spies* KAITLIN) Oh, no. There she is. Come dance, Beau. Be nice to us old empresses.

BEAU: You want to dance, Kaitlin?

KAITLIN: (*Plays restlessly with her sweater*) No one expects you to live in a funny sort of limbo.

SOUND: *A tango plays.*

BEAU: You know I love to tango.

KAITLIN: Well, don't just slip a look. Buy.

BEAU: (*His face set in headstrong denial*) A tango, Miss DeBango?

RORY: In a matter of minutes, I'm important, all of a sudden. To get ahead you've got to be a good dancer.

(RORY *dances upstage with* BEAU)

KAITLIN: An old-fashioned holiday on the river.

IRENE: (*Glancing at* KAITLIN) You work so hard to go to these reunions to hide your marriage from looking like itself. Luisa! Come dance.

LUISA: (*Joining her*) Two women?

IRENE: If I wait for the right man, I may never dance. Who made up those rules anyway?

LUISA: There are plenty of nice men.

IRENE : I don't want to share my room. I look in my bed and say get out.

BUNKY: The champagne's so thick, it's cresting over.

LUISA: I wish I could put words together like you, Bunky.

IRENE: One reason celebrities talk so well is they've learned to talk money out of people. Big dog personalities in brains the size of gnats. *(Crosses to the railing, catching her breath)*

BUNKY: My songs haven't got real value, until I die.

IRENE: *(Watches BUNKY relishing the champagne)* Bunky acts like his dad. He was a gangster.

BUNKY: Gambler.

IRENE: In the horse business in Virginia. Breakfast at noon, dinner at ten.

BUNKY: He accommodated my grandmother by dying right on schedule.

IRENE: I went to the funeral to make sure he was dead.

LUISA: *(Touching his shoulder)* I would like to have known your father.

BUNKY: Me too. There was something hard but important about him.

LUISA: I'm glad I got to meet your mother. I see where you get your dreamy eyes and—

BUNKY: Being a singer has turned me into a sly person. Deaf in one dear. *(BUNKY coughs)* I lived for those moments of glory...

(BUNKY refills their glasses, his eyes strangely soothed by the fizz of the champagne. LUISA hovers by him, high with adoration)

BUNKY: You got me thinking too deep.

LUISA: Humph. About your daddy?

BUNKY: *(Pouring another glass)* I'm thinking about…*(Yells out)* Mus-ic. Hear the echo. Mus-ic.

LUISA: Ooooh!

BUNKY: I'm trying to discover the essence of New Orleans in music? But it's not commercial. *(Shouts)* Com-mer-ci-al. See. No echo.

LUISA: Hmmm. Why sing, if it makes you feel so bad?

BUNKY: I've wanted to be a musician all my life. I'm dependent on it. If I don't have musicians about me, I become depressed.

LUISA: Music's a neurosis?

BUNKY: To freeze time.

LUISA: *(Her eyes bright with champagne)* Cause it's moving too fast?

BUNKY: Right. Yeah.

(IRENE crosses to KAITLIN, buried in a book, CREATING LOVE. Throughout the sequence, BEAU and RORY dance by flirting playfully. The characters' lines overlap in the fury of tango dancing)

LIGHTS: Shadows of darkness.

KAITLIN: Where're my sunglasses? The wind blows specks into these lenses. A—a-a-h. Like slivers of glass.*(SHE puts on her sunglasses)*

IRENE: I'm not used to sitting on the Promenade Deck with my eyes closed.

KAITLIN: *(Motioning to a box)* Tea? There's Tropical Escape, Wild Forest.

IRENE: Try some Siberian ginseng. The herb for energy.

ROSARY HARTEL O'NEILL

KAITLIN: If I were any more alive, I'd be dead. *(Shielding her eyes from the glare)*

IRENE: I've Spanish news for you, baby. Real love is not like that.

RORY: *(Dancing by KAITLIN)* Yes, next to elegance and class will be your wife's picture.

BEAU: *(To RORY)* I'm a nursemaid to Kaitlin.

RORY: If you just stand and sway from side to side, I can do everything else.

IRENE: *(Shrieks out)* How old are you, Rory? Forty, fifty?

RORY: I make forty look good.

IRENE: *(To KAITLIN)* You're heading full tilt toward disaster.

BUNKY: *(Dancing by)* When you play with other musicians in front of an audience, you've this experience of living through more feeling than you can capture in words.

LUISA: Aaaah!

IRENE: *(To KAITLIN)* He's going to do that to you after you've been the... the—

KAITLIN: Love giver. Women have had to live on a deeper level to survive—

IRENE: Run away with a gal with higher tits—

BUNKY: *(Twirling LUISA)* It's like being inside a tidal wave. A wall of water engulfing you. It's that many sounds from all sides.

LUISA: Wow.

BUNKY: Like a roar pulling you into forgetfulness.

RORY: *(To BEAU)* Some clients can work things out on the fee couch.

IRENE: Only a fool would stay and watch. *(Storms out)*

RORY: *(To BEAU)* Meet me on the lower deck. I don't just look. I buy. *(Exits)*

KAITLIN: *(Removes a cigarette but doesn't light it)* I smoke only at night. It's the best I can do. Women smoke more than men because we've…

(BEAU moves behind her, his hand to her neck)

BEAU: *(Grabs KAITLIN's chin intensely)* I'm no longer your lover, but I still feel like— Must you smoke?

KAITLIN: I'm just holding it. Scandal's titillating.

BEAU: *(Removes a handkerchief)* That's what you wanted, Kaitlin. A husband as a kind of accessory.

KAITLIN: I like the math of it, the figuring out of it. The juggling.

BEAU: *(Sits next to her, removing the glasses, blotting her cheeks)* I don't want another woman. I want my wife.

KAITLIN: If I'm not doing it, I can't complain about others doing it.

BEAU: *(Rises suddenly, walks to the railing)* How many parties do I have to attend alone? I'm not a machine. Christ, I wish I was. Since the hospital, I touch you, you're ice. To be naked and fail is one of the most gruesome things you can do.

KAITLIN: You're the one who works all night.

BEAU: *(Pause)* Are you for or against talking? I hoped this cruise might—

KAITLIN: Change things?

BEAU: Is it going to be a slow spiral downward or everything is fine, and then bam?

KAITLIN: You work yourself into a white heap. And leave me the shell.

BEAU: I spent four weeks, seven and a half hours a day with my editor, cutting one hundred pages from my novel. I had every sentence put on trial for its life. The writing is so hard. The tyranny now is that the work be good.

KAITLIN: Why do you push yourself?

BEAU: Because like being married… *(Shaking his head)* … writing is also a prodigious joy. Writing makes you aware you're a thinking person and you can impose some order. When a story is rolling, you can forget time. Last week, I wrote for hours without knowing the room had gotten dark. *(Affectionately)* And you've been like my shadow. The first reader who shares the vision. Remember when you read the opening chapter aloud to hear what caught, and I solved it in your presence.

KAITLIN: Vaguely.

BEAU: You're the person I write for, whom I trust. Sometimes I think if I write well enough I can make you live forever. *(Grabs the railing)* Come here *(SHE draws away.)* Haven't I been punished enough? Each night *(Turning to her)* I lie there watching you. "Your head, your gesture, your hair. Are beautiful as a beautiful landscape."

KAITLIN: Baudelaire.

BEAU: "The smile plays on your face like a fresh wind in a clear sky."

KAITLIN: Muse.

BEAU: "Thus I would wish one night when the voluptuary hour sounds."

KAITLIN: Love poet.

BEAU: *(Embracing her)* "To crawl, like a coward, noiselessly, Towards the treasures of your body." *Voulez-vous coucher avec moi?*

(KAITLIN's hands flutter to her mouth confusedly. She crosses downstage, confiding to the audience.)

KAITLIN: My husband's a master at deflecting women because he's been doing it so long. For our fifth anniversary, he brought me back this Faberge locket. Gold with a coral rose. It's got a tiny watch inside, circled with diamonds. But it's got no face. *(KAITLIN removes the crystal, swings it)* Beau's getting back at me beautifully. The new woman's exotic. Carbonated bubbly.

Help me, Baudelaire. See what I must see. *(Sits down)* I'm asking for power, not permission. *(Pause)* Don't beg anybody but God. *(Exits)*

ACT 2

(Later that night. The deck is dressed with holiday lights, tinsel, party favors for the countdown at midnight. KAITLIN is costumed as the nineteenth-century poet Baudelaire. Elegantly boyish in her slacks, vest, jacket, and cravat, KAITLIN talks to the audience.)

KAITLIN: I'm dressed for the masquerade party. Charles Baudelaire. The ex-dandy. Gentleness isn't going to get me anywhere. *(Grasps a Virginia Slim cigarette)* A cigarette. For what do I want to live my life wanting something? So I die ten years sooner. *(Holds up a book reverently)* For Christmas, Beau gave me a first edition of Baudelaire's poetry, *Les Fleurs du Mal*. When you benefit from a corrupt relationship, it's hard to complain about it. Listen. That's my poem, *"La Vie Anterieure,"* or "Previous Existence." I'm an old soul. I was Baudelaire in another life. I'm serious. I haven't told my family yet, but I can see on a higher plane, so I'll tell you. I am Baudelaire. He—I—I was a mean desperate person, so they sent me back. Tonight I'm supposed to learn something about love. An epiphany? *(KAITLIN withdraws with her book)*

LIGHTS: The scene shifts to a side deck.

SOUND: Let Me Call You Sweetheart.

(RORY stands in a sequined dress, flashing a camera at BEAU)

RORY: Smile. When you're alone, you bring a camera. It gives you such a sense of belonging. *(Squats to take a photo)* Yeek! You want to have a miserable night? Put on a sequin skirt. It sticks to your stockings. When you sit down, the sequins crunch. I've always got something on me somewhere that's uncomfortable. My feet, my hips, my face. I thought about becoming a nun, but I changed my mind when they gave up their habits. The pope didn't give up his costume, did he? I want to dress simply and wear a long strand of pearls between my legs.

BEAU: *(Touching RORY'S ring)* What a weird ring.

RORY: I like the fact that it's a stag, being a stag most of my life. The only man I've got is on the dollar bill in my pocket. Might as well have fun with your money now. Kaitlin's going to have a party after you're divorced.

BEAU: You're dangerous.

RORY: *(Turning away)* This is the first New Year's in five I haven't spent in a cemetery. I come from a family of six girls. The town where we grew up is empty. Now that my mother has died, there's no place for us to meet. So we gather twice a year at the cemetery, on All Soul's Day and on the day she died, January first. It's difficult, but we're around the tomb for a week. The will of my mother was to keep us together.

BEAU: *"La vie c'est la mort. Parlez-vous français?"*

RORY: I bet the hook in your line is better than your sinker.

(BEAU and RORY exit. LUISA wheels in IRENE in a Queen Victoria costume, a basket of delicacies on her lap)

IRENE: That dinner wasn't worth it. Tasteless sauce on stiff meat. I wore my queen's mantle. Talked French with a Southern accent. And the captain asked if I was from the Amazon. Shush!

LUISA: *(In Spanish, randomly)* Oh Lord! There's nothing more menacing than the old lady with a train. Merciful heaven.

IRENE: I was queen of Mystic Ball. Quiet!

LUISA: She's old, and she has to drag animal skin.

IRENE: Buy rich and you buy once. Buy cheap and you buy forever. *(Glaring at LUISA)* Out! Spaniard!

LUISA: Merciful heaven!

(LUISA exits. KAITLIN stretches out with her book, Germaine Greer's THE CHANGE)

IRENE: It's a constant job, traveling with an Hispanic. *(Regarding the book's title)* Feminism's passé in this day and age.

KAITLIN: The woman's story has yet to be told here. How love can go majorly wrong.

IRENE: You used to love to chat.

KAITLIN: We were united in our hatred of Daddy and my first husband. (KAITLIN clutches the crystal on a chain) A higher power... is punishing me.

IRENE: Whom are you talking to?

KAITLIN: Baudelaire. Most people have to be taught by their personal psychic to use these.

IRENE: I hate anything that begins with a p-s-y.

KAITLIN: I didn't, because I'm, I'm kind of... a witch. (Breathing quickly) Oh. Baudelaire just corrected me. I'm a sorceress.

IRENE: Have you lost your mind?

KAITLIN: (Laughs) I became a psychic and offered to do Beau's readings to seduce him. (Changes her voice) "You don't want that girl." I'm serious. Ask it a question. (Swings the crystal in a circle) It'll swing one way for no. Another for yes.

IRENE: (Holds the now-lifeless crystal) One misconception of life is that you need straight answers to your concerns.

KAITLIN: It doesn't work when you hold it, Mama, because people have different energies. I've had plenty of lives. While people were fighting the Civil War, I was eating the good French food of the nineteenth century. In fact, this is my first time as a Southerner and a wife.

IRENE: No point in being a wife, if you're a convalescent. Beau's had his children—

KAITLIN: From a previous marriage.

IRENE: He's got the income now, and he wants some action.

KAITLIN: G-a-w-d.

IRENE: As time passes—it's important to offset the loss of beauty with energy. I spent a lot of years being young. I woke up one morning, and I wasn't young anymore. So I bought myself a floor-length mink. Turtlenecks in every color. Gold bracelets. And I never wear red. Look at you lying around in a man's suit. Men can talk about the women who keep the best houses, raise the best children, and cook the best pies. But it's the beautiful women they come home to. It's true, for everybody—the Chinese, Spanish, Africans—unpleasant, but true. Southern men. They want trophy wives. Second wives, I'm sure they torture them daily. They tortured the first wife; why would they stop after that?

KAITLIN: A war is being waged against wives, and it's being led by their m-m-mothers. You know when we lost? I'll tell you. We lost two hundred years ago when m-m-mothers said, "You need someone to take care of you."

IRENE: (Chuckles) Now Kaitlin, Beau serves many functions for you—

KAITLIN: I don't care who knows I'm forty-three. (Shouts) Just forty-three.

IRENE: Shh! I don't trust anybody who tells their age. If you tell your age, you'll tell all.

KAITLIN: (Vaguely) My son's out there, and my husband's inside. Talk to them.

IRENE: The more you act like you're on your honeymoon, the better. Otherwise, mother Beau. Let each episode pass. I'd say, "Who's in this house?" The help would never say, "Her." They'd say, "Nobody. Mrs. Dubonnet, you know that." Brutal. I think the best mistresses always are.

KAITLIN: There's the amicable divorce, M-m-mama.

IRENE: I've passed these fiftyish ex-wives at garage sales in their plastic shoes. Hungry for a third part-time job. Without a man, a woman better have family.

KAITLIN: Not everywhere. In Paris, women are very secure—

IRENE: Restrict yourself to worrying about Beau ten minutes a day. The rest of the time, enjoy life. Book a weekly facial. Dine exquisitely, alone. Or remarry, if it's convenient. You should get a bigger ring on round three. What gives sense to life is that it's short. It will end. Don't expect so much, and you won't be disappointed. It took one hundred fifty years for women to vote. So equality in marriage will probably take another hundred years.

(BUNKY enters with LUISA)

BUNKY: Luisa's divine in white. It's like Mae West white. When she walks she sparkles.

(LUISA removes her cape. SHE is wearing a simple gown)

LUISA: That cape from the thrift store's probably a dead woman's.

BUNKY: Let's practice Black Jack. Want to play, Mama?

KAITLIN: I've always been warned not to play Black Jack.

IRENE: Black Jack's the one game you can win at. We need a crowd. Kaitlin's not big on giving the house a cut. Count me in.

BUNKY: The ace and the jack. That's the winning hand. Or an ace and a face card.

KAITLIN: (To herself) I keep having these terrible thoughts. Sometimes, I'm on another planet where nothing is human.

IRENE: (Overlapping) Kaitlin's hardly any fun anymore.

BUNKY: Will you shut up?

IRENE: Happy people don't think deeply.

KAITLIN: The only time I was happy was when I was expecting Bunky.

BUNKY: You've a grown-up son. That counts for five.

KAITLIN: I wanted to give Beau a child. But my eggs weren't normal, and a baby wouldn't grow.

IRENE: Beau doesn't need more babies.

BUNKY: None of my friends want children.

IRENE: They're taking away the crutches that made it bearable. *(Motions to the others)*

LUISA: Pills for morning sickness.

BUNKY: Plastic bottles.

IRENE: Diaper service.

KAITLIN: I didn't want the surgery.

IRENE: Did you tie off your tubes, girl?

KAITLIN: But I trusted Beau.

IRENE: You're strange.

KAITLIN: Gave myself over to believing someone.

BUNKY: *(Calls out)* Black Jack.

IRENE: Didn't you prepare for the operation?

BUNKY: Will somebody defang Mimi?

IRENE: I work harder every day to be ignored twice as much. And I never win at Black Jack.

(IRENE and LUISA exit)

BUNKY: Here's to relatives. All the pretty people on all the pretty cruises.

KAITLIN: *(Coldly)* I want to go home to my three dogs.

BUNKY: *(Yells)* Life sucks. *(Smiles, looking into her eyes)* I feel better. Your turn.

KAITLIN: Life—life?

BUNKY: Flare out! Life sucks.

KAITLIN: I can't remember what to say.

BUNKY: *(Howls)* Life sucks.

KAITLIN: Life—I can't. I can't.

BUNKY: Shh. Open your mouth, and I'll scream for you. *(Shouts)* Life sucks.

KAITLIN: You should have been the first of many boys.

BUNKY: A line of kings.

KAITLIN: Your dad had money, but he didn't want more kids. And sons were all I wanted. Back then, you got pregnant at eighteen, you got married.

BUNKY: I should know these things.

KAITLIN: Can you forgive me? Sending you off with Grandma when I knew how mean she was.

BUNKY: It's what I wanted, Mama.

KAITLIN: When you say, "M-m-mama," it sounds funny. M-m-mama, that's the name for the woman who raises you. My body was the machine. Last night, I dreamed, I was back in that gorgeous white nursery at Mama's with the canopied cradle. You were a beautiful baby. "Beauty boy," I used to call you. Remember? Such a handsome little man.

BUNKY: We don't need to talk about this.

KAITLIN: I still remember Mama's Cadillac driving you away. I thought you'd join Beau and me later in Paris…

BUNKY: *(Inhales deeply and looks away)* So what's your point?

KAITLIN: If I hurt you, I want to know—

BUNKY: When I told you I wanted to live with Grandma, it was a test… to see how much you'd fight for me. The day I left, you answered the phone right

ROSARY HARTEL O'NEILL

in the middle of when I was leaving. Afterward you didn't even come to the door. Look, I don't want anything from you. I don't need anything from you.

KAITLIN: I can't talk to you when you're angry.

BUNKY: God. It's not that I have this all thought out. It's just a feeling. You got what you wanted, and I got seconds. The best I could do was place a Band-aid over my mouth.

KAITLIN: Did you miss home much?

BUNKY: One night in three. I wanted to protect you even when I couldn't see you. So I kept this blank medallion. Only I know what's on it. I found it under your rug after you left.

KAITLIN: My high school charm. Lord, I feel so— after all the letters, the unanswered calls.

BUNKY: You fly around saying how much you love everybody, when the only person you really love is yourself. I'm supposed to forget the years of silence. Mimi and I didn't enter your room until ya'll called from Paris. The next day she piled your things in a heap in the yard, lit a match to them. Books, papers, clothes.

KAITLIN: I phoned every day.

BUNKY: I never knew.

KAITLIN: Didn't Mama tell you?

BUNKY: All that time Mimi and I were destroying your stuff. Clearing your room. Painting the walls red. I felt that was part of being in a family. (Looks at her) A strand of hair's stuck to your cheek. I don't want to spend the rest of my life punishing you and myself. I can reach within my heart and see you're still a good person deep inside.

(As BEAU enters, surveying the water, we hear the ship's radio)

RADIO: IF A LATE SNACK SOUNDS GOOD, WE'LL SET UP A BUFFET FOR YOU TO SEND YOU OFF ON A NIGHT OF SWEET DREAMS.

BUNKY: *(Exits)* The moonlight buffet. Yum.

BEAU: *(Secretively)* Think I'll try out the brass bed in the stateroom. You?

KAITLIN: From time to time, I like to sleep less.

BEAU: *(Cautiously)* You've been dreaming again—

KAITLIN: Each night I float higher…

BEAU: About the—

KAITLIN: Until I'm a thousand feet off the ground.

BEAU: The baby—

KAITLIN: I see everybody and descend when I want. I float in front of the moon, but she sees right through me.

BEAU: I've behaved badly.

KAITLIN: *(Gesturing to the sky)* With a moon, it'll never be pitch black. Ooh. See those cracks in the moon?

BEAU: I didn't mean to hurt you.

KAITLIN: Men once believed that the dark spots were oceans, and the bright ones, continents.

BEAU: I'm sorry.

KAITLIN: Everyone wants to do what comes naturally and hope he's absolved.

BEAU: You think I did something?

KAITLIN: *(Laughs.)* I'm sure there're one or two people who were faithful, but they must be in a mental institution.

BEAU: I just played Black Jack.

KAITLIN: Alone? To be safe, a woman must be attractive to a man. The

ROSARY HARTEL O'NEILL

prettier you are, the safer you will be.

BEAU: Actually, I flirt to see if you still think I'm a machine—

KAITLIN: I would have to drink liquid for a year to look like I did ten years ago. I saw you with Rory—

BEAU: If you would've said, don't talk to—

KAITLIN: But to follow her like Daffy Duck.

BEAU: You're mad at your mother. You take it out on me—God. I understand what you're going through and why... you... you feel so bad. Chri— You can't make a move worrying how your mother is going to come down on you. Her remarks hit you with the force of delayed bombs. I've seen too many husbands in their tuxedos with the smell of mothballs and camphor. Men beaten into submission. Fossils from a time of manners and good breeding. Is that what you want?

KAITLIN: Baudelaire says, "You lie."

BEAU: You know I hate it when you speak like that—

KAITLIN: *(Yells)* Marriage sucks!

BEAU: You're so ungrateful.

KAITLIN: You're a filthy rotten cheat.

BEAU: Act adult—

KAITLIN: Am I a grown-up; I forget. I lie in bed at night, telling myself what a stupid fool I am. What about that girl in Cannes? She sent the letter to our house. And the one from Berlin? Y'all never came back before three a.m.

BEAU: We don't need to talk about this.

KAITLIN: Should I haunt the singles bars for a younger man? Exhaust myself in volunteer work? Go to bed earlier and earlier 'til I get too old to notice? Should I have surgery? Wear something fashionable. Designed for an anorexic with no breasts!

(LUISA enters with IRENE. KAITLIN breaks away, pulling a bell out of her pocket, rushes downstage as SHE chants a Buddhist prayer)

KAITLIN: "We're alone and we're entangled." Buddha.

BEAU: Marvelous.

IRENE: Kaitlin, get that bell out of your face.

BEAU: It's a Buddhist ritual.

(KAITLIN rings the bell.)

KAITLIN: The past isn't real.

LUISA: Women don't adapt well to "the change."

IRENE: I say, "Hawk that bell."

BUNKY: *(Rushing in with a drink)* I was in the Blue Moon Saloon. An eighty-seven-year-old blind man is tending bar with no liquor license. The guy said, "You want a bourbon ditch." I though the guy meant bitch. A bourbon ditch. You mix bourbon with water, it looks like a ditch! *(Somberly to KAITLIN)* What happened?

KAITLIN: I'm gossiping with my angel, Baudelaire.

BEAU: The poet.

IRENE: And opium addict. Why not admit yourself to a nice hospital for a rest. I volunteer in a ward with lots of—

LUISA: Smiling faces.

IRENE: Old candy stripers—mostly women over forty. Trying to connect to something.

KAITLIN: *(Puts a hand to her chest)* Oh Lord. My heart's beating twice as fast.

IRENE: Last week, there was that fiftyish woman. A bird person.

KAITLIN: A dark soul's entering my body. Ooh.

IRENE: But she had had eight children.

KAITLIN: I remember being in a hospital in Paris. A pink room. When the door cracked open, you could see people with balloons. Sometimes, you'd hear carts rushing down the hall. They couldn't find Beau.

BEAU: *(Returning)* You're blaming me?

KAITLIN: My nurse looked everywhere.

BEAU: You knew I had to do that tour.

KAITLIN: I'm recalling the operation now. Yummy sedatives. It feels soft. Marshmallow, white soft all around me.

BEAU: Stop.

KAITLIN: There's something I've got to tell y'all.

BEAU: Do you have to?

KAITLIN: I'm remembering it now. The abortion.

BEAU: No.

KAITLIN: Talking freely. Not stopping myself.

IRENE: You had an abortion? At how far along?

KAITLIN: About... five months, M-m-mama.

BUNKY: Christ!

LUISA: It could have lived.

BEAU: They told us it was only three months.

KAITLIN: Baudelaire moved through me. He drove Beau to push me to—

BEAU: I suggested… Kaitlin have it because Doctor Peters said the pregnancy could—

KAITLIN: Beau said to save our relationship, I'd have to kill the damn baby.

BEAU: That's a lie. I said, "An infant with serious problems would pose—"

KAITLIN: When the contractions started, it felt like I was in labor. They gave me ice to suck like—I was so weak. It took all my effort to raise my eyelids. Pools of blood. And sheets of glass. I heard the doctors say I had a forty-five percent chance of living. *(Fast, cold)* "Where in the hell is my husband?"

BEAU: No one called me.

KAITLIN: Shut up! *(Quietly)* I came as close to dying as you can come and still be alive. While I lay on the table, I floated out of my body. It happened during the two or three minutes when I was right on the threshold of death. Grandma, Uncle Jack, and others came from the other world. They came to lead me.

IRENE: Grandma Malter?

BUNKY: And Uncle Jack?

KAITLIN: He and Grandma kept talking about death, but they never used that word. "The crossover," they said. "Don't be afraid of the change."

LUISA: The passage?

KAITLIN: Behind them stood a group like a choir in gray robes. They didn't speak, but you could tell they were friendly. I said, "Do we have to come now?" Because I was standing next to this tiny boy.

BEAU: *(Insistently to KAITLIN)* Keep silent.

KAITLIN: The boy was pointing downward, saying, "Look what I can do as a human." So I repeated, "Do we have to come now?" And they said, "The little one, yes. But you? That's not up to us. That's up to you and God."

BUNKY: Incredible.

KAITLIN: "We're just here to let you know the transition is easy," they said. "It's peaceful and calm." *(Sharing a great secret)* And I learned something. People do not die alone. Even when they are murdered, they die with great love around them. These blessed ones are still watching over us. *(Matter-of-factly)* They showed the baby to me... before they took it away.

BEAU: God, I'm so sorry—

KAITLIN: A perfectly formed boy. Beau pressured me, but I killed it. It was part of my body, and I hated it. I don't want more things hanging on me, f-f-f-fussing at me.

BEAU: You panicked, sweetheart.

KAITLIN: Don't minimize it. For God's sake. It was a deliberate act. There is no good reason for what I did. But there's an ugly, wise part of me that's relieved.

(KAITLIN exits, and BEAU and IRENE follow)

BEAU: Kait-lin! Kait-lin!

IRENE: Kaitlin was too vain. So she waited until it was dangerous.

LUISA: Quick. Go talk to your mom.

BUNKY: *(Sniffing back tears)* Lousy allergy.

LUISA: She needs you.

BUNKY: *(Grabs open a pack of cards)* One thing I've inherited. Lousy allergies. Hang around this climate too long, your head will bust open. *(Empties the box, spilling cards)*

LUISA: Go comfort your mother.

BUNKY: *(Leans over, picks up a joker)* A joker. Being a joker has certain advantages. A joker's not needed for most games. And you can avoid players in distress. *(Collects the cards and deals)* Shoosh, that was a joke. Oh... geez...

Now, in Black Jack, a joker's never dealt.

LUISA: What're you doing?

BUNKY: Folding back the cards for Black Jack. Dealing imaginary hands.

LUISA: I'm trying to get you to help your mother.

BUNKY: (Pushes his chair back abruptly) Shoosh! Mama's more of a problem than she has a problem.

SOUND: Puts on some loud Tom Waite music.

LUISA: How can you say that?

BUNKY: What? (Turns music down, catches his breath) Look, I make absolutely no difference here.

SOUND: The ship bell rings.

You hear those ship bells? Can I control when they'll ring? (Turns up the sound)

LUISA: (Loud) Go talk to her. (Turns the music down)

BUNKY: You know how much you'll be missed when you're gone? Pour a drop of water out of a bucket that's full. That's how much.

LUISA: Your mom could kill herself.

BUNKY: Geez… My father died of a heart attack after trying to overdose for twenty years. Mama looks better now than ever before. My saying something would only give her ammunition for… for… later. God, let me concentrate.

SOUND: BUNKY turns up the music.

(HE grabs his forehead, sniffs) Christ, my allergies are… pouring cement into my head. I wanted to protect Mama. Embrace her scars. No big deal. Big and little murders occur daily. Oops. Ha.

LUISA: That's not funny.

ROSARY HARTEL O'NEILL

BUNKY: How do I know you're not a spy? A smiling face, then zap. You're at my throat.

LUISA: *(SHE snaps off the music)* Your mother has been punished for wanting–

BUNKY: Shoosh! I understand why she's upset.

LUISA: Starting today you will have responsibilities as a son. *(Leaning over him)* Because you've seen her pain.

BUNKY: Fine. I don't know the truth of her life, and you... You damn sure don't know it. You see these stones? They're nothing but glass.

LUISA: They're not real?

BUNKY: Counterfeit sparklers from tinseltown. Props from a video that was scrapped when my songs didn't hit the charts. They shine like real under the light and they're just as heavy. See? Don't talk to me about my mother heading for catastrophe because I live there. You think I'd take this free trip if I had other options? I haven't eaten this well all year. Breakfast, lunch, dinner and the seafood buffet. That's what I like about a cruise up the Mississippi. Babe, we ain't going nowhere.

LUISA: You've such a mellow voice, just like your mother's. And you've got her big eyes. *(Staring into his eyes)* I used to envy how your mother looked.

BUNKY: All right. All right.

LUISA: In that debutante portrait in the front parlor. Then when I heard she was married to Beau Ellis.

BUNKY: God, you find it hot? *(Sniffs)* Why me?

LUISA: Who else? If there is love around her, she will have the desire to live. In any case... you don't want your mother to die. Before you've a chance to do something for her? *(THEY kiss)*

(KAITLIN enters wrapped in a white blanket, her shoulder bruised. SHE is followed by IRENE.)

KAITLIN: I wanted to throw myself in the Mississippi River. But I skidded. Some tourists rescued me.

IRENE: You hurt?

KAITLIN: No. I slipped near the gangplank. Aborted the mission. *(Laughs)* No pun intended.

LUISA: I'll get a robe.

(LUISA exits.)

KAITLIN: In the old days, when an infant died, the mother veiled her head and withdrew from society.

IRENE: Don't think so deeply.

KAITLIN: After an abortion, friends don't hasten to comfort you. *(Tightens the robe across her chest)*

IRENE: Learn to say, "Who cares." I said, "Who cares," fourteen times yesterday, and I felt a lot better.

SOUND: *We hear the Preservation Hall band playing "When the Saints Go Marching In."*

IRENE: *(Opens an umbrella, does the cakewalk)* My mother after eighteen years of a childless marriage produced me. This left her with a permanently bemused expression. I don't think she was ever happy again.

KAITLIN: Hold me, Mama. I feel so bad.

IRENE: Don't fuss about me. It's time you come home to New Orleans and stop feeling sorry —

BUNKY: Mimi. Please!

IRENE: *(Pulls out a handkerchief for the cake walk)* Laissez les bons temps roulez.

(IRENE exits. LUISA enters with a robe. BUNKY breathes deeply, then smiles as he drapes it over KAITLIN)

ROSARY HARTEL O'NEILL

BUNKY: For some reason, Ma, you're never prettier than when you're sad as hell.

KAITLIN: What consoles me is I've a beautiful robe—

LUISA: To me, you're perfect—

KAITLIN: It's not a good day, Luisa.

BUNKY: *(Laughs uneasily, pours his own drink)* I've decided to take a break after this cruise.

KAITLIN: Shh. You've got to be quiet to hear the river.

BUNKY: Go... go to the Gulf Coast. Enjoy those blue skies and pink sand. Forget my Faustian pact for the all-American dollar.

KAITLIN: The great Mississippi. The river says, "God loves artists."

BUNKY: But I was never actually —

KAITLIN: Shh. You're always going to do the work of a great artist. *(SHE removes the crystal)*

BUNKY: Come to the Gulf Coast.

KAITLIN: *(Laughs and clutches the crystal)* Why now?

BUNKY: Mystical people are inspiring. You're my mother and you're... you're all soul. I appreciate Baudelaire, the crystal. All these things you like, I like.

KAITLIN: Yes.

BUNKY: I'm glad you'll spend time with me and Luisa.

KAITLIN: Lu—is—a?

LUISA: But we're just friends.

KAITLIN: *(Pushes the couple into an embrace)* Make something happen,

Luisa. He'll be sweet to you, if you'll be sweet to him.

(LUISA and BUNKY embrace.)

KAITLIN: *(Cont.) (Smiling as SHE turns away)* A minute ago Bunky was starting school and now—

BUNKY: *(Crossing away)* Ma, the next song's for you.

(BUNKY and LUISA exit.)

KAITLIN: I think it's ancient, this fear of abandonment. You don't want to love your sons too much, because you've got to give them to younger women. And you could become the enemy.

RADIO: THERE ARE ONLY FIVE STEAMBOATS LEFT. AT ONE TIME, THERE WERE OVER TWELVE THOUSAND. THE LARGEST IS THE DIXIE QUEEN.

(KAITLIN opens her copy of Baudelaire's __The Flowers of Evil.__ RORY enters, tipsy)

RORY: *(Chuckles, then points inside)* I haven't found "de-mand." De man, get it? I'm not interested in those dancing dudes. Designated dancers. Two gay men in the middle of a darkened dance floor, perfectly surrounded by white-haired women. *(Laughs)*

KAITLIN: Not me.

RORY; *(Chuckles to herself)* You're such a frail canary. You can sing, but don't take you out of your cage. *(Leans back)* Why not let Beau do his little party thing? The thinking wife's not a happy one. I know. I'm in taxes.

KAITLIN: Rory, did you read The Flowers of Evil?

RORY: I'm not a flower person. I don't care much for things that die.

KAITLIN: Then you don't know tropical flowers. Morning glories kill everything, and they're gorgeous. Crepe myrtles, the hotter it gets, the more they bloom. *(Carefully)* I saw you talking with my husband.

(KAITLIN lifts up her robe pocket and aims a gun under it at Rory)

KAITLIN: I'm going to let out my rebel yell. And shoot a tiny hole through your head.

RORY: Another pistol-packing mama.

KAITLIN: *(Lifting the covered gun)* I'm going to blast it off at midnight. A woman in the French Quarter got killed that way. They don't know which of the thousands of bullets did it. I could bat you upside your head. Through all that teased hair. And no one would see it.

(RORY pulls out her Mace, aims it at KAITLIN)

RORY: It's my fault your husband's...on the prowl?

KAITLIN: In Louisiana, the girlfriends are entertainers. The governor has a stripper. Beau has a stand-up comic. *(SHE aims the gun.)* What should I do as the good wife? Blow off an earring? Whack your big toe? I'm going to get me some guts, buy me a whip, and wring your neck like a chicken. *(SHE screams)* Get out, Rory. Get out.

RORY: I got two legs, remember. *(Exits)*

SOUND: *Calliope plays* Daisy.

(BEAU enters with a bouquet. KAITLIN hides the gun.)

BEAU: That calliope's got a player piano like the one my mama had at her plantation in Saint Ursula. Kaitlin, come see. You're watching the barges?

KAITLIN: I guess. One day the Mississippi will be nothing but cement.

BEAU: *(Hands KAITLIN the bouquet)* Truce?

KAITLIN: Gorgeous camellias with petals like tissue paper.

BEAU: And inside, a DEAREST pin.

KAITLIN: Goodness.

BEAU: Diamonds, emeralds, amethysts, rubies, emeralds, sapphires, topaz. Spells DEAREST.

KAITLIN: *(Handing the pin back)* Keep it. I'm remembering everything and not crying. We're young, that's the best memories. Baudelaire says we'll never have our own child.

BEAU: Never's fine.

KAITLIN: Sometimes, he says you're inside my soul. I feel each suggestion that passes through you. But Baudelaire says, you like fast women. You watch them to escape me. I've been in nobody's life, Beau. I can no longer trade on my appearance. I lie awake at night worrying what will become of me.

BEAU: To me, you're like Psyche, the embodiment of inner life.

KAITLIN: I'd rather be a witch. Roam on winter nights with bats and glow worms for company. Witches and female saints are a lot alike. They both prophesy and read hearts. They live in cloisters. Fly off to a higher perch. Cackle a little. *(KAITLIN pulls out a paper gun, shoots it)* Happy New Year!

BEAU: Kaitlin, you scared me. I think you owe me an apology? *(SHE turns away)* I know you're struggling for your identity, sugar. Fine. I'm living an ordinary life. On this cruise, I see a roomful of people who've found marriage highly entertaining. Are they happily married?

(KAITLIN stares at the Mississippi)

KAITLIN: I hoped a baby could… bring us together.

BEAU: It will take time to rebuild trust, but I'm willing to give us another chance.

KAITLIN: *"Le Grand Pan est mortal."*

BEAU: The god Pan is mortal? Is this some sort of a test? To taunt me out of my brain?

KAITLIN: It's not easy for me to talk straight, Beau. I've been groomed to manipulate…

BEAU: I need you to set limits for yourself and me.

KAITLIN: It's over, Beau.

BEAU: You think your decision's the right one, by God.

KAITLIN: I've got to think I'm going to live forever. That way I can do anything. I'm sure one can even acclimate to being divorced a second time.

BEAU: But why? For God's sake, why?

KAITLIN: There's a one-word answer even to why questions. *(Screams out)* "Because."

BEAU: I know I was wrong about Rory—

KAITLIN: It's not about whether or not you cheat.

BEAU: I know, if you stay we can work it out.

KAITLIN: When we get together, there's no direction.

BEAU: I feel like a dam is breaking. You've been an obsession for me. In the hospital… when I was standing by your bed… You were more beautiful to me than ever. Where will…?

KAITLIN: I dread telling you because it would give you hope.

BEAU: Can I call you?

KAITLIN: I'll write.

BEAU: This is so humiliating.

KAITLIN: You don't have to wait.

BEAU: I don't want this cruise to be about the marriage I lost.

KAITLIN: *(Softly)* A marriage is not the final product.

BEAU: *(As HE exits)* So the final product is?

KAITLIN: Us. You and me—truthfully together.

LIGHTS: *Fireworks flash, streaming red and purple through the mauve sky. The glare grazes KAITLIN's face as she roams the deck with another unlit cigarette.*

RADIO: ON THE RIGHT ARE BONFIRES LIGHTING UP THE LEVEE. AND THAT'S NOTTOWAY PLANTATION IN WHITE CASTLE, LOUISIANA. CLAIMING TO BE THE LARGEST PLANTATION IN THE SOUTH, NOTTOWAY BOASTS SIXTY-FOUR ROOMS.

KAITLIN: *(Suddenly "gets it")* Not a way! You feel like you could have fun in a plantation like that. It says, "Come play in me." Giant doorways. Distant ceilings. And extraordinary oaks. They make an unreal entrance to those high, high windows. Strange houses. People are too little for them. The river keeps devouring their front yards. And lightning strikes trees in warm climates. Funny, how I thought it'd be marvelous to live in a planta-tion. *(Laughs)* I'm from the superwoman generation. We were told we could have it all. A terrific husband you never saw. Great kids someone else raised. A perfect body you could push forever. They were hiring women every-where. A temporary boom in the marketplace. And every man was a self-professed liberal. You have to do a reality check when you release a gorgeous, rich husband. But sometimes solitude is a way of finding God that still exists, but that is so far away. Isn't that right, Baudelaire?

SOUND: *The countdown to midnight begins. Ten, nine, eight, seven, six, five, four, three, two, one. Happy New Year. Auld Lang Syne plays...*

(BEAU crosses over and kisses KAITLIN.)

KAITLIN: Wouldn't it be wonderful if you could be true?

CURTAIN

NEW ORLEANS COMEDIES

Turtle Soup
A ONE ACT

CAST OF CHARACTERS

UNCLE GENE SONIAT, age 69
LUCILLE, his niece, 29

(Noon, the present time, April 1st, in New Orleans. A stark light glares into the master bedroom of a mansion. A clever man, UNCLE GENE SONIAT, 69. lies on his sickbed. Deaf, HE stares blankly ahead, and breathes through a partially opened mouth. When HE speaks, HE shouts. His pregnant niece, LUCILLE, 29, enters with a tray of soup and calls out nervously over his rough breathing.)

LUCILLE: Uncle Uncle? I'm coming in? I brought you turtle soup from the Country Club. It's marvelous to think someplace still makes great soup. Turtle soup was a specialty of the late-nineteenth-century café society. It contains a strained broth and turtle flesh. Are you breathing? Don't die while I'm here! *(Calls out)* Nurse! Nurse! Where did the nurse go? *(Puts the soup on a table with legal documents; picks up one; talks to herself)* What's this? A new will?

UNCLE: It's hot!

LUCILLE: Oh, Uncle! You scared me! *(Slips the paper back)* No, fever. But you're sweating. I'll fold back these sheets. It's ninety degrees outside. The humidity creeps in.

UNCLE GENE: Have you seen the helicopter?

LUCILLE: You've been dreaming, Uncle. Eat something.

UNCLE GENE : Helicopter's landing.

LUCILLE: Some turtle soup.

UNCLE GENE: What?

LUCILLE: *(Hollers)* From the Country Club!

UNCLE GENE: You didn't charge that to me?

LUCILLE: They don't... take cash. This delicate soup with flesh will restore your strength. No other soup is finished with sherry.

UNCLE GENE: Huh?

LUCILLE: If you dined in Victorian society, you'd likely start with turtle soup. It's event eating like going to a three-star restaurant in Paris. I got the Club recipe from Cook. Take the flesh of one shelled, skinned, and cleaned turtle. About two pounds of flesh. In a soup kettle, cover with four— *(UNCLE GENE spits it out)* Oh. Don't spill it. Good Lord. Nurse!

UNCLE GENE: *(Shouts)* Did you put my car up?

LUCILLE: I didn't drive it.

UNCLE GENE: Where're my keys?

LUCILLE: Where I left them yesterday.

UNCLE GENE: Who's got my keys?

LUCILLE: They're the most famous keys lost in New Orleans. Twenty people looked before finding them. I bet they're where I left them—

UNCLE GENE: What's that?

LUCILLE: We'll try some later. *(Swallows hard, wipes her brow)* Uncle… Uncle Gene, I need you to… improve… so you can help with the baby.

UNCLE GENE: Huh?

LUCILLE: The pregnancy's fine. I've the doctor's advice in this book. *(Holds up a book)* We're naming the baby after you. But I don't know where to put the nursery? I thought we might use that sewing room for—

UNCLE GENE: What's that?

LUCILLE: *(Screams)* The baby!

UNCLE GENE: I don't want a baby. Don't bring it here. Southerners worry me. We're dealing with a smaller and smaller gene pool. Hah! So much soup, and none for me. *(Pointing)*

LUCILLE: Sure. You don't want more fresh soup? By the twentieth century, most turtle soup is canned. It stopped being a big American soup 'cause the soup's popularity endangered turtles. But a private organization like the Country Club could—

UNCLE GENE: Huh?

LUCILLE: *(Shouts)* Make turtle soup!

UNCLE GENE: Since I knew your dead mother and father, I take the liberty of telling you, you've soup on your teeth. Hah!

LUCILLE: Well? I'll… just wipe my… mouth… Uncle? My husband… asked me to speak to you. I need your help… with finances. Can I talk to you… Would you explain these… You've never told me about your investments, securities?

(SHE takes out some papers. UNCLE GENE hits his hand against the bed. HE makes an awful grunting sound.)

UNCLE GENE: Arf. Arf. I can't hear a word you're saying!

LUCILLE: Money's due on these—insurance policies.

UNCLE GENE: What's that?

LUCILLE: *(Shouts)* Premiums. Am I authorized… to pay them?… I don't have power of attorney.

UNCLE GENE: Debutantes. You don't go to the bank. The money's supposed to appear in your purse.

LUCILLE: I'm trying to… to manage the household and medical expenses. Upkeep is costly. The chairs need reupholstering. The doorknobs should be replated, and the ceiling medallions—The entire house needs painting…

UNCLE GENE: I just gave… the Dominicans… ten stained-glass windows… in honor of… my mother and father… and the deceased… Soniat-Nix family… members. Arf! Arf!

LUCILLE: Are you choking? Nurse! Shouldn't someone be here? Where's Father Boileau? Doctor Jayne? Uncle… I hate to bother you with my troubles, but I lost that teaching post. I pray to God the delivery's easy because I've no medical insurance. We have my husband's unemployment, thank God, though it's running out. He auditions—but in a freelance business, the question is, "Who wants to work with you?" An actor—

UNCLE GENE: Huh?

LUCILLE: *(Shouts)* An actor!

UNCLE GENE: All that effort for temporary work. Hah! What's he done? A couple of movies people are afraid to see.… They place his films in the rear of the store! That ought to tell you something.… You'll be lucky if you don't get a disease. What will it take to bail you out?

LUCILLE: Your attorney says you've… added a codicil… to your will.

UNCLE GENE: I can't hear what you're saying.

LUCILLE: Oh, your hearing aid is in the wrong ear. It's the left ear, not the right. Why did you do that? *(Fixes the hearing aid)* Can you hear me now? You hear?

UNCLE GENE: Don't shout.

LUCILLE: Your lawyer is concerned…

UNCLE GENE: My lawyer.

LUCILLE: She says you've… left all your money to the Dominicans.

UNCLE GENE: You came here to weasel your way—

LUCILLE: Did you give my inheritance—

UNCLE GENE: To bother me… with your selfishness?

LUCILLE: I want to know if you've cut me out… before I see you… in your casket!

UNCLE GENE: I can leave my money to whomever I want.

ROSARY HARTEL O'NEILL

LUCILLE: It's not that I want the… the money. It just makes me feel…If I didn't know better, I'd think I was a stranger… and that my life had been a dream. I would care for you… even if you lost everything. But you do nothing for me.

UNCLE GENE: Don't get worked up!

LUCILLE: I think of you as my father and since I've moved up here, I've admired you.

UNCLE GENE: I took you off the street. Isn't that enough?

LUCILLE: Yes, but living here you made me feel I was your daughter.

UNCLE GENE: I never adopted you.

LUCILLE: I'm your only living relative.

UNCLE GENE: I raised you and gave you a house.

LUCILLE: Which is falling apart. My father was your only brother!

UNCLE GENE: Come on. My estate's not worth much… after taxes… hospital charges… about…

LUCILLE: Nine million.

UNCLE GENE: I'm a millionaire. What do you know?

LUCILLE: Don't mock me.

UNCLE GENE: Has your no-count husband been tracking my assets?

LUCILLE: He talked to an estate specialist.

UNCLE GENE: Did he? Why don't you give me the name, so I can find out how wealthy I am.

LUCILLE: We promised not to…but it's the most reputable firm.

UNCLE GENE: What's its name? Hah!

LUCILLE: They estimated the value of this house, your country home, your French Quarter apartment, your commercial properties: Pizza Hut, the phone company, the post office, that Canal Street parking lot—conservatively at ten million.

UNCLE GENE: How did they inflate their figures? Here's how I see it. Your actor husband walks into this big house on Exposition Boulevard and finds a sick old man and a plain young girl. This actor's well has run dry, and his future is behind him. *(Clutches his chest)* Bad indigestion. So the actor takes a look at the ugly girl and considers marriage. "What's wrong with her?" he thinks. She ought to be fun. Did she stop ovulating? Change zip codes? At first, the thought of marriage hits hard. He doesn't want a "bouder" wife. A pretty, pouting wife, but he thinks he does. He's not broke, you see. He's having a hard time meeting the standards he's developed. And he likes that house. He thinks, "Why not marry this girl and take the old man's money? The fellow can't last that long."

LUCILLE: Liar!

UNCLE GENE: I'm cutting you out of my will. I don't owe you a damn thing. And I hate this darn soup! *(Dumps the bowl of soup upside down)* Get out, and get my nurse. I would hate to meet my maker after treating me so unfairly.

LUCILLE: May you burn in hell.

UNCLE GENE: *(Points to heaven)* I'm going up. The Dominicans are getting me in. And when I go there I'll be right next to St. Peter. There are no places in heaven. Now I may have to fry longer in purgatory. But when I arrive, I'll have Christ on my left and Saint Peter on my right. *(Clutches his chest)* My chest! I can't breathe. Call Doctor Jayne... Father Boileau. I need to say my Act of Contrition. Get a priest... you idiot! *(Coughs and laughs uncontrollably)* I didn't change the will. April Fool!

CURTAIN

AUTHOR'S NOTE

Turtle soup is a late-nineteenth-century soup. It contains a broth base that is strained. Take the flesh of one shelled, skinned, and cleaned turtle (about two pounds of flesh). In a soup kettle, cover with four quarts of water, add two medium carrots, peeled and quartered, two stalks of celery with tops quartered, one medium-sized peeled yellow onion, quartered, about six grinds of white pepper (no salt yet), and one-eighth teaspoon of ground allspice, one small Greek or Turkish bay leaf, one-half bunch washed but whole curly parsley, two tablespoons fresh lemon juice. Bring to a boil and immediately lower to a simmer, cover, and simmer for one hour. Strain and reserve all liquid, discard all of the vegetables and the bay leaf, cut the turtle into bite-sized pieces and return to the reserved broth. You may refrigerate for up to 24 hours. To finish the soup for serving, return to clean soup kettle, and add one scant teaspoon salt and one-half cup Amontillado sherry (Dry Sack). Bring to a simmer uncovered for ten minutes. Serve in soup plates, each garnished with about a teaspoon of minced fresh curly parsley or diced fresh tomato flesh.

Turtle soup equals a clear delicate broth, not just water, delicately spiced, with the particular accent of flavorful dry sherry. Turtle soup always has sherry, and no other soups classically have sherry. A clear delicate broth, lightly spiced, finished with sherry. If you went out to dinner in a fine home in the nineteenth century, your dinner would likely be turtle soup. This was a soup for the cafe society, people who had money. It was event eating, like going to a three-star restaurant in Paris. You dressed for this soup. The assumption was a delicate soup with flesh in it and well-flavored was restorative of strength. By the time you got to the 20th century, the turtle soup was canned. The quality deteriorated. It stopped being a big American soup when turtles became endangered because the soup was so popular. The canning of turtle soup became outlawed, but a private organization like the Country Club could do it. Getting the flesh out of the turtle was labor intensive, which was probably why it was an upper-class food.

The kind of menus that came out of those Victorian societies were labor-intensive meals. A gallon of turtle soup would cost $80.

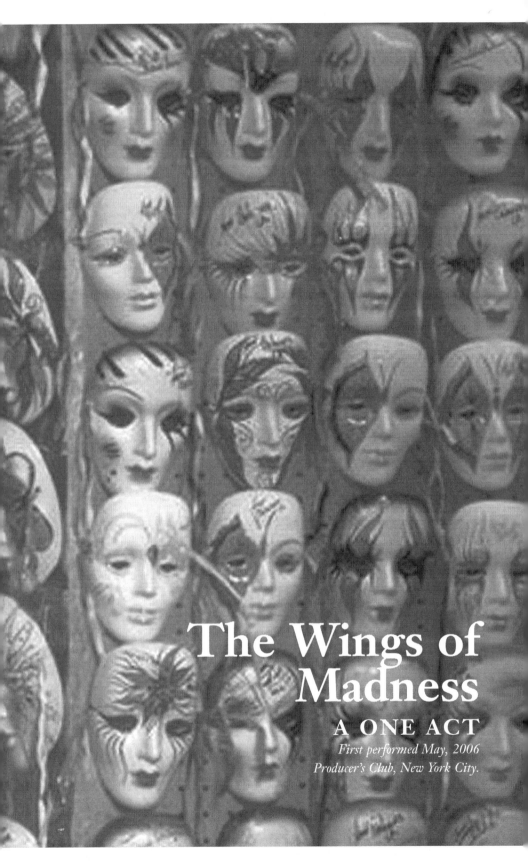

The Wings of Madness

A ONE ACT

First performed May, 2006
Producer's Club, New York City.

Claudia, a beautiful woman of uncertain age, pale-faced
with long blonde hair. Her voluptuous figure is sheathed in
moonbeam silk.

SETTING

The interior of a Spanish-type mortuary on Veterans
Highway outside New Orleans, the type with fake brick,
too much wrought iron, and lanterns with amber glass or
possibly glass in several colors. Tackiness is felt in the
details: an overdone sign-in table, metal folding chairs, a
pressed wood end table with Kleenex and plastic roses, and
a coffin. (The coffin may be placed in the audience.)

*(A forbidding July night. It is raining; claps of thunder rumble the cheap building.
Outside, the highway is full of sinister noises, gusts of wind, the slush of water, car
brakes, muffled screams. The interior of the room is in complete darkness except for
the vigil lights on the sign-in table. Candles flicker in their ruby glass cups.
CLAUDIA appears, framed in the doorway. A wispy chiffon scarf floats free in the
breeze which blows from behind her. CLAUDIA points to her gown.)*

CLAUDIA: What's this? The latest in shrouds. *(Turns around, shows her
half-covered back and bare feet)* No back. No shoes. I don't worry how I dress
because people don't look at you long inside a casket in New Orleans. This
is the city that care forgot!

LIGHTS: CLAUDIA flicks on a light.

There's a young man laid out in parlor B, who won't say a thing. Those
moody people from the Ninth Ward. I've to accept I've more education
than he has. We're not going to speak. He'll never be from uptown. Why
couldn't I have been buried from Bultman's—the mortuary on the avenue
that's like a plantation? They know how to showcase a body. *(Somberly)*
When I think of it pouring on my tombstone... my little patch of dirt.

SOUND: A truck approaches, then passes.

Trucks racing outside. A Taco Bell next door. I don't know anyone who uses
a mortuary on Veterans Highway. *(Inspecting the parlor)* Tigerlily Kleenex

boxes on every table, a blanket of plastic roses. *(Points to her casket)* And cheap lining, flamingo pink. *(Gingerly picks up the sign-in book)* Well, who do we have here? Death brings all the relatives out. *(Sadly)* Even in the rainy days of July.

SOUND: *Noises, hushed talking, and approaching footsteps.*

My family's at the door. They're sure enough late.

SOUND: *Muffled noises, talking, a harsh male laugh.*

My husband, Elliot. He smiled once or twice, and he was nice once or twice. If he gets any fatter, he'll lose his looks. They call him the walrus 'cause he flops about. Elliot was homeless once, for seven or eight months, but it's okay now, he drives a Mercedes. He's got that jaundiced eye, from listening to the funeral director tally up the expenses. It was an extensive make-over. The man's got money, but he's not used to giving it to a mortician. *(To ELLIOT)* Come here, my hubby. Up close, you can see my eyelid wrinkle. My hair's still growing. Death's so messy. *(To MARGUERITE)* There's my little girl, Marguerite. Behind her daddy. That haircut looks awful. Marguerite. Never show those ears. *(Sadly)* Remember when I plaited your hair in ten thousand itty-itty braids, and I left it like that for the whole summer. Stay back. Better not see me up close. You've got my pictures. All those Christmases and Easters when I looked so pretty. Elliot, take her away.

SOUND: *The startled soft cry of a child, which intensifies as CLAUDIA speaks.*

Stop the sniveling, Marguerite We need gentlemen and ladies, even at the mortuary. Pretend graciousness. You'll always be missing something, Marguerite. A mother who's weak is no role model for a daughter. I'm just a little stone in the river that you pass to move on. Look, I want you to stand over there by the wall. Think pleasant thoughts. I'm experienced in dealing with grief. That's my strongest point. Life's going to sling disappointments at you. So if you start out sad, you're already in trouble. Stay back. We mothers have got to go one by one. Perfectly normal procedure. God can't kill everybody at once. It's too expensive.

SOUND: *Whirl of cars passing. Heavy rain. A little girl shrieks.*

(CLAUDIA raises her hand as if admitting a secret to quiet the child.)

Your father said I fell off the roof of that six floor building. But I didn't. *(Pause)* I was pushed. However, fair's fair. I provoked him first. Never touch a man in anger, sugar. They always hit back. Hard. It's not their fault, really. It's a testosterone thing. Can't have the little woman shoving them around. Carelessness has become so rampant. *(Pause)* I dove like a winged chariot. No back-up. No props. Someone carted my remains over here. The soul is left to linger after a violent death. Spirits don't come and carry you aloft.

SOUND: *Bolt of lightning. Crash of thunder.*

(MARGUERITE howls.)

LIGHTS: *Lights rattle off and on.*

Stop crying, Marguerite! I don't want to live again. Marriage is a curse. It both lifts you up, and gives men a vantage to shoot you down. Once you make marriage everything, you have the smell of desperation.

SOUND: *Mozart's "Requiem" is played.*

(CLAUDIA laughs hoarsely, running her fingers wildly through her hair, enjoying the music and moonlight.)

How lovely. I've such energy under the moon. Daddy told me he was faithful, again and again until I believed him. Before I go to Hell, I've one chance to avenge him. To have someone's name is to have some control over his soul. So, I'll roam around. Then, on an ugly night when Dad's got his hands on some pretty young thing, I'll appear like a phantom wife, clutch his throat with my cold, withered hands and choke out his life. *(With a nervous chuckle)* Rain's stopped. Time to slip inside my mahogany box. Close the lid. Waiting's a tedious job, but I'll be back.

CURTAIN

APPENDICES

THE PLAYS

ROSARY HARTEL O'NEILL

Wishing Aces

A PLAY IN ONE ACT

APPENDIX

Total Characters now 7 women 2 men

**Make new scene (Scene 3) right after BUNKY'S LINE:
BUNKY: Hey Beau, an ace is flipped up.**

SCENE 3

(Silence. Moment of peace)

(NOISE of people approaching.)

FEMALE COP: State police for Bunky Legere.

(CAPTAIN GATEMOUTH enters. SHE is a mottled giant in a ripped T-shirt, shouts)

CAPTAIN: Bunky Leger.

BUNKY: Yes.

CAPTAIN: You others from that train?

ALL: Yes.

CAPTAIN: Got orders to take you to the Mississippi sheriff. Picked up two engineers and a blind sheepdog a ways back.

BUNKY: The dog's mine.

BEAU: You the state police?

CAPTAIN: I'm an Iranian catastrophe specialist--

(TWO INDIANS with rattlesnake boots, bird feathers, and tattoos on their biceps

bound inside.)

CAPTAIN: This here is Cochise--a recovering heroin addict. And Pocahontas. They can find anything or anyone in the swamp.

COCHESE: *(To BEAU)* State police notified your folks--

POCAHONTAS: Your daughter got us--

COCHESE: Don't worry. We'll get y'all out of--. We can bust through anything.

CAPTAIN: *(Gesturing to boat)* More guns on this baby than a battleship.

POCAHONTAS: *(Speaks into a cell phone)* Yeah, we got them.

(INDIANS and COP exit. BEAU takes the phone and braces HIMSELF.)

BEAU: Hello? *(Stammers)* Marcelle! God … where are you? They found us … Thank God. *(Holds phone out)* You did what!!!

MARCELLE: *(Entering talking on the phone)* I charged twenty thousand dollars to Elsa's visa! *(HE looks up and spots his daughter, drops the phone, goes and hugs MARCELLE)*

BEAU: Marcelle! What are you--Thank God you're okay.

MARCELLE: Oh Daddy! I'm so--Yes I'm fine.

(BEAU flashes others a smile.)

BEAU: Everybody this is my daughter? She's . . .she's fifteen.

(ALL hug and scream for joy)

(DOG barks in the distance.)

BUNKY: My dog!

CAPTAIN: *(to BUNKY , MARCELLE and HETTY)* Boat's a ways away. We'll take you three first.

(BUNKY and HETTY start belting and MARCELLE joins in:)

HETTY AND BUNKY: "Louisiana, they're trying to wash us away, wash us away. To wash us away . . . "

(ALL exit except BEAU and KITTEN.)

(BEAU and KITTEN stand in the doorway, their faces luminous.)

BEAU: The Bayou seems a radiant place, glossy leaves, marsh phosphores-
cent. Going to write a novel set here... Wed a damsel in distress.

KITTEN: I've no time for that now.

BEAU: Tut. Tut. I don't date the woman I love I marry them... How about
a ceremony at Saint Alfonsus Church?

KITTEN: That awful area.

BEAU: We could be alone. With only those friends who dared to come..
Let's celebrate what's good at the start. "If Winter comes, can Spring be far
behind."Shelley. Better yet: "And life would be all spring." Emily
Dickinson. There's a quote to begin a life with.

(BEAU cradles KITTEN's face. Impatience creeps into his kiss.)

(SOUND of BUNKY and HETTY singing in the distance, "Louisiana. They're
trying to wash us away. Wash us away." Music gets louder till --BLACK OUT)

THE END

White Suits in Summer

A PLAY IN TWO ACTS

APPENDIX

Replace the opening scene with this text.

Total Cast 2 men 14 women

CAST OF CHARACTERS

BLAISE SALATICH, a handsome, out-of-work actor, 28

LUCILLE, his serious wife, an at critic.38

SUSANNE DUPRÉ, his ex-lover a famous painter, 28

TED CLAPPER, her frustrated manager, 26

NURSE

3 METER MAIDS

FEMALE COP

COOK

6 DOMINCAN/SINGING NUNS

SCENE: A mansion on Exposition Boulevard, New Orleans. We are in a big, finely-proportioned parlor with a high ceiling, Orientals, a crystal chandelier. The atmosphere is that of a grand sanctuary, where the landowner can view Audubon Park as a superior. Floor-to-ceiling windows, sometimes used as entrances, open onto a gallery overlooking a wide lawn, which tumbles onto Audubon Park. During the daytime one has the feeling of a semi-tropical park, and at night of an oak garden, which climbs into the stars.

TIME: The present. Sunshine, already hard on the windows, fills the room with a sharp light.

ACT I

SCENE 1

SETTING: A summer day. Noon. The present. Several suitcases line the stage.

AT RISE: *LUCILLE, 28, runs onstage. SHE's very healthy with a mass of hair and deep-set hazel eyes. There is a curious blend of country carelessness and intelligence. Her husband, BLAISE, enters, buttoning his shirt. He is handsome, about 26, but his carriage makes him appear older. HE is tall, long-limbed with a wide forehead, thick brown hair, and fine sensitive eyes. HE wears conservative dark clothes, obviously expensive, and HE wears them well. Harsh sunlight falls over the gallery as TED CLAPPER, in a rumpled white suit, approaches. HE checks back for fear his car will be towed. An effusive businessman, HE's in his twenties, but his face looks older.*

TED: Anybody home? *(Crosses to BLAISE)* Teddy Clapper.

LUCILLE: Who?

TED: New Orleans Country Club? Southern Yacht Club? Now I'm managing Susanne Dupré.

LUCILLE: Susanne Dupré. *(Screams in delight)* Oh my. Oh God. Oh, no.

TED: *(Searches about)* My glasses broke. I've a second pair.

LUCILLE: I'll fix them. You know my husband. *(To herself)* Oh my God. Susanne Dupré.

BLAISE: Can I help you with something?

TED: Mom and I want you to host an exposition of Susanne Dupré.

LUCILLE: *(to BLAISE)* This is the miracle we've been waiting for.

(Three METER MAIDS walk across the stage talking loudly over their ipods)

TED: *(Looks out)* They're not giving me a ticket? I double-parked by a fire hydrant, then barged into the curb...

BLAISE: You should move your car.

TED: Like I said, we're looking for patrons to do an exposition of...

(Phone rings. TED searches for phone, gives up when ringing stops.)

TED: *(cont.)* Mom might phone. I've rough car trips calling her. She fired the night watchman and bought me a phone. My mother is the sweetest, panicked person on earth. I advanced up to escort when Dad departed this world...

LUCILLE: I saw it in the obituaries.

TED: A show on Exposition Boulevard could be an important event. Susanne's a young legend.

LUCILLE: A practitioner of the—

TED:Nobler forms.

LUCILLE: Her show in Berlin left me—

TED: Ecstatic as did her show at the—

LUCILLE and TED: *(Together)* Guggenheim in New York.

(TED's cell phone rings. HE waves it off.)

TED: We'll ignore that. All Mom's friends are dying, so it's not great for her. Her two best friends died within weeks. What with her heart surgery and the cataracts...

(Phone stops ringing. HE searches for the scrapbook and pictures.)

TED: *(cont.)* Mom made a scrapbook of your wedding. She keeps saying, "Why couldn't you've married Lucille." *(to LUCILLE)* Every boy at Jesuit High School was in love with you.

BLAISE: *(to TED)* Thanks for the gift.

LUCILLE: *(to TED)* Your glasses fixed.

TED: Amazing. *(Phone rings, TED answers it)* Hello there. *(to BLAISE)* If I don't respond instantly, Mom calls the cops. *(talks into the phone)* Yeah, Mom. I gave Lucille the clippings and the...no. *(To himself)* Where are those grapefruit spoons? *(Checks about; to LUCILLE)* Mom had them replated. *(to*

Blaise) My family's in fine jewelry and heirlooms. *(into phone)* I got them. *(hangs up)*

LUCILLE: *(Peeking in the box)* Another priceless treasure from Uncle.

TED: Mom says ya'll have the finest art collection.

BLAISE: He gave it to the museum.

(Phone rings, but TED ignores it, looking for an outlet to recharge it.)

TED: If I'm gone long, she'll find me—hunt me down. My sister came for a month with her kids—wild, exhausting six, seven, and twelve-year-olds. After she left, it required weeks of down time to revive Mother.

LUCILLE: Wouldn't it be wonderful to have kids 'round the house?

TED: Little Lucilles and—

BLAISE: We're not having children yet.

LUCILLE: I didn't mean today.

TED: Where's that outlet?

BLAISE: With Uncle Gene's illness and—

LUCILLE: Blaise's goal is to become a great actor, get fame, start his own production company.

TED: *(Interrupting, to BLAISE)* Say, weren't you and Susanne schoolmates at—?

BLAISE: Berkeley.

TED: Right. I told Susanne a political edge would move her ahead faster. She started her triangle series in Berlin.

(BLAISE guides him to an outlet.)

LUCILLE: Splendid.

TED: I organized this smashing opening at the Mary Boon in New York. She constructed and deconstructed Naughty Marietta and the Casket Girls at the Whitney. *(TED's phone rings)* Mom gets foggy and keeps calling. *(Speaks into the phone)* I'll pick you up for dinner.

(HE hangs up. Phone rings again. TED throws up his hands.)

TED: *(cont.)* Each time, it's an earnest pitch—when can I expect you? Mom's got a housekeeper, a chauffeur, and a cook, but she's essentially alone. Eating out and her poodle, "Bootsy," are all that keep her going. Pardon me. *(Picks up the phone and talks to his Mom)* Yes, I gave them the— no, no. I'll do it. More gifts—certificates for silver frames for your wedding portrait and invitation, and for baby rattles, cups, brushes, diaper pins, cutlery, and dishes. All to be engraved later.

LUCILLE: How extravagant.

TED: We've tons of wedding and baby gifts—never bought or returned— and Mom wants you to have them all—in case something... She should never have had heart surgery of that magnitude. *(Into the phone)* Yes. She's got it. Goodbye, Mom. *(Hangs up the phone)* I handle Mom's expenses, the understatement of the year. Time's coming when I'll have to move in—

BLAISE: *(Checks his watch)* Excuse me.

TED: Wait. About the show—

LUCILLE: 'Course we'll sponsor it. We'll use the side gallery.

TED: Excellent.

LUCILLE: Uncle will contribute. I've got great ambitions for Blaise.

(3 METER MAIDS enter the street yelling and writing up tickets)

TED: Is that a meter maid out there?

METER MAIDS: You get that clunker. Up on the curb ? Fire Hydrant.

(A FEMALE COP joins THEM)

COP: No Parking and Handicapped Zone!

TED: *(Hearing their voices)* What? They-ve got a—Stop!

LUCILLE: Don't leave.

TED: Three shapes of them are ticketing my car. Bat women from hell. *(to LUCILLE)* I'll be right back.

BLAISE: Take your time. I'm going for a smoke. *(Exits)*

(Moments later. LUCILLE, high-strung, turns up a baby-minder, a ritual SHE deals with continually.)

(SOUND: Uncle Gene, moaning in his room. LUCILLE speaks into the machine.)

LUCILLE: Nurse?

(LUCILLE gets up and paces, looks out the window, to where TED has gone then back upstage.)

NURSE: *(entering)* Yes. Miss Lucille

LUCILLE: Can't you ease Uncle's pain?

NURSE: Got a call in to the doctor. I've been having a time—. The man won't—you try getting him to—

LUCILLE: *(Dismissing her)* Tell Cook to serve some condiments.

NURSE: She don't like to leave that kitchen!

LUCILLE: Tell her!

(NURSE exits)

(SUSANNE, 24, enters, quietly with her portfolio and paint box. SHE is dressed casually in seductive clothes. Hollows shadow her cheeks and her slender neck. There is a quality of nervous tension, the mental strain of an artist who puts unrelieved pressure on herself.)

SUSANNE: Hi. I'm Susanne Dupré.

LUCILLE: Oh my. Oh my Lord. You're an absolutely brilliant artist. I'm Lucille, Blaise's wife.

SUSANNE: Hello. Ted sent me in.

LUCILLE: Anyone in love with painting admires your work. *(Looks about)* Where's Ted?

SUSANNE Parking the car. Is this a bad time?

LUCILLE: Sorry—I'm in such a tether.

SUSANNE: I understand. My challenge is to discern reality.

LUCILLE: Ah. To paint things the way they truly are—

SUSANNE: Not through false glasses.

LUCILLE: New Orleans must be quite an interesting study when—

SUSANNE: Viewed as an outsider. *(Stares at her)* You're lovely. *(Overcome with disappointment)* I don't think I can exhibit here. It's too—fussy.

(SUSANNE looks out, her face hot and sweating. Music floats in from the Cathedral. Isaiah 6: "Here I am, Lord. Is it I, Lord? I have heard you calling in the night. I will go, Lord, if you lead me. I will hold your people in my heart.")

LUCILLE: Choir practice from Holy Name Church. I can hear them even better from my classroom at Tulane.

SUSANNE: *(avoiding LUCILLE'S face)* You teach?

LUCILLE: Art history. At Tulane.

SUSANNE: What a view. The sun sifting through Spanish moss. And the park dancing all around. I feel like I'm being reborn, nourished by Utopia. People would be calmer if they lived in beauty. Marvelous house.

LUCILLE: It's been in my family for generations.

SUSANNE: And will stay there.

LUCILLE: These houses are great 'cause they keep memory alive.

(Moaning through baby-minder)

My uncle has cancer.

SUSANNE: Sorry.

LUCILLE: I use a baby-minder. It's sad.

SUSANNE: With a certain—

LUCILLE: If you need to buffer entropy, this is a good training ground.

SUSANNE: My presence feels inappropriate.

LUCILLE: I adored your Berlin exhibit. "How the Feminist and the Archetype Intersect."

SUSANNE: What did your husband think?

LUCILLE: Right. You met Blaise.

SUSANNE: Well?

LUCILLE: He framed my article comparing your painting to Beckett's drama. *(Hands SUSANNE the article)*

SUSANNE: "Apocalyptic Isolation." Some title.

LUCILLE: You're a prodigy.

SUSANNE: People get noticed if they do something unusual and live in New York in their twenties.

LUCILLE: You're welcome to stay—

SUSANNE: There is motion here, but again—it's not the house I was hoping for.

LUCILLE: We could paint the walls, redo some lights.

SUSANNE: *(Shaking her head)* No.

LUCILLE: Blaise needs to meet people in the arts.

SUSANNE: It won't work.

LUCILLE: He wants to do leads in film and theater, the whole panoramic portrait.

SUSANNE: Not tiny parts, shards in the mosaic.

LUCILLE: We can create projects for you both from here.

SUSANNE: *(Picks up a large white album)* Your wedding album.

LUCILLE: There's Blaise kissing me at the altar, feeding me cake.

SUSANNE: You're still newlyweds. Love hasn't changed to respect.

(SUSANNE fidgets with a cigarette. TED enters.)

TED: I can't stay. I promised to take Mom to Antoine's.

LUCILLE: Don't worry. Susanne and I can discuss the exposition.

SUSANNE: If we have one.

TED: Don't mind her. *(Whispers to SUSANNE)* You'll do what I say.

SUSANNE: I don't know. *(to herself)* Change carries consequence.

TED: I'm off.

(LUCILLE ushers TED to the door. BLAISE enters from the park, brushes past SUSANNE, walks to get liquor.)

BLAISE: Oh, Susanne.

LUCILLE: Right. You knew each other. Kiss me, dear. *(HE kisses HER)* We're still honeymooning.

BLAISE: Excuse me. *(Leaving)*

LUCILLE: Don't be rude, darling. I need your input on the exposition.

SUSANNE: Maybe you shouldn't have it, just enjoy the park, and—

BLAISE: Can I get you a drink? Every Southern home has a recovery shelf. *(to SUSANNE)* A Bloody Mary?

SUSANNE: Perrier. Might as well drink with class.

LUCILLE: You'll let us host you?

SUSANNE: Not sure. I feel mostly good about what Ted and I are doing— It's simply a desire for a real home—that the other galleries can't fulfill.

BLAISE: Maybe this need is invalid.

SUSANNE: I think not—

(BLAISE wipes his forehead, which has broken out in a sweat. COOK enters with

a tray of condiments. Plots them on a table.)

COOK: This ain't part of my job!

(COOK exits. LUCILLE chuckles in the embarrassed silence and passes condiments.)

LUCILLE: *(to SUSANNE)* Your use of triangles intrigues me. We must include "Shakti's Heart"—your triangle symbolizing the Hindu Goddess.

BLAISE: It's too Gauguin for me. Actually, that piece depresses me the least.

LUCILLE: Blaise!

BLAISE: *(to SUSANNE)* Weren't you supposed to search out dark, lugubrious triangles?

SUSANNE: The easy expositions are over, and the tough ones just begun.

LUCILLE: Showing here will not be as difficult as you think.

(BLAISE starts to exit.)

LUCILLE: *(cont.)* You're not leaving? Relax, dear. This is for you.

BLAISE: I like to pace. If I sit, I might miss something.

LUCILLE: *(Clears her throat)* Tell us about your recent work.

SUSANNE: I've been correcting energy-draining behaviors.

LUCILLE: That affects your painting.

SUSANNE: And life. Confusion won't divert me from seeing reality.

LUCILLE: Your paintings are sharper.

SUSANNE: Painting is about paying attention in a Buddhist way.

BLAISE: That's hard to do.

SUSANNE: I slip into the skin of people I see—even if it hurts.

LUCILLE: You paint "fruitful blank spaces" which life fills in.

SUSANNE: When I smile...I'm thinking of something enticing.

LUCILLE: You're smiling now? Isn't she, honey?

SUSANNE: You can use art to heal, to face a part of yourself you hate.

LUCILLE: Go on!

SUSANNE: In my last triangle series, I saw myself in the colors and mended my ways.

LUCILLE: *(to SUSANNE)* How do you know when a painting is finished?

SUSANNE: *(to BLAISE)* When you love it.
(A moan through the baby-minder. A bell rings. LUCILLE rises to leave.)

LUCILLE: Uncle calls every five minutes.

BLAISE: Nurse is there.

LUCILLE: Yes, but he waits for me. *(to BLAISE)* Darling, get Susanne's press agent, mailing lists. Talk strategy.

SUSANNE: I don't know.

LUCILLE: We'll give you two an outrageous reception: jazz band, oysters etoufees, mint juleps.

SUSANNE: But does the world need another show?

LUCILLE: 'Course. Artists make dreams. *(to BLAISE)* Kiss, kiss, love bug.

(LUCILLE adjusts the baby-minder and flutters off. BLAISE gives SUSANNE a hard look.)

SUSANNE: Love bug.

BLAISE: When did you move to New Orleans?

SUSANNE: Before your wedding.

BLAISE: You came to our wedding?

SUSANNE: *(Removes newspaper notice)* I sat in back of the church. Didn't make the reception.

(Doorbell rings.)

NURSE: *(OFFSTAGE)* The prescription. I've got it, Miss Lucille.

(BLAISE turns down the baby-minder.)
SUSANNE: Lucille is, like a mother... You think about California?

BLAISE: I recall lots of dead things. *(starts to leave)*

SUSANNE: After your wedding, I slept all day. I felt like a part of me was melting—

BLAISE: Now you've seen me and I've seen you.

SUSANNE: Why did you move here? For the?

BLAISE: Restaurants—You can be a starving artist in your teens, but in your twenties you like to dine out occasionally.

SUSANNE: When I started painting, I didn't worry about sales.

BLAISE: As long as you work for your soul, it's great.

SUSANNE: Sometimes I can't—sleep.

BLAISE: You need to—

SUSANNE: I'm not taking pills or fooling around.

(LUCILLE enters with mail to get a bottle of gin.)

LUCILLE: The mail came.

BLAISE: My headshots!

LUCILLE: Why send them? Soon, we'll produce you here. Money's the crucial factor.

SUSANNE: And talent.

LUCILLE: Persistence. I won't let Blaise fail. *(Pause)* Uncle wants a Ramos Gin Fizz made of orange flower, water, and gin.

BLAISE: I'll get it.

LUCILLE: *(Checks the baby-minder)* You plan which paintings to hang.

(Moaning through the baby-minder; SHE starts to go)

Everything's an argument with Uncle. Is there any nutritional value in gin?

SUSANNE: *(to BLAISE)* Joy and celebration.

LUCILLE: Mm. I can hardly get one job done when something hits me. *(Kisses HIM boldly)*

BLAISE: I should help you.

LUCILLE: Give me a kiss, pumpkin. A bear kiss. *(Pause—exits)*

(A breeze rises. BLAISE gazes at SUSANNE so the light from the great porch lanterns catches her face with streaks of brightness. Distant thunder. The gallery is blanketed with a golden coppery light. A hymn floats from the Cathedral: <u>On Eagle's Wings</u>. "And he will raise you up on eagle's wings. And hold you in the palm of his hand.")

SUSANNE: *(Sings)* "And he will raise you up. And he will raise you up. And he will raise you up...on the last day." I love rain on an unexpected day. Every pore opens to the wind.

BLAISE: Nice.

SUSANNE: That's what I remember about New Orleans. The music—and the rain.

BLAISE: I don't have time for this.

(Thunder.)

SUSANNE: There's a sense of romance about the rain. The sun is around us, but the rain is within us. *(Removes her sketchbook, draws)* When I got here, the rain seized me. Mind if I draw you?

(SHE moves closer, drawing him. Footsteps inside. BLAISE calls out.)

BLAISE: Who's there?

SUSANNE: I'm putting you in a triangle—

BLAISE: Lucille? *(Picks up a book)*

SUSANNE: Using weightlessness to let your image soar.

BLAISE: Five minutes is all.

SUSANNE: You've a wonderful body.

(With a flickering smile, BLAISE clutches his book like a Bible.)

BLAISE: I read one self-help book a week—

SUSANNE: Dressed or undressed—

BLAISE: *The Greatest Salesman Alive*, takes a year to finish 'cause it's—

SUSANNE: Self-hypnosis.

BLAISE: You read one chapter three times a day for a month.

SUSANNE: What contacts do you have here?

BLAISE: None. I'm competitive with people.

SUSANNE: Hold that pose.

BLAISE: I forget how I'm supposed to behave.

(BLAISE gives SUSANNE a hard, silencing look.)

SUSANNE: When I saw you in "Hamlet", you defined the word, star.

(SHE takes out his picture as Hamlet. LUCILLE hurries onstage.)

LUCILLE: We've lovely watercress sandwiches and crab soup. Give me a kiss. *(LUCILLE kisses HIM)* Oh Lord. She's painting here.

BLAISE: Stay and watch.

LUCILLE: Ooh. Uncle won't eat 'less I join him.

BLAISE: *(to LUCILLE)* I'm tired. Let's go nap.

SUSANNE: I should let you two alone.

LUCILLE: Don't be silly. Uncle cries out for attention. His paper is damp. His milk is warm. There's dust on the floor. The new maid is lazy. She barely came in the month we were gone. Then I've got to prepare the shopping list.

BLAISE: Let me help you.

LUCILLE: No. Sit for Susanne. You know how Uncle treats the nurse when I'm not there.

(LUCILLE buzzes off. BLAISE follows uneasily, stands in the doorway as the night turns black. SUSANNE toys with a palette knife. Seeing it, BLAISE trembles. SUSANNE speaks maliciously.)

SUSANNE: You've broken out in a sweat.

BLAISE: New Orleans is melting me.

SUSANNE: How long have you been unemployed? Eight months?

BLAISE: Warm.

SUSANNE: Nine?

BLAISE: Warmer.

SUSANNE: A year? Two?

BLAISE: "Regret not the glitter of any lost day." Tennessee Williams.

SUSANNE: What happened in Hollywood?

BLAISE: Nothing.

SUSANNE: You told Lucille you'd talk—

BLAISE: I thought I'd make a bundle.

SUSANNE: Doing what?

BLAISE: Selling chunks of my soul at varying intervals.

SUSANNE: Did you?

BLAISE: I auditioned weekly for months.

SUSANNE: That's a lot of no's.

BLAISE: I was holding on for the word, yes—

SUSANNE: *(Slyly)* To lose yourself in the play?

BLAISE: Right.

SUSANNE: You went to interviews with producers?

BLAISE: Yes.

SUSANNE: Casting directors?

BLAISE: So.

SUSANNE: Ah, Blaise Salatich. You've played all these parts blah-blah-blah.

BLAISE: Exactly.

SUSANNE: Finally, a director of a major picture hires you and he gets fired!

BLAISE: Who told you that?

SUSANNE: Did you go back to the old ways?

BLAISE: No.

SUSANNE: Numbing yourself with—?

BLAISE: No. I wanted to, by God.

SUSANNE: But you didn't.

BLAISE: I kept busy, worked out. Ran.

(HE feels for a cigarette. SHE takes it out for him.)

SUSANNE: You didn't slip once after so many months?

BLAISE: Never.

SUSANNE: So you auditioned for special parts.

BLAISE: Right.

SUSANNE: You were a hand model? A parts model? What?

BLAISE: Soft porn is what they call it. So.

SUSANNE: What happened on your last audition?

BLAISE: Producer arrives in this enormous barrel-like hat.

SUSANNE: He asked you to his hotel room.

BLAISE: Devouring pistachio nuts, telling me his tale of woe.
(SHE hands HIM a drink.)

BLAISE: *(cont.)* Asks me to sit on the bed and unbutton my shirt... This can't be happening, I thought. I was anxious, but it was a lead. "I'd like to cast you," he said. So, I took off my shirt. He stared till my ears got hot. This can't be happening, I thought. He made me lie on the bed. Then he undid my belt and unzipped my pants. This can't be happening. I backed off. There was this screaming, this hotness. He came at me with a knife. Blood everywhere, drenching his shirt, pants, the floor. Looked like he was coming at himself with the knife.

SUSANNE: He died.

BLAISE: I'm trashed in California.

(SUSANNE adds ice to his drink. The song, <u>Here I am, Lord</u> is heard from the church.)

LUCILLE: *(Entering)* Uncle wants ice chips for his drink. Your sketch is rapturous. *(Looking at SUSANNE's drawing)*

BLAISE: *(to LUCILLE)* Stay, sweetheart.

LUCILLE: Did Susanne agree to—

SUSANNE: I do!

LUCILLE: Glorious.

(LUCILLE exits.)

SUSANNE: You have an agent here?

BLAISE: She calls herself one. The only help I ever got was from other artists. They taught me how to face guerilla warfare, to be outspoken, aggressive.

SUSANNE: You can't be an artist unless you plunge ahead. Courage brings peace. Dream big. Fight back. Nirvana awaits. When you march forward, you stand up for the weak, the old, the silenced poets of the world.
(A car horn toots. SUSANNE starts, and crosses to BLAISE.)

SUSANNE: *(cont.)* I have to go. Ted gets impatient.

BLAISE: I've missed you.

(BLAISE smiles sadly. The car toots again. SUSANNE hurries out. LUCILLE enters with an envelope.)

LUCILLE: Good news. Uncle's financing the exposition.

BLAISE: *(Sarcastically)* Victory is ours.

LUCILLE: Ours? Did you drink all this gin?

BLAISE: It's a negotiable indulgence. *(Hands her an envelope)*

LUCILLE: Oh dear.

BLAISE: Why does Uncle send you business letters? You talk all day.

LUCILLE: He's a Soniat. Soon as they have an opinion, it becomes a legal document.

BLAISE: Throw it away.

LUCILLE: Wait, it's a lien on this house. He didn't mention—

BLAISE: He was annoyed, you said—

LUCILLE: With your career and our stay abroad.

BLAISE: But he gave us the house.

LUCILLE: Before he did—he took out a mortgage—

BLAISE: "You don't have to be rich," he said, "when your relatives are rich."

LUCILLE: To pay some of his insurance.

(Doorbell rings.)

(Six DOMINICAN NUNS arrive in full habits. NURSE lets them in.)

NUNS: Good evening. Is our patient's sleeping?

NURSE: Finally. I've never seen so many habits!

NUNS: The good priests sponsored this call—

LUCILLE: *(to BLAISE)* Dominicans slinking about...badmouthing you to Uncle.

COOK: *(Poking in)* I ain't cooking for more people!

(LUCILLE goes to the NUNS.)

LUCILLE: You'll have to come back—

NUNS: We're here to sing for your Uncle and leave our music!

(The NUNS hand NURSE an envelope and burst into a jazzy rendition of "Amazing Grace." BLAISE tries to usher them out)

BLAISE: Good night—

LUCILLE: Thank you~

NUNS: And we brought pictures of the our new music hall that your Uncle wants to sponsor—

COOK: *(Poking in)* I'll bring him supper and—

NUNS: Put our folder by his food tray. With our blessing.

(BLAISE seizes the envelope, opens it, and reads)

BLAISE: *(Reads)* "Addendum to the will and testament of Gene Soniat. I hereby leave the Dominican order—"

LUCILLE: Y'all are writing Uncle's will?

NUNS: We put in a sentence for what he wants to give to the convent. And a rosary blessed by the Vatican and a large print Bible—*(to LUCILLE)* Of course you are the major heir although he is upset about your husband. *(Pointedly)* He keeps asking for you, Blaise.—It would be wise to visit with him.

BLAISE: *(Starting to leave)* I'm not going to be two-faced—

NUNS: *(to LUCILLE)* We brought Gregorian chants for when he—

BLAISE: Get out! Just get the—

NUNS: He says you married Lucille for his money, that acting is for—

BLAISE: For parasites?

NUNS: —if you can't get your own sponsors, you should quit.

BLAISE: Everyone wants to be a performer or—. Then we have religious institutions grabbing the money. Crappy singers working for free and alienating a dwindling public.

LUCILLE: Don't lose patience. . . .

NUNS: The lord is bountiful. Help your uncle to understand you. Visit him. Say you're interested in sales.

BLAISE: I'm not getting in that pot. The last man who got in there got eaten.

(Laughs, but LUCILLE doesn't join in.)

NUNS: *(Looking at LUCILLE)* We promised your wife we'd get you to chat with him.

BLAISE: Honey... have you been talking to these... these—sisterss!

LUCILLE: You know Uncle's... sick. That's why he's irritable, and can't be with anyone more than five minutes. I love him. I remember how he was when I was a little girl. I can't think of life without— He's not himself—

NUNS: Now he's dying.

BLAISE: Are we sure? God!

NUNS: We moved him to our final rites list.

LUCILLE: Lord, I can't take it.

NUNS: Has he signed a living will? *(To BLAISE)* Poke your head in the door. Go talk to him! Or Lucille may be disowned.

(We hear UNCLE moan through the baby monitor)

NUNS: Let's go to him!

(LUCILLE exits with the NUNS who intone "Amazing Grace" as they bow their heads and head toward UNCLE'S room)

(BLAISE gazes after THEM, breathes deeply. We hear wind from a summer rainstorm, sweeping over the park. HE picks up the book, and exits. Lights fade.)

A Louisiana Gentleman

A PLAY IN TWO ACTS

APPENDIX

Appendix scene for A LOUISIANA GENTLEMAN with a cast of 11 women and 1 man.

Replace Act One / Scene 4 with scene below that includes a cast of 8 girl MARDI GRAS REVELERS

ACT ONE
SCENE 4

(Two months later. Early March, Mardi Gras time. The living room is strewn with DALE'S objects and Mardi Gras decorations and costumes. SARA enters in a long coat and is talking into a cellular phone. SHE walks before the set as if down a street.)

SARA: Blaise. Are you there? Pick up … No, I don't want to leave a message so you can wave my laundry over the Quarter. I'll call back. *(Hangs up and dials again)* This is your aunt. Remember? The one who is financing your education. I don't like the role, but I've got to play it. Pick up. *(Slams the phone and dials again)* Blaise, I know you're there. Medical school's over, and it's five-thirty. I got your exam grades. Need I say, I'm horrified. I don't want to be hectored by F reports showing up in my mailbox. When I said medicine was a social art, I didn't mean it was a party. You have my brother's reputation to consider. *(Coughs)* I know the roots of stupidity are complex, but I want you to get your brains and life out of hock. Learning is a slow system of osmosis. Eavesdrop on the smart fellows. Write a longer paper. And please do brown-nose your teachers after class. *(Coughs)* Remember the golden rule. She who has the gold rules. I'm not financing a failure.

(Blackout. Toward the end of SARA'S speech, DALE enters in a sorcerer's costume with her astrology chart. SHE is followed by eight girl REVELERS, in grotesque carnival costumes.)

305

NEW ORLEANS COMEDIES

(The REVELERS dance with home made instruments and whistle, playing drums, hitting spoons, singing)

REVELERS: "All because it's carnival time, it's carnival ti-me, it's carnival ti-me, everybody's drinking wine . . .". . . .Oh, oh you know what it's about time to do. We're going to--Everybody put your hands together. We're going to take you to a Mardi Gras parade.

(Girls clap hands and whistle, Sing and dance)

Yes, I'm going to New Orleans. I want to see that Mardi Gras.
See the Mardi, Mardi Gras. See the Mardi Gras.
Yes, I'm going to New Orleans. I want to see that Mardi Gras.
See the Mardi, Mardi Gras. See the Mardi Gras.

When I get down dere, I'm going to see the Dirty Dozen Band.
See the Mardi, Mardi Gras. See the Mardi Gras.

I'm going to stay right dere, down on Rampart and Dumaine.
See the Mardi, Mardi Gras. See the Mardi Gras.
I'm going to stay right dere down on Rampart and Dumaine.
See the Mardi, Mardi Gras. See the Mardi Gras.
I'm going to stay right there untill I see that whole parade.
See the Mardi, Mardi Gras. See the Mardi Gras.

I got my tickets in my hand, I'm going to go to New Orleans.
See the Mardi, Mardi Gras. See the Mardi Gras.
I got my tickets in my hand, I'm going to go to New Orleans.
See the Mardi, Mardi Gras. See the Mardi Gras.

When I get down dere (hoot),
I'm going to show you what it's all about.

(Music and cavorting perhaps a CD blaring with trumpets as REVELERS and DALE dance.)

Yes I'm going to New Orleans, I want to see that Mardi Gras.
See the Mardi, Mardi Gras. See the Mardi Gras.
Yes, I'm going to New Orleans, I want to see that Mardi Gras.
See the Mardi, Mardi Gras. See the Mardi Gras.

When I get down dere, I want to see the Dirty Dozen Band.

I got my tickets in my ha-nd, I want to go to New Orleans.
I got my tickets in my ha-nd, I want to go to New Orleans.

I'm going to stay right dere, till I show you what it's all about.

We're going to jump and shout. We going to turn this club about.
We're going to jump and shout. We going to turn this club about.
We going to turn this club about.

(Music: trumpets, brass. REVELERS do a second line dance back and forth to the balcony)

(GILLIAN enters, goes to a corner to rehearse her nurse's role in the television series. BLAISE follows, going to another part of the room, studying.)

GILLIAN: Who are those people?

DALE: Friends. They are using our balcony to watch the--

GILLIAN: How long will they stay—

DALE: Till the parade passes! *(To GILLIAN)* You're so . . .so rude!

(DALE motions the REVELERS over by BLAISE and lifts her chart)

Blaise has the most wonderful astrology chart.

REVELER # 1: There's so much creative giftedness around him--

REVELER #2: *(Continuing thought)*--I've been inhaling.

GILLIAN: *(Calls out)* Ssh. I'm working on my lines.

DALE: Still?

REVELER # 3: You have to make art --

REVELER # 4: --as if you had eternity.

GILLIAN: *(Studies her script)* "The doctor will be making rounds in a half an hour if you'd like to freshen up."

BLAISE: *(Puts headsets to his ears and opens a book)* I'm going under. Do you know the Australian box jellyfish is the most poisonous one alive? Toxins, that's the theme of the night.

DALE: *(To REVELERS)* Look. I did a watercolor of Blaise's sun sign.

REVELER #5: Maybe finished, maybe not.

REVELER # 7: Blaise's an old soul.

REVELER # 8: He's had twenty-five hundred lives.

GILLIAN: Get that out of his face. Go outside.

BLAISE: *(Rises)* Come on, girls! *(To REVELERS)* Y'all will have to leave right after the parade.

(BLAISE shows the REVELERS to the balcony. Noises from street. DALE waves the chart in GILLIAN'S face.)

DALE: Mama studied at the School des Beaux Arts, and lived on Beethoven Street—in Paris.

GILLIAN: *(Ignoring HER)* "What are these pills doing on the table. You were supposed to take them—"

DALE: Across from the Eiffel Tower. Her apartment once belonged to a Cavalier poet from the seventeenth century.

DALE: "Gather rosebuds while you may and while you're young go marry, for having once lost your prime, you may forever tarry."

GILLIAN: *(Reciting her lines)* Where was I? Oh yes. "You were supposed to take them with your milk—"

DALE: *(To GILLIAN)* Do you want me to do your chart?

REVELERS: *(From balcony)* Throw me something mister!

GILLIAN: Quiet!! I need to concentrate.

REVELERS: *(From balcony)* Hey mister! Mister up here!

GILLIAN: *(Grabs stomach)* Ugh. I've got these awful cramps.

DALE: *(To GILLIAN)* You want a heating pad?

GILLIAN: Get away.

DALE: *(To GILLIAN)* Something to drink? A Coke?—

(BLAISE returns. Tries to distract DALE with his textbook)

BLAISE: Here, sugar. Did you know the cure for a jellyfish is to pour vinegar on the tentacles? Don't pull them off because they release the poison. A brown recluse spider bites you, it can kill you. See the fiddle on its back? A black widow, you spot that, you better squash it.

DALE: Oh. No. Stop. *(Crying)* I'm an Aquarius. We're the sign of the most emotion. I feel for others you see. I believe in non-injury to living things so they can roam free.

REVELERS: *(O.S.)* Hey throw us some beads. Up here!

GILLIAN: *(Puts in ear plugs)* Time for ear plugs. Where was I ? "Supposed to take them with your milk after breakfast—"

(Police whistles. Sirens getting louder)

REVELERS: *(O.S.)* Parades coming! Hoo-ray! Hoo-ray!

DALE: *(To BLAISE)* Take a break.

BLAISE: I've got exams the Monday after Mardi Gras—

DALE: I'll quiz you --. On ways to die from poison.

BLAISE: I've got those big tests coming up!

REVELERS: *(Poking in)* Parade's here y'all!!

DALE: *(To REVELERS)* We're not watching! *(To BLAISE, intimately)* Oh look at your chart? Astrology shows you the potential genius of yourself. I'm Aquarius with a moon in Virgo, and you're Virgo with a moon in Pisces.

GILLIAN: Quiet—

DALE: Your horoscope is . . . a "fortunate" chart.

REVELERS: *(O.S.)* Throw us something!

GILLIAN: *(Memorizing)* "After your breakfast." No. "After your lunch."

DALE: *(To BLAISE)* You'll always be able to get whatever money you need, and you'll be protected from the worst life can throw at you. For you have the sun in Virgo and the moon in Pisces. Johann Wolfgang von Goethe, born in 1749, had the sun in Virgo and Count Tolstoy, born in 1828, had the moon in Pisces. Moon in Pisces means the aim of your life is to be in tune with the infinite.

GILLIAN: She puts me in a state—

DALE: Something of the magician hovers about you.

GILLIAN: With. . .strangers, useless banter.

DALE: (To BLAISE) For you've a guardian angel, at your side. And she will give you the power over the world that the Magic Lamp gave to Aladdin.

(Sirens blare outside as a parade approaches. Throughout the sequence music blasts in from the street)

REVELERS: (O.S.) It's coming! It's coming!

GILLIAN: Shut up! (Rising) Get rid of… those… those freaks! Weirdos! Tramps!

DALE: You ruined my reading. … I have no friends … you--

GILLIAN: Blaise, do something.

BLAISE: It's so exhausting—

DALE: (To GILLIAN) Go to your room.

BLAISE: To have to be an evangelist.

DALE: Witch.

GILLIAN: She's off on a rage again.

DALE: Gillian's so mean.

GILLIAN: You hear her, Blaise?

BLAISE: (Packing his books) I'm looking for quiet.

GILLIAN: When I've suffered the—

BLAISE: The quiet I can't get.

REVELERS: *(O.S. singing)* Hey!! Hey rock and roll!!

GILLIAN: *(Pointing toward REVELERS)* The degradation of strangers . . .a sister-in-law who's a...a--

REVELERS: *(O.S. singing)* Hey!! Hey rock and roll!!

GILLIAN: Oh, my stomach hurts. Your sister's constantly misbehaving a worthless—Restless anxious—being—Oh, my stomach hurts so bad. Ah. Oh.

(REVELERS enter with handkerchiefs and napkins doing a second line.)

ALL REVELERS: We're about to do the indoor second line.

REVELER # 7: *(Explaining to GILLIAN)* The second line is a dance we do in New Orleans--

REVELER # 8: Whenever there is a reason to celebrate.

REVELER #1: We celebrate anything.

GILLIAN: My period's so screwed up.

BLAISE: Lie down.

DALE: She wants attention.

REVELER # 2: You wave that handkerchief in the air--

GILLIAN: Oh. These cramps.

REVELER #3: Put your back deal in motion--

BLAISE: Is that blood?

REVELER # 4: So get on up babe. Get on up.

GILLIAN: God. Help me.

REVELER #5 AND #6: *(Screams)* "Talking about hey now--

BLAISE: Get a towel.

DALE: Where?

BLAISE: Towel!!

REVELERS #2 and #1: *(Chanting)* Talking about *hey now hey now aiko aiko one day.*

BLAISE: There. Call an ambulance.

DALE: Streets are roped off.

REVELERS #3, #4, #5: *(Chanting) Cha qua mo cha qua mo fille anne.*

GILLIAN: I can't stop the bleeding.

REVELERS #6, #7, #8: Feel that music I been told. It's good for your body and good for your soul…

BLAISE: A damn ambulance.

REVELERS : Now everybody say "I done got over. . . I done got over . . .I done got over. . . your love. Everybody sing! Hey. Hey. Hey. Hey Hey Hey. Hey Hey Hey Hey--

(A band blares outside as REVELERS dance. DALE runs toward the balcony)

DALE: Parade's here!

(DALE is on balcony. BLAISE hovers over GILLIAN and REVELERS take over singing as lights fade.)

END OF SCENE 4

END OF ACT ONE

Black Jack

A PLAY IN TWO ACTS

APPENDIX

Appendix replaces end of Act One with following, which adds in 12 VULTURES—Vegas/style singer dancers.

Total Cast 16 women 2 men

This should come right after Kaitlin's speech around page 257 that ends with "No! Ha. Marriage is a complex activity. It both connects you and underscores your solitude."

(SOUND: A steel-drum band plays Yellow Bird with vibrato-heavy, metallic pinging. RORY charges in, flaunting a vulture headdress and Cleopatra robe. She is followed by 12 dancer/singers, the VULTURES. They do a Vegas-style production show. With a theme of "Riding the Nile," it's a medley of everything Egyptian — a "snake dance," a belly dance, a strut with feathered headdresses, to the words of "What Ever Lola Wants, Lola Gets." And ends with all the girls singing Sea Cruise by Frankie Ford: The show has an abundance of laser lighting effects, videos. And ends with much taped applause.)

VULTURES: *Laissez les bon temps rouler!* Let the good times roll.

(VULTURES come down from the stage. RORY takes the microphone.)

RORY: YOUR STEAMBOATIN' VACATION CONTINUES WITH THE MISS CLEO COSTUME CONTEST. *(Pause)* My vultures and I will mingle and check out your attire.

VULTURES: I gave my asp to the captain and my bangle to the bartender. That just goes to show that men are interested in mature love affairs. *(Parading around in their costumes) (Pointing to RORY)* She is Cleopatra. The Egyptian queen. At mating time, vultures perform exciting displays.

RORY: They will shoot upward, and join claws in midair.

IRENE: *(To KAITLIN)* There's always one in every group that's the strangest.

VULTURES: We were born on June 23. It's a mystic day when women went mad in the heat of the night. We're not nice girls. The first thing we read is the lists of the departed. That's where the money is. And you've no client to negotiate with

(BUNKY enters costumed as Hamlet, followed by LUISA, dressed as Ophelia. BUNKY waves a bottle of champagne)

BUNKY: A round of bubbles for anyone? For any two? I'm Hamlet and she's sad Ophelia.

IRENE: You look bad, but she looks worse. *(Assessing BUNKY)* For any beverage, use real crystal, darling, never plastic. You can't buy class, but you can be very visible with your money.

RORY: *(Glancing around)* Beau's lost his wife. Good. *(Spies KAITLIN)* Oh, no. There she is. Come dance, Beau. Be nice to us old empresses.

IRENE: Speak for yourself.

RORY: I've danced seriously without ever taking it seriously. The one thing I have and Kaitlin doesn't is energy.

BEAU: You want to dance, Kaitlin?

KAITLIN: I'm sure someone else will dance with you. *(Plays restlessly with her sweater)* No one expects you to live in a funny sort of limbo.

(SOUND: A tango plays. VULTURES tango about)

BEAU: You know I love to tango.

KAITLIN: Well, don't just slip a look. Buy.

BEAU: *(His face set in headstrong denial)* A tango, Miss DeBango?

ROSARY HARTEL O'NEILL

RORY: In a matter of minutes, I'm important, all of a sudden. To get ahead you've got to be a good dancer. That's all. Everyone says they can, but most women can't.

(RORY dances upstage with BEAU. VULTURES line dance.)

KAITLIN: An old-fashioned holiday on the river.

IRENE: *(Glancing at KAITLIN)* You work so hard to go to these reunions to hide your marriage from looking like itself. Luisa!
Come dance.

LUISA: *(Joining her)* Two women?

IRENE: If I wait for the right man, I may never dance. Who made up those rules anyway? Nobody I know.

LUISA: There are plenty of nice men.

IRENE: Where? *(Looks around)* I don't want to share my room. So a man can say when to turn the lights out. I look in my bed and say get out.

BUNKY: The champagne's so thick, it's cresting over. It's the privilege of champagne to make you happy, sleepy, and dreamy.

LUISA: I wish I could put words together like you, Bunky.

IRENE: One reason celebrities talk so well is they've learned to talk money out of people. It's something in these investors. Big dog personalities in brains the size of gnats. *(Crosses to the railing, catching her breath)*

BUNKY: My songs haven't got real value, until I die.

LUISA: I like money, I just don't want to devote my life to it.

IRENE: Well, don't go into medicine.

(A distant band plays Sailing by Christopher Cross: We hear the words: "It's not far down to paradise / At least it's not for me / And if the wind is right you can sail away / And find tranquility." Ahhhhh.")

NEW ORLEANS COMEDIES

IRENE: *(Watches BUNKY relishing the champagne)* Bunky didn't taste champagne until he was seventeen. After that he became a lush.

LUISA: She's a fast talker.

BUNKY: You speak the language, but you don't understand the rapid fire?

IRENE: Bunky acts like his dad. He was a gangster.

BUNKY: Gambler.

IRENE: In the horse business in Virginia. Breakfast at noon, dinner at ten.

BUNKY: He accommodated my grandmother by dying right on schedule.

IRENE: I went to the funeral to make sure he was dead. Bunky had a difficult childhood. His parents were millionaires.

LUISA: *(Touching his shoulder)* I would like to have known your father.

BUNKY: Me too. There was something hard but important about him. Almost bulletproof.

LUISA: I'm glad I got to meet your mother. I see where you get your dreamy eyes and—

BUNKY: Being a singer has turned me into a sly person.

LUISA: Auool.

BUNKY: Deaf in one dear. So many musicians are. We've blown our hearing out.

(BUNKY coughs)

LUISA: You feel terrible?

BUNKY: Well, I'm above ground. I lived for those moments of glory . . . So when a song is never born, it' like bearing a dead child.

(BUNKY refills their glasses, his eyes strangely soothed by the fizz of the champagne.

LUISA hovers by him, high with adoration. We hear music in the distance <u>Sloop John B</u> by the Beach Boys and words, "I feel so broke up / I wanna go home.")

BUNKY: *(Laughs)* You got me thinking too deep.

LUISA: Humph. About your daddy?

BUNKY: That jerk? *(Pouring another glass)* I'm thinking about … *(Yells out)* Mus-ic. Hear the echo. Mus-ic.

LUISA: Ooooh!

BUNKY: I'm trying to discover the essence of New Orleans in music? But it's not commercial. *(Shouts)* Comm-mer-ci-al. See. No echo.

LUISA: Hmmm. Why sing, if it makes you feel so bad?

BUNKY: I've wanted to be a musician all my life. I'm dependent on it. If I don't have musicians about me who excite me, I become depressed.

LUISA: Oh. Music's a neurosis?

BUNKY: To freeze time.

LUISA: *(Her eyes bright with champagne)* Cause it's moving too fast?

BUNKY: Right. Yeah.

(IRENE crosses to KAITLIN, buried in a book, <u>Creating Love</u>. VULTURES dance in place. Throughout the sequence, BEAU and RORY dance by flirting playfully. The characters' lines overlap in the fury of tango dancing)

(LIGHTS: Shadows of darkness)

KAITLIN: Where're my sunglasses? The wind blows specks into these lenses. A—a-a-h. Like slivers of glass. *(SHE puts on her sunglasses)*

IRENE: Beau's unbearable. I'm not used to sitting on the Promenade Deck with my eyes closed.

KAITLIN: *(Motioning to a box)* Tea? There's Tropical Escape, Mint Magic,

Wild Forest.

IRENE: Try some Siberian Ginseng. The herb for energy.

KAITLIN: If I were any more alive, I'd be dead. *(Shielding her eyes from the glare)* It's basically a matter of figuring where to look.

IRENE: You're not the sharpest knife in this family's drawer. You want to live in a fairy tale? I've Spanish news for you, baby. Real love is not like that.

RORY: *(Dancing by KAITLIN)* What attracts me to you, Beau, is you've such a good relationship with your wife.

BEAU: I'm happy if I can keep her amused. Between the long hopeless litany of disappointments—

RORY: Yes, next to elegance and class will be your wife's picture.

BEAU: *(To RORY)* I'm a nursemaid to Kaitlin. We fight all the time.

RORY: It's called marriage, Beau. If you just stand and sway from side to side, I can do everything else.

IRENE: *(Shrieks out)* How old are you, Rory? Forty, fifty?

RORY: I make forty look good. *(Dancing, she laughs huskily)* I used to date men older than me, but I kept getting older.

IRENE: *(To KAITLIN)* You're heading full tilt toward disaster.

BUNKY: *(Dancing by)* When you play with other musicians in front of an audience, you've this experience of living through more feeling that you can capture in words.

LUISA: Aaaah!

BEAU: Kaitlin doesn't mind. Isn't that right, darling?

IRENE: *(To KAITLIN)* Speak up, moron. He's going to do that to you after you've been the . . . the—

KAITLIN: Love giver. Women have had to live on a deeper level to survive—

IRENE: Run away with a gal with higher tits—

BUNKY: *(Twirling LUISA)* It's like being inside a tidal wave is. A wall of water engulfing you. It's that many sounds from all sides.

LUISA: Wow.

BUNKY: Like a roar pulling you into forgetfulness.

RORY: *(To BEAU)* Some clients, if they are active enough, can work things out on the fee couch.

IRENE: Presenting her bosoms, on a platter. Well, I'm leaving. Only a fool would stay and watch. *(Storms out)*

RORY: *(To BEAU)* Meet me on the lower deck at six o'clock. I don't just look, I buy. *(Exits)*

(Music: Band plays and a man with a lizard voice, croons, "I'd love to get you / On a slow boat to China / All to myself alone")

KAITLIN: *(Removes a cigarette but doesn't light it)* I smoke only at night. It's the best I can do. Women smoke more than men because we've *(BEAU moves behind her, his hand to her neck)* … more anguish.

BEAU: *(Grabs KAITLIN's chin intensely)* I'm no longer your lover, but I still feel like—

KAITLIN: I don't want to be teased.

BEAU: We may not have been successful literally, but we've been successful sexually. We could pretend again.

KAITLIN: I don't know my husband tonight. For me he doesn't exist.

BEAU: Must you smoke?

KAITLIN: I'm just holding it.

BEAU: I did a professional thing. I acted out the definition of the word "scandal." I did another professional thing. I dropped it.

KAITLIN: Scandal's titillating.

BEAU: It's diversion. *(Removes a handkerchief)* That's what you wanted, Kaitlin. A husband as a kind of accessory.

KAITLIN: I like the math of it, the figuring out of it. The juggling.

BEAU: *(Sits next to her, removing the glasses, blotting her cheeks)* I don't want another woman. I want my wife.

KAITLIN: If I'm not doing it, I can't complain about others doing it.

BEAU: *(Rises suddenly, walks to the railing)* How many parties do I have to attend alone? I'm not a machine. Christ, I wish I was. Since the hospital, I touch you, you're ice. To be naked and fail is one of the most gruesome things you can ever do.

KAITLIN: You're the one who works all night.

BEAU: I realize I've been callous. I put my writing before our relationship. *(Pause)* Are you for or against talking? I hoped this cruise might—

KAITLIN: Change things?

BEAU: Is it going to be a slow spiral downward or everything is fine, and then bam?

KAITLIN: You work yourself into a white heap. And leave me the shell.

BEAU: This is my first day out of prison. I spent four weeks, seven and a half hours a day with my editor, cutting one hundred pages from my novel. I had every sentence put on trial for its life. The writing is so hard, the rewards are so few, and the loneliness is intense.

KAITLIN: The doors are open for you everywhere.

BEAU: The tyranny now is that the work be good. I'm in a constant state of terror as to its quality.

KAITLIN: Why do you push yourself?

BEAU: Because like being married . . .(*Shaking his head*). . . writing is also a prodigious joy. Writing makes you aware you're a thinking person and you can impose some order. When a story is rolling, you can forget time. Last week, I wrote for hours without knowing the room had gotten dark. (*Affectionately*) And you've been like my shadow. The first reader who shares the vision. Remember when you read the opening chapter aloud to hear what caught, and I solved it in your presence.

KAITLIN: Vaguely.

BEAU: You're the person I write for, whom I trust. Sometimes I think if I write well enough I can make you live forever. (*Grabs the railing*) Come here. (*SHE draws away*) Haven't I been punished enough? Each night I sleep with this heaviness. (*Turning to her*) I lie there watching you. "Your head, your gesture, your hair. Are beautiful as a beautiful landscape."

KAITLIN: Baudelaire.

BEAU: "The smile plays on your face like a fresh wind in a clear sky."

KAITLIN: Muse.

BEAU: "Thus I would wish one night when the voluptuary hour sounds."

KAITLIN: Love poet.

BEAU: (*Embracing her*) "To crawl, like a coward, noiselessly, Towards the treasures of your body." *Voulez-vous coucher avec moi?*

(*KAITLIN's hands flutter to her mouth confusedly. Music: Band plays Beyond the Sea by Jack Lawrence. We hear "Somewhere beyond the sea. Somewhere waiting for me. My lover stands on golden sands and watches the ships . . ." as the VULTURES run downstage and surround BEAU.*)

VULTURES: We want your autograph. You won the costume contest.

BEAU: But I'm not dressed.

VULTURES: Come get your prize.

(THEY crown HIM with a gold laurel wreath and lead him upstage. Music: Beyond the Sea continues to plays as KAITLIN crosses downstage, confiding to the audience.)

KAITLIN: My husband's a master at deflecting women because he's been doing it so long. For our fifth anniversary, he brought me back this Faberge locket. Gold with a coral rose. It's got a tiny watch inside, circled with diamonds. But it's got no face. That's the best kind for a wife. *(KAITLIN removes the crystal, swings it)* Beau's getting back at me beautifully. The new woman's exotic. Carbonated bubbly. Something bad is happening. And I've got to look, but I don't want to. Help me, Baudelaire. See what I must see.

(Sits down. Distant Band plays My Heart Will Go On, the love theme from Titanic)

I'm asking for power, not permission. *(Pause)* Don't beg anybody but God.

(Lights fade as MUSIC swells.)

"Knowing and working with Rosary O'Neill is to experience her infectious joy at the miracles of theatre. Her astonishing skills and indomitable writer's spirit place Rosary in the pantheon of great American women playwrights. A unique, international star."

> *Saul Reichlin*
> *London. Artistic Director, Lone Star Theater LLC*

"Aside from grace and charm, Rosary has a great literary talent I admire deeply. This great quality exists not just in her many superb plays but in the way she created the Southern Repertory Theatre of New Orleans and led it over many years to its superb final home in Canal Place. How fortunate that lately she has moved her high talents to New York and her country home in Rhinecliff."

> *Robert Kornfeld*
> *Co-chair, Literary Committee of The National Arts Club*

"It was a privilege to receive Rosary O'Neill as a Fulbright Senior Scholar at the University of Paris in 1992-93. A prize-winning playwright, and authentic voice of her native Louisiana, she was an outstanding ambassador for contemporary American culture. The quality of her craftsmanship, speaking for one of America's most richly diverse regions, was a demonstration to often skeptical French audiences that a distinctively American cultural tradition does indeed exist, and continues to flower."

> *Genevieve Ramos Acker*
> *Deputy Director 1984-1996*
> *Franco-American Commission for Educational Exchange*

With her deep sensitivity to artists and to the artistic process, Rosary O'Neill's plays unfold. Against a background of a doomed and resonant South her characters take life onstage. The author shows us their conflicts and their ultimate nobility. Deeply rooted/uprooted in New Orleans, Rosary O'Neill makes us understand what, in art as in life, must irrevocably be lost, and also, what can be saved.

> *Kathleen Spivack*
> *Writer, Visiting Professor, American Literature and Creative Writing,*
> *University of Paris, France, 1991-present*

ROSARY HARTEL O'NEILL is the author of fourteen plays produced internationally by invitation of the American embassy in Paris, Bonn, Tibilisi, Georgia, Budapest, Hungary, London and Moscow. Her play UNCLE VICTOR was chosen Best New American Drama by the Cort Theater, Hollywood, and celebrated in the Chekhov Now Festival in New York. BLACKJACK was selected for Alice's Fourth Floor Best New Play Series. She was founding artistic director at Southern Rep Theater from 1987 to 2002. She has been playwright-in-residence at the Sorbonne University, Paris; Tulane University, New Orleans; Defiance College, Ohio, the University of Bonn, Germany and Visiting Scholar at Cornell.

Other fellowships include the Virginia Center for the Creative Arts (VCCA) Playwrighting Fellowship to Wiepersdorf, Germany, and two fellowships to the Playwriting Center, Sewanee University. She also received a play invitation to the Actors Centre, London, as well as residences in playwriting at the VCCA, Ragsdale, Dorset Arts Colony, Byrdcliff Arts Colony, and the Mary Anderson Center.

She was chosen outstanding artist in Paris and awarded a Fulbright to Paris for her play WISHING ACES. She was a finalist in the Faulkner Competition for New American Writers; a finalist for outstanding artist for the state of Louisiana 2002; and a finalist in the Ireland Tyrone Guthrie Residency in playwriting with the VCCA 2002. She was awarded a Senior Fulbright research specialist in drama to Europe, 2001-2006, and received first invitations to the *Conservatoire Nationale du Drame* (leading acting-training center in Paris) and the *Conservatoire Nationale de la Danse* (leading dance-training center outside Paris).

Recent professional achievements include: DEGAS IN NEW ORLEANS, which was invited to the New End Theatre (a heralded theater for contemporary plays) in London and featured in the Best New American Play Oktoberfest of the Ensemble Studio Theatre (a leading theater for new work) in New York City and in the Reading Series of the Abingdon Theatre, New York. She is playwright-in-residence at the National Arts Club, where much of her recent work has been developed.

Author photo by DC Larue.

For more information about the work of Rosary O'Neill,
visit her web site at:
www.rosaryoneill.com

PRODUCTIONS AND PUBLISHING

FOR PLAYS:
ENGLISH LANGUAGE RIGHTS
Samuel French, Inc.
45 W. 25th St., 2nd Floor
New York, NY 10010
212.206.8990

FOREIGN LANGUAGE RIGHTS
The Marton Agency, Inc.
1 Union Square W. Suite 815
New York, NY 10003-3303
212.255.1908

FOR NOVELS:
Edythea Ginis Selman Literary Agency
14 Washington Square Place
New York, NY 10003
212.473.1874

Manufactured By: RR Donnelley
                    Breinigsville, PA USA
                    June, 2010